The Mammoth
Book of
Love and
Sensuality

The Mammoth
Book of
Love and
Sensuality

Edited by
Caroline Rey

CARROLL & GRAF PUBLISHERS, INC.
New York

Carroll & Graf Publishers, Inc.
19 West 21st Street
New York
NY 10010–6805

First Carroll & Graf edition 1997

A copy of the Cataloging in Publication Data for this title is available from the
Library of Congress.

ISBN 0–7867–0374–1

Note

This book is not a substitute for your doctor's or health professional's advice, and
the publishers and authors cannot accept liability for any injury or loss to any
person acting or refraining from action as a result of the material in this book.
Before commencing any health treatment, always consult your doctor.

Printed and bound in the EC

10 9 8 7

Contents

CHAPTER 1

Learning to Love

A sexual journey with a new partner is a voyage of discovery which has a vast potential for excitement, sensuality and promise. Of course, the route will vary from time to time and the sex will vary from the ecstatic and memorable to the routine and predictable. For, in any couple's life together, there are sexual milestones and each new phase brings forth rewards of its own.

The time from first meeting to actual intercourse varies enormously from couple to couple. But whatever their situation, the first time they make love is a unique experience and one that they will remember all of their lives.

The first few months of a relationship between lovers are often described as the "honeymoon" period. This is the period when a couple cannot have too much of one another. Often every moment spent apart is regarded as wasted. And it is during this period that a couple lay the foundations of the kind of sex life that they will have together.

Each partner will have different expectations for when they make love, for each human being's sexuality is unique and individual. What they will be united in is the hope that it will be a perfect experience, perhaps with each of them coming together at the same moment.

For many lovers, however "good" they are technically, this is unlikely to be the case. The chances are that both will be over-anxious to impress the other and to please them, all of which is a potential recipe for sexual disaster.

And because each of them is not yet familiar with the other's sexuality, the chances are that they will misjudge the other's feelings. The woman may believe that the man is more sexually experienced than he really is, and the man may be surprised to find a more, or less, sexually assertive woman than

Reassurance is an important part of first-time sex. Both the man and the woman will have expectations based on past experiences, so it is worth talking things through and examining each other's feelings.

he had imagined. Also, both may be tempted to try techniques that pleased previous partners. And what pleases one person in bed will not necessarily please another.

Humour should be handled with care, especially at the start of a relationship. A man's ego, particularly, is fragile at the best of times and a loud guffaw or hysterical giggles if he fails to achieve an erection, or he ejaculates prematurely, is not going to do much for his confidence. Equally, a man who finds something in his partner's sexual technique amusing is going to dampen the whole experience. Remember that tickling sensitive spots, or nibbling an earlobe, can both do much to diffuse what might turn out otherwise to be a disastrous experience.

It is important not to place too much emphasis on the "first time". If a couple recognize that it is the first of possibly thousands of lovemaking episodes together, a first-time disaster can easily be put into perspective. If it does go perfectly, then that should be regarded as a bonus. One of the joys of sex is that it can be practised almost any time, any place and as often as a couple wants.

The first time you sleep with someone is not the best time to experiment with sexual techniques and try out little tricks you may have learned from previous partners. It is assumed that you are emotionally involved with each other and that you want to give the maximum pleasure possible to your partner. Sex between you then has almost infinite possibilities. Casual sex may have an excitement value of its own without responsibility, but the potential for exploring possibilities is, of course, severely limited. And with the rate of AIDS cases increasing all the time, casual sex now carries a risk that many people will wish to avoid.

It is through sensitive and sensual foreplay that arousal becomes possible – for both partners – and orgasm becomes both pleasurable and intense. If the feelings and the foreplay are right, the rest will follow. And it does not matter if it does not succeed this first time. A couple can always try again, later.

Be prepared to take time arousing your new partner. And be adaptable in your approach. If the other person wants to take the

FIRST-TIME SEX

The decision to have sex with someone for the first time should never be taken lightly, and most people, however experienced, will find themselves somewhat nervous, embarrassed and concerned when faced with it.

There is no general rule on whether or not to wait but the big issues to consider and discuss with your partner are contraception and sexually transmitted diseases, particularly AIDS.

This is especially important in short-term sexual relationships which may be exciting but carry the risk of infection with sexually transmitted diseases, including the HIV virus that causes AIDS. The risks can be reduced by employing "Safer-Sex" procedures like these:

❤ **Avoid sleeping around.** *The more people you sleep with, the more likely you are to meet someone with the HIV virus and become infected. Think extra carefully about whether to start a new sexual relationship.*

❤ **Think before having sex.** *Don't have sex if you or your partner has an inflammation, sores or an unusual discharge around the genital area. Avoid oral sex if either partner has cuts or sores around the mouth.*

❤ **Use a condom.** *It gives some protection against infection if used properly. For women, using a diaphragm or cervical cap can help to protect the cervix from infection.*

❤ **Tell your partner if you have an infection.** *It may be that your partner has passed the infection on to you in the first place and may be reinfecting you without knowing.*

For more information and advice about sex and contraception, see your doctor or other medical staff.

initiative, let them; if they want you take control, then do so. But above all, keep things simple. And if you choose to massage, for example, keep the rhythm slow and sensual.

Don't worry too much about your own orgasm, particularly so for the men – and do not, in your eagerness to satisfy your partner, make her feel pressurized to have an orgasm. And for her, in an effort to please her partner, the worst possible thing she can do is to fake an orgasm. This may work in the short term, but for a couple's sex life together, it could become a habit that will become impossible to break. The man will feel that he is doing everything right to please her when in fact he is not. And in the long term the woman who fakes her orgasms will be denying herself her true sexual potential.

Overcoming inhibitions

Sex in any relationship, whether first-time or otherwise can fall prey to sexual inhibitions. There is no denying that these are personal, but at the same time, they are learned and very much governed by fashion. For example, fifty years ago oral sex was considered a perversion and to be inhibited about it was not only acceptable but normal. Today, however, many women are branded as inhibited simply because they have not taken this new message on board.

Fortunately, given that sexual inhibitions are, in the main, learned, even something as simple, yet deep-rooted as a fear of making love with the lights on, can be overcome if the individual is willing.

Perhaps surprisingly, the best starting point is to discuss with your partner what each of you means by love. During such a session, both partners usually reveal that they have their own ideas about the subject and their own stereotypes which they expect their partner to fulfil.

Just because a woman cannot go along with something sexual does not necessarily mean that she does not love her man, yet "any woman who really loved me would do…" is a common cry. This can be a very false and damaging definition of love.

On the other side of the coin are those women who realize only too well what their needs are, yet say nothing for fear of appearing "tarty" in their partner's eyes. It is a sad fact that, in millions of homes, one partner may be fantasizing about something he or she would like to do, and which their partner might very well be prepared to do, yet the subject is never discussed.

Try making a list of sexual subjects which cause problems to you in your relationship and put each on a small slip of paper. Suitable subjects might include penis size, oral sex, breast size, occasional impotence, PMS, semen, talking during intercourse or who initiates sex.

Take it in turns to pull one out of the pile unseen and share your thoughts about it. Say what you think about it and honestly try to be understanding about your partner's point of view.

Invest more time and care in your love life generally. If you want your partner to be less inhibited in a particular way, a good start is to ensure that he or she is being made love to in a way that is really pleasing them.

An individual who feels taken for granted, is bored, or frankly turned off much of the time, is very unlikely to want to behave in an uninhibited way.

Make a positive effort to act more sexually in general. To at least some extent, we can "act" in a more uninhibited way and

WHO DO WE LOVE?

The question of how we choose our partners is one of great personal interest and occupies much of our daily thoughts. If we are single, we spend hours dreaming of the person we will live with or marry. But what makes a particular man or woman attractive to us?

Personal preference in partnership is a modern Western phenomenon. It is uncommon in many parts of the world where marriage serves more of a legal than personal purpose, the nuptial agreement acting as a kind of cement which holds together land titles and family businesses. The majority of the world's marriages and partnerships are still arrranged by parents or village elders.

Unconscious chemistry

In most of Western society we are able to choose our partners on the basis of our own sexual preference, rather than having someone else make the decision. But how much conscious choice do we really have?

Although in Western society many people have a greater choice of partner due to increased mobility, the most enduring relationships tend to be with those whose background has a close degree of similarity to our own.

Chances are we will live with or marry someone from the same social, economic and religious group, with a similar level of intelligence and who resembles us in many personality and physical traits.

Class systems vary from culture to culture, but people tend to get involved with someone they consider to be of their own class or caste. Liaisons beyond these invisible barriers are usually frowned on by one or both sides, and the "intrusive" partner is often considered an outsider, ignorant of the other's language and habits.

The same is true for many religious communities. Thus, it is vital for a Muslim to marry into the faith.

Most of us consider similarity in level of intelligence to be fairly important. We can talk more easily and effectively to the potential lover who speaks the "same language" and who takes the same views and opinions for granted. Similarly, our personality type plays an important role in who we choose to fall in love with, and this is shaped mainly by our family structure and early emotional and learning experiences.

"Chemistry" between two people is often largely due to the unconscious recognition of certain shared personality characteristics. From our dress to our facial expressions, we are constantly giving out unconscious and detailed personal information.

Defining attraction

Sexual preference in humans has been found to be established before the age of six. When we start our search for Mr or Ms Right, we are looking for someone who resembles our "search image" – a montage of the physical features of family members and childhood friends.

So the man or woman we find attractive now unconsciously recalls someone who we admired as a child.

We are also unconsciously conditioned to find certain physical characteristics desirable. Fashions in beauty change quite dramatically over generations and in different cultures – what is considered beautiful varies enormously according to what is in demand at the time.

achieve what we want. At first this may seem a little false, but with practice it could become second nature and at least gets you over the first hurdle.

As time passes, reveal more and more of yourself (and not just your sexual self) to your partner and you will be amazed how it lessens your inhibitions. We all want to be fully understood by somebody, preferably by our partner, but this cannot happen in a vacuum. Both partners need to make an effort to share more of themselves.

Drawing the line

Accept that everyone has a "final position" on certain things – a line beyond which they will not venture. Although these lines can be extended a little, this is often the most that can be expected. What every loving couple should aim for is to be sufficiently mature to be able to come to terms with their respective "final positions" and not to make an issue out of them.

One useful mechanism for overcoming inhibitions is thought-stopping. This is a simple do-it-yourself psychological technique that uncouples negative thoughts such as guilt and anxiety from your thinking and substitutes instead positive, helpful thoughts. It works because the brain can only cope with one emotion at once. Thinking of one emotion will flood out another.

The moment a negative thought comes into your head that makes you feel anxious, fearful, or guilty and which inhibits you from doing something you or your partner want to do, shout "STOP" loudly and crash your hand down on something. Quickly replace the thought with another, positive one that pleases or excites you. To do this you will need a bank of exciting and pleasant thoughts ready.

Try thought-stopping eight or ten times a day, or whenever a negative thought enters your head. Over a few weeks, the number of negative thoughts you have should reduce and you will become better at flooding them out.

Step-by-step desensitization is another psychological game that alters the way you behave and is based, like all behavioural therapy, on the notion that if something can be learned it can be unlearned.

A woman, for example, is too inhibited to make love with the lights on. She recognizes her problem, and wants to change, but every time she tries to overcome it, her anxiety level rises, so that she either will not have sex at all with the lights on, or gets no pleasure from it when she does.

To expect her to jump straight from that fear level to actually live out her goal is unrealistic, and no amount of blackmail or shouting will alter that.

What she needs to do first and foremost is to read the signs – to learn the signs of fear and anxiety so that she can recognize what is happening when she's faced with a difficult situation. The following sensations are all feelings that a woman who is going to make love with the lights on may have, and it is essential to score the ones she is really feeling and not to deceive herself:

0 *Completely relaxed.*

1 *Slight anxiety. Sweating a little, and wondering if you have to go through with it.*

2 *Moderate anxiety. Tension building up. Butterflies in tummy.*

3 *High anxiety. Heart pounding and profuse sweating.*

4 *Unacceptable anxiety. Want to run away.*

5 *Total panic.*

The next thing to do is divide the problem on a ten-point scale with a very easily achievable goal that produces no anxiety at all. A scale plan for learning to make love with the lights on that could work for some people might be as follows:

1 *Lie on the bed, fully clothed alongside your partner, reading a sexy book or magazine showing women and men in bed together naked.*

2 *Lie in bed naked under the bedclothes with your partner with the lights on, reading the sexy magazine.*

3 *Lie in bed naked under the bedclothes with your partner, keeping the lights on, without the magazine.*

4 *Lie in bed naked with your partner with no covers and the lights off.*

5 *Lie in bed naked with your partner with no covers and the lights on.*

6 *Undress in front of your partner with the lights on.*

7 *Walk around naked in front of your partner.*

8 *Take a bath or shower together.*

9 *Make love with the lights on.*

10 *The fear is gone!*

The first step in this technique is to relax and raise your level of sexual arousal by cuddling, kissing, reading a sexy book or magazine together, or whatever turns you on. When you are aroused and feeling happy and relaxed, do the first item on the list. On the proven principle that pleasure and sexual arousal reduce anxiety, use the nice feeling to help you.

If you feel totally relaxed and there are no signs of anxiety, you can go on to the next stage and so on until you arrive at the step that makes you anxious. Stop here. Do not go on. Use your thought-stopping techniques to flood out anxious thoughts and calm yourself down until you feel relaxed and happy again. On this, or on another occasion, try that step again, perhaps when you are more sexually aroused or when you are feeling exceptionally loving.

Work up the list step by step so that over a few weeks you are able to go right up to the last one without any signs or feeling of anxiety.

You will probably find that as you climb the list your sexual fantasies will change too. This is good. Build on it. Let your mind jump about on the scale during masturbation, with or without your partner, so that you have rehearsed in fantasy what you want to achieve in practice. You must not actually do anything, though, unless you have worked carefully up to it, step by step, or you may find yourself disappointed.

Step-by-step desensitization can be used for a number of other sexual anxieties such as fear of oral sex, deep penetration and so on.

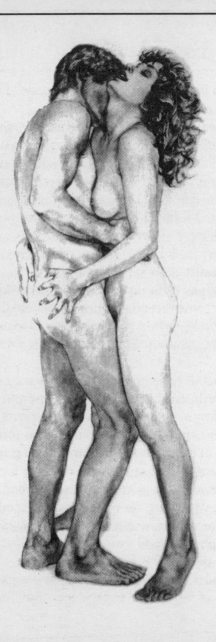

Begin foreplay with cuddling as it will help develop an intimate knowledge of your lover's bodily contours.

Foreplay

The value of foreplay to increase the breadth and scope of love-making has been recognized for thousands of years.

The Ancient Chinese recommended that the man should delay his orgasm until after the woman had experienced hers – even if it meant that it did not happen at all. This was largely for religious reasons, but the principles of anticipating your partner's needs rather than your own still hold true today.

Making love is more about what goes on in a person's head than what happens biologically. That is why illicit affairs can be so appealing. Yet so often the sex in an affair – heightened with danger and guilt – is unsatisfactory for both parties.

For the couple who have difficulty in finding time to do this, it is as well to remember those early days when they could always find time for each other. The sex was probably less satisfactory – but there was more emphasis on touch, loving words, gifts and surprises.

Any of these can act as an appetizer to love if the mood is right: a shared hobby, such as sporting activities; wine and food (a glass of wine before lovemaking can relax both partners, and good food can be a real aphrodisiac); erotica in the form of books, magazines, films or art; verbal flattery or the odd gift; and sex games, such as dressing up and acting out imaginary scenes.

Great lovers are made, not born. Lovemaking demands constant practice, like any great art. An open mind, a willingness to give sexually as well as receive, and a sensitivity towards our partner's needs, both physical and emotional, are all that is required to enhance the quality of your pleasure.

For men in particular – and for most women – orgasm is the expected outcome of all sexual experiences. But for the creative lover it is only one feature of sex – it is an end rather than a means.

The quality of an orgasm can vary with each sexual episode. By putting your energy into creative foreplay – to stimulate and entice your partner, exploring the sensuality of their bodies for delicious stimulation – the sexual experience can improve almost beyond imagination. And with the trust developed through familiarity, and an increased knowledge of a partner's needs, each can anticipate the kind of foreplay the other will respond to and enjoy.

If you want to make your partner feel good about being loved, wanted and needed – tell them. Your voice is a tool of great erotic expression. "I love you" or "I want to feel your skin against mine" at the right moment can make your partner melt into a state of expectant bliss. Some people are turned on by street language in bed.

"I can't wait to fuck you" whispered to your lover at a formal dinner party can start them longing for dessert well before the first course. A long play of double-entendres and stolen touches may follow, slowly kindling desire until you get home.

The accomplished seducer knows the value of compliments and flattery. It is not so much what is said, but the fact that some-one we are attracted to has made an agreeable comment. And if we are told that we look good, we are not going to disbelieve it.

Part of foreplay involves knowing what makes sex memorable for your partner, knowing what they know and like best, and putting it into action.

Many women tend to be more influenced by the place in which they make love than are men. So if your partner loves romantic, candlelit evenings for two at home, prepare one for her, or if she likes making love in unusual places, do your best to

You can bring your partner to the brink of orgasm using your hands or your mouth. If she raises her legs back towards her shoulders you can insert your fingers deeply into her vagina.

accommodate her. If she likes flowers or small presents then give them to her. And if she likes you to dress in a certain way, you should indulge her in her fantasy.

The majority of men are no less influenced by mood when it comes to lovemaking. It is just that their sexual parameters are slightly different – they tend to be more visually stimulated. It is your body, and often the way you are dressed that can make sex memorable for him, so dress for him periodically. If he finds you seductive as a "tart", dress and behave like one.

Tease him almost unmercifully. If you decide to wear no underwear, tell him that this is what you have done. Treat sex unselfishly, concentrating on making it memorable for him and, by so doing, memorable for yourself.

For the man who wants to bring his partner to the brink of orgasm, take time removing each of her garments, using your hands to run up and down her back, her legs and her stomach. Nibble her feet and calves and behind her knees. Encourage her to stretch out and abandon herself to you.

When she is totally naked, use oil all over her but do not touch her breasts or vulva. Instead, lightly brush over them as you caress her less erogenous zones.

When you caress her breasts, pour oil onto them and knead it in. Then use the tip of your penis to trace a path around each nipple. If she tries to touch you restrain her. Then use oil on her vulva with the other hand, first of all circling it before gently using a finger on her clitoris. When she is ready, insert as many fingers as she likes into her vagina and use your thumb on her clitoris. Do not let her come just yet.

Another way of bringing her to the brink of orgasm is by using a vibrator – one of the most versatile and variable sex aids for a woman. There are a number of ways you can use it in foreplay: use it on her breasts and her buttocks as well as her vulva. If she likes it, insert the tip into her anus as well, although remember not to put it into her vagina afterwards as this may transfer anal bacteria.

Vary the speed setting as you alternate, using it inside her and on her clitoris. Make sure that you keep your other hand busy all over her body. And don't forget to use your mouth too.

Men love to be caressed and fussed over as much as women. The only difference is that, because they are more genitally oriented, they tend to require less time to become aroused. So although the quality of arousal should be memorable for him, it should not take too long, otherwise he will come too soon which may be fine for him but not so good for you.

Use your hands and your body to caress him. Trace a path along his back, from his feet to his neck, first with your hands and then your breasts.

Then turn him over and pour a little oil onto his stomach and the tops of his legs. Rub it firmly in and then pour some onto the top of his penis, gently rubbing it in with both hands.

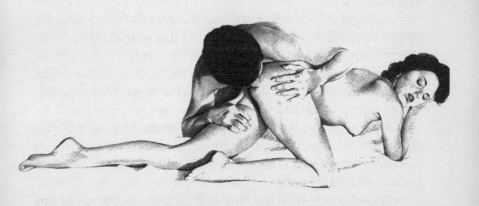

Foreplay can be an exciting and intimate part of lovemaking.

Kissing should never be restricted to the mouth. Try kissing and caressing your partner all over – from the toes upwards. A slow and sensual build-up to foreplay will increase her pleasure in lovemaking tenfold.

Here are some other suggestions for getting a woman in the mood for love, and remember the key to all of them is not rushing.

Slowly remove your partner's clothes, kissing and caressing her as you do so, then lead her to the shower. Wash and rinse her hair as sensuously as you can. Soap each leg in turn in your lap, lather her breasts and buttocks, then using a small amount of soap, wash her vulva. Applying the shower nozzle close to her skin, rinse her with tantalizing jets of warm water. Rub her down with a warm towel.

You could lie your partner down and using your eyelashes or hair, trace a carpet of sensation over her body. Then, with your penis, trace a path around her lips and breasts, then her buttocks and perineum.

Many women's breasts are very sensitive during arousal. Ice can be wonderfully shocking if rubbed around each nipple. Your partner can dangle her breasts in your face as you kiss them, or you can even lick wine, yogurt or ice cream off of them. Some women like semen on their breasts, so if you masturbate yourself, you can then direct the fluid over her.

Most men can be brought to orgasm in seconds, but with skilful foreplay it can be delayed for ages.

Bath your partner, soaping his front down gently, then the backs of his legs. Use light strokes and slow persistent pressure. Now wash his penis and testicles; pull back the foreskin if he has one, and briefly simulate masturbation. Then dry him with a warm towel and take him to another room to make love.

Use your breasts to trace a path over his body, then move one breast around his penis. Turning to his back trace a path from head to toe and run an erect nipple along his perineum. Apply a little oil to your breasts and flatten them over his penis, taking it between them. With rhythmic movements, bring him to the verge of orgasm.

Use your lips to kiss him all over. Work your way up his leg, bypass the genitals, and kiss his nipples. Then descend slowly to his penis, breathing close to his skin as you do so. Take his testicles into your mouth one by one. Perhaps the most intimate form of kissing is to use your vaginal lips, again starting from the feet and working your way up, close to his face.

Food

Dinner is often a prelude to sex. A good meal in an intimate setting can definitely create the right mood for an evening of lovemaking. It's a chance for you to be alone together, to really talk and appreciate one another's company.

Going out to eat is great when you can afford it. The chances are, if you've already been seeing your partner for some time, you'll have a favourite restaurant where the food, the wine, the staff and the atmosphere combine to get you in the mood for an evening of sensuous pleasure.

The disadvantages of eating out are that you have to choose from a menu that may not include exactly what you had in mind, and of course, no matter how worked up or excited you get about the prospect of imminent lovemaking, there's nothing you can do about it until you're both home. No matter how effective your oysters and champagne were, you might just find yourself struggling to sustain the mood through a twenty-minute wait at a bus stop or in bad traffic on a wet night.

All of which, of course, makes a romantic evening (or afternoon) for two at home the best possible option for combining food and sex.

Invite your partner to dinner for two in your own private restaurant. Lay the table prettily, light some candles and dim all the lights to create a romantic atmosphere. Take care choosing and preparing the food: combine some of your favorites – things you normally only have as treats on special occasions – with things you can have fun with, and splash out on a bottle of wine, champagne or your favorite liqueur.

Some foods can be eaten in an incredibly suggestive way. Try asparagus with melted butter. Feed it to each other using your fingers and then lick them clean. Other finger foods – chicken

Exciting foreplay and your favourite food and drink may put you in the mood for sex that is much raunchier than usual.

legs, prawns or fruits – can also be eaten sexily, in an almost animal way, and can be fed to one another.

Certain foods have a reputation for being aphrodisiacs;
whether they are or not is debatable but just for fun you could
include them in your menu. Some get their reputation simply
because they look like the part of the body they are supposed to
stimulate. Oysters resemble the vulva and are also extremely
sensuous when they slip down the throat, and olives and broad
beans look like the testes.

Other foods – like freshly picked tomatoes, fish and onions
– stimulate our sense of smell and some spices have been
recommended through the ages to cure sexual problems like
impotence and premature ejaculation.

Chocolate, the traditional lovers' gift, was considered a
potent aphrodisiac in the seventeenth century because it was so
rare and exotic. Research in recent years, however, has shown that
there may just be some scientific basis to its reputation, as
phenylethymine, the chemical found in chocolate, produces
feelings of elation, euphoria and energy. The taste and texture of
chocolate is regarded by some as a good substitute for sex but
why not have both?

As well as eating food you can use it during lovemaking to
enhance one another's pleasure. Why not plan a naked picnic in
your bedroom? Put a rug or blanket over the bed, or on the floor,
and serve easy-to-eat food.

Take it in turns to feed one another – you could have fruit
salad dipped in cream or yogurt. Serve chilled wine or champagne
in a bucket with lots of ice. You could try feeding each other
mouth to mouth or dribbling cold wine over each other's bodies.

Your partner could stroke cream over your breasts and lick
it off or you could cover his penis with cream or yogurt and do

SEX SIGNALS

Unconsciously, we all respond to body language cues – tiny signals which we observe and put together to make a general impression of what another person is thinking. If we learn which signals to look for and how to read them accurately, it can be a great advantage.

❤ *Eye contact: repeated eye contact shows that a person is interested in us, probably – though not necessarily – sexually. Men will look directly into a woman's eyes, maintaining the eye contact for longer, whereas women are more likely to snatch glances, looking away self-consciously when caught.*

❤ *Dilated pupils: the important detail to look for is the size of the pupil – the small black area in the center of the eye. When we look at someone we find attractive, the pupils of our eyes dilate. This in turn seems to make us more attractive to the person looking at us – in one test, a group of men were shown two apparently identical photographs of the same woman. When they were asked which one was most attractive, all the men chose the photograph where her pupils were dilated.*

❤ *Smiling: when talking to someone who attracts us, we tend to open our eyes wider than usual, while our eyebrows are held slightly higher. We are also likely to smile more often with the mouth open, and use increased tongue-play in moistening our lips frequently.*

❤ *Touch: a man may put his arm around a woman while introducing her to friends, guiding her across a room or into his car. And when the body contact is actually necessary, the warmth with which it is done can betray a good deal. Likewise, a woman may adjust a man's tie, button his shirt, dust his lapel or brush the hair away from his eyes.*

❤ *Tone of voice: many of us are too shy to come straight out with what we feel, or believe that a direct approach would seem too forward. In these cases, tone of voice provides a good deal of information. Affection is usually transmitted by soft, low resonant sounds. When someone of the opposite sex starts to talk to you, listen for a slightly slurred or purring voice with a regular rhythm and upward inflexion – a rising note rather like a question.*

❤ *Preening: preening behaviour is the term used to describe the largely unconscious attempts to make oneself more attractive – flicking hair off face, straightening the tie, pulling in the stomach and so on.*

❤ *Stance: someone who is attracted to you usually stands close to you in such a way as to signal openness and accessibility. Their arms will be relaxed and in an open position, and their feet, if they are standing, will be pointing in your direction, leaving the body undefended.*

the same. Why not try placing a strawberry, grape or even a piece of chocolate at the entrance of your vagina and get your partner to eat it? Massage one another using crushed soft fruits, cold custard, spray-cream or even ice-cream.

Your partner could tip a little ice-cold champagne onto your breasts or stomach and lick it off, and don't forget that honey, syrup and jam feel (and taste) delicious poured all over the breasts or penis and sucked or licked off.

The ice from the ice-bucket can be stroked all over one another's body or your partner can put it against your genitals and move it around with his tongue; the contrast between his

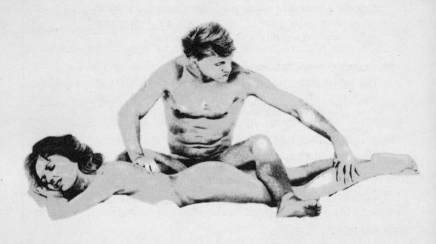

Massage each other, taking it slowly and rhythmically. It will awaken feelings and sensitivity all over.

warm mouth and the cold ice should feel exquisite. Try cooling your mouth with an ice cube and fellating your partner, drinking a mouthful of piping hot herbal tea and doing the same, then do it in turns. Remember to let each other know what feels best.

The pattern of arousal can be simple or complicated. One day it may last a whole afternoon and begin with just a word, a touch or a glance. A couple may feel like a lingering, gradual build-up to lovemaking or they may just want to have sex in a passionate frenzy. Follow your instincts and respond to your lover's desires.

Sensual massage

Touch is the sense that registers heat and cold, pain and pressure. But as every lover knows, touch is far more than this. Through touch, we communicate feelings, give and receive pleasure, and express our needs and desires.

But although touch is a natural sense, its full expression does not always come naturally. It may be something we need to re-learn if our lovemaking has gradually become increasingly focused on intercourse alone.

The "arrival" at sexual intercourse does not mean that the other stages in the touch sequence are no longer important. But in any long-term relationship, there will be times when we forget to touch. Taking a step back in the sequence can actually be a step forward in lovemaking.

Sensual massage between lovers is an extremely erotic, intimate laying of hands on skin. Sometimes it may be part of a prelude to lovemaking, while at other times, it is a form of love-making in itself.

WHICH OILS TO USE

Vegetable-based oils are best for massage – and many "essential" herbal oils have highly acclaimed benefits. Avoid baby oil – it is mineral-based and soaks into the skin too quickly. Always dilute "essential oils" with vegetable oil unless they are packaged for direct use on skin. Pregnant women should avoid undiluted oils.

❤ **Sweet Almond oil:** *contains vitamins E and F*

❤ **Apricot oil:** *contains vitamin A*

❤ **Lavender oil:** *eases pain*

❤ **Sandalwood oil:** *moisturizes dry skin*

❤ **Peppermint oil:** *is an aid to painful joints*

❤ **Geranium oil:** *reduces swellings*

❤ **Juniper or Rosemary oil***: tones aching muscles*

The secret of sensual massage is that one partner can be completely passive, while the other makes all the decisions and is the pleasure-giver. A heady sensation for either partner, a massage can provide even greater feelings of closeness and more complex exchanges of lovemaking.

Once you understand the art of sensual massage, it will help you learn how to release and enjoy both your own and your partner's body by relaxing tight muscles and freeing pent-up emotions.

Massage is the rhythmical application of pressure on the body using the hands, thumbs and fingers. Blood and lymph vessels – the body's drainage channels – run through muscles and as muscles relax, the gentle pressure of the massage helps stimulate the circulation and clear away toxins. It is important, therefore, that all the long strokes, called effleurage, apply pressure towards the heart.

It is also important not to lose contact with the body, so you should apply the pressure upwards and then lightly drag your hands back down the body.

As massage is often a preliminary to more direct sexual stimulation, you should avoid touching the genitals, and breasts until your partner is feeling totally relaxed, yet refreshed and full of energy.

Keep the movements steady and slow. Jerky movements will leave your partner feeling edgy. How much pressure you apply is a matter of preference. Many people like to feel some weight behind each upward stroke without it being too fierce or rough, while others prefer a lighter touch. Generally, though, try to put your body weight behind your strokes rather than just using your arms and shoulders. This makes it possible to lean into the upward strokes.

It is important that your hands slide easily over the skin, so use a light application of talc or an oil to the palms. Some people do not like talc as it can dry the skin, but an oil will leave the skin feeling wonderfully soft and smooth. Do not use hand cream or body lotion as this will disappear into the skin too quickly and the skin may become sore when you rub.

Always apply the oil to your hands first and then lightly distribute it over the area of the body you are going to massage. Do not use too much oil as your hands will slip and it will be difficult to work all the oil into the skin. Place a towel under your partner to prevent any excess oil marking the floor or bed covering underneath.

You can massage your partner on the bed or on the floor. The floor will provide a firmer resistance to your pressure and will allow you more freedom of movement. Placing cushions or pillows under your partner makes massage more comfortable and relaxing. A pillow placed under the stomach when lying face down or under the thighs when lying face up helps release the lower back.

Cover the parts of the body that you are not working on. Allow plenty of time to massage each other so that you do not feel hurried. You need not go through the full sequence every time, but choose just one area which seems particularly tense or pleasurable. You can take ten minutes or an hour or two – it's entirely up to you. Let your partner unwind and talk about what feels pleasurable, or just allow the sensation of touch to find its own way.

Remember that massage should be highly pleasurable and not painful. The more you practise, the more proficient you will become.

There are a number of basic massage techniques which may be alternated to provide a soothing and relaxing experience:

● **Effleurage:** *always begin and end your massage with this stroke. It is a light, soothing movement. Stroke up both sides of the spine, then out across the shoulders, down the sides and back to your original position.*

● **Hacking:** *a chopping movement made with the edges of the hands to tone up the muscles. Take care not to come down too hard with your hands as you could hurt your partner or yourself.*

● **Cupping:** *similar in speed to hacking, this is a light rhythmic movement using alternate hands. Cup your hands, keeping fingers together and thumbs tucked in, so that they make a hollow sound.*

● **Kneading:** *this uses just the same action as working on dough. Keeping your hands in a relaxed curve, pick up and roll the areas of soft tissue over the bone smoothly and rhythmically.*

● **Tapotement:** *a quick, light tapping movement made with the fingertips or clenched fists.*

● **Petrissage:** *a small, circular movement made with the balls of the thumbs or fingers, particularly effective on the back moving up from the base of the spine. Work only on the muscles on either side of the spine and not over the spine itself.*

Generally women are more responsive to touch than men, as their pleasure zones extend over more of the body. But everyone, everywhere finds the lips and genitals sexually sensitive, and stimulation of them may lead to an orgasm in some people.

Other sensitive areas include the breasts, buttocks and ear-lobes, the inner arms and legs and the nape of the neck; these are all very sensitive to touch and can be used to heighten sensuality during lovemaking.

Seducing your partner

It is almost a cliché that onlookers can tell whether a couple are in love by the way that they look at each other. And the couple who want to re-establish the "honeymoon" period later on in their relationship need look no farther than the lessons learned in the early days of their courtship. Then, they exchanged gifts, touched one another, held hands and made time for each other.

More importantly, their lovemaking was an unselfish act, where it was important to give sensations and not merely receive them.

After a few years of marriage, however, some couples find that day-to-day lovemaking lacks imagination and excitement. As they get to know each other and see their weaknesses for what they are, the result is often a reduction of the sex drive of both partners.

While there is no doubt that this is quite common there is no reason why an established couple cannot "engineer" a resurrection of the "honeymoon" effect with each other. There are all sorts of techniques which can help a couple rediscover former intimacy.

While familiarity can be said to breed contempt in many respects, it is a powerful weapon in seduction and the man or woman who knows their partner's body can give them maximum pleasure.

When planning to seduce your partner make a list of all the things you intend to do. Prepare one of his favorite meals (a cold supper will mean that you can eat at any time), then take time to decide what you will wear. The way you dress and look are the most obvious means of arousal. You might also consider hiring a sexy video from your local video shop the day before the event.

If your partner has sensitive breasts, spend some time leisurely licking, sucking and kissing her nipples.

This is his special evening so choose an outfit that will turn him on. Some men like women in stockings, garters and high-heeled shoes, others may prefer pure white, virginal underwear.

Make sure that whatever you choose is easy to remove. Many an ardent lover has lost control, or even his erection, while undoing rows of tiny buttons.

After a hard day's work, a fragrant bath is one of the most sensuous ways of relaxing, so run a hot bath for your partner.

When he arrives home, greet him at the door, then pour him his favourite drink. Escort him into the bathroom, undress him, help him into the bath and leave his drink within easy reach.

Remove your dress so you don't get it wet. This will let him see what you are wearing underneath, and should give him a hint of what is in store.

THE PSYCHOLOGY OF SEDUCTION

Seduction is like a game of chess – it's all a question of strategy, making the right moves, countermoves and, eventually, persuading one of the players to surrender. To achieve their goal the seducer must select the opportunity, choose an available partner, get them interested, sustain their interest, introduce the idea of sex and finally – and for the would-be seducer, more importantly – make them willing to have intercourse.

The way in which we seek out sexual partners is significant. For some people the thrill of seduction is all in the "chase" not the eventual conquest. They love wanting someone and pursuing them. Such lovers tend to be fairly self-confident. They believe in themselves, in their charms, and in their likelihood of success. Almost certainly, their confidence has an effect on the outcome.

Time and place

Two of the main points about starting a sexual encounter are the choice of the appropriate opportunity and the right person to approach.

Some situations are not suitable for sexual advances – the place is wrong, the time is wrong, sex is not "in the air". But those that are suitable have two features in common: they increase a person's arousal – although not necessarily sexual – and preferably both partners' excitement. For this reason, any occasion that increases physical excitement can be a useful preliminary to a sexual encounter. The most instinctive signs as to who looks interested and available come from a careful reading of body language – our unconscious or non-verbal cues.

While assessments about someone's availability can be instantaneous – based on snap judgements about very tiny clues such as gestures or tone of voice – taking availability to the point of seduction is a much more complex affair.

Sensitive seduction

It is important to be sensitive to the signs of rejection or acceptance as things progress. Seduction is a game that involves two people and no fixed rules. The only reassuring factor for the would-be seducer is that most people do enjoy having sex, so the odds are not all against you if you learn how to play the game.

Flirtation serves to keep the partner aroused and excited but has a side-benefit as well. It can be used to indicate that you are available to others also and consequently need fairly serious wooing.

Unavailability is a time-tested part of the seduction game. Being too readily available can be as off-putting as being completely unavailable.

The skin is highly sensitive. Try licking your partner all over to find his or her most pleasurable zones.

Tell him to close his eyes and then take his penis in your hands. Gently rub each testicle and run your hands up and down the penis shaft, gradually building up the speed.

Tell him how desirable you find him. All he has to do is lie back and enjoy it.

When he has reached orgasm, and recovered, dry him off and help him into a bathrobe – there will be no need for him to dress.

During the meal, spoil him thoroughly. Keep his wine glass full but don't overdo the drinks for either of you. Once you have finished the meal, take him by the hand to the living room and switch on the erotic video.

Nestle up to him as you both watch. When you find a scene particularly exciting, place your hand inside his robe and absent-mindedly rub his penis. If you feel aroused yourself, place his hand under your dress so that he can feel your clitoris. At this stage resist any temptation to make love.

When the video is finished, put on his favourite piece of music, dim the lights and take your clothes off in front of him. Take your time and move to the music. When they are all off, touch yourself and stimulate your clitoris. Move up to him and use your breasts to tease and tantalize him. Let him touch you briefly, moving away if he becomes too insistent. Move up behind him and kiss him. If he likes it, pay special attention to his ears.

Kissing, particularly on the ears, eyelashes and neck, can make all the difference between routine lovemaking and an explosion of sexual sensations.

Massage and oral sex may play an important part in your seduction, ensuring that you and your man will be highly aroused and ready to make love.

For many men, seducing a woman is a challenge, but when that woman is his long-term partner, it can bring even greater rewards.

A good warm-up to an evening of seduction is to do something non-sexual together in the afternoon. Go to a romantic movie, perhaps have a walk in the country together – all these work wonders for building up a level of intimacy between you as you unwind from the pressures of family and working life. The evening can begin with a candlelit dinner, either at a favourite

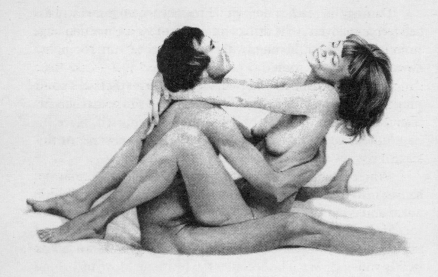

Sitting in each other's laps allows complete visual contact with both hands free to explore each other's bodies.

restaurant or at home – as long as you keep the preparation simple, to avoid spending hours in the kitchen! During the meal do not drink or eat too much. No one feels very seductive or, indeed, likes being seduced if they have drunk too much alcohol or have indigestion.

Be sensitive about what you eat. Certain foods are especially sexy to eat and a seductive man can make the most of this. Give your woman little tastes of your dishes and get her to do the same. Compliment her frequently.

Only now does the sexual side of the seduction begin but the job is already more than half done.

Dancing is really a form of foreplay when it takes place between two lovers, so if the restaurant you choose has dancing, so much the better. If you are dancing at home, turn the lights down low, put on some favourite music and just spend time dancing closely and being in one another's arms. Kiss a lot and snuggle into one another. Take it gently and do not go straight for intercourse.

Slowly undress her as you dance and compliment her on her beautiful body. Tell her how much it turns you on.

At this point, you will probably both want to retire to the bedroom. Remember to leave the heating on so that the room is warm and cosy.

If she is still has some clothes on, put on some music and ask her to strip for you. This should be a real turn-on for her as well as you.

Once she is undressed, you can present her with some sexy underwear, and ask her to try it on. Get her to model it as if she were in a fashion show. At this stage, resurrect any sexual games you played in your courtship days. Many couples remember them with affection.

If the seduction is going well, now is the time to take things a stage further.

Ask her to lie back with her legs apart and slowly caress her body from top to toe. Massage her, if she likes this, preferably using some scented massage oil. Tease her breasts and nipples and intimately massage all the parts of the body that you know excite her.

Now caress her vulva and clitoris so that she is highly aroused. All the time encourage her to do to you whatever you know she enjoys best. Remember that you are seducing her and enabling her to get the best out of it.

When she is highly aroused and well lubricated, insert first one finger and then two in her vagina and do whatever she likes best with them.

As the tension mounts she may welcome the introduction of a vibrator. Use it exactly as she wants and be guided by her body movements and unspoken messages as to what she best likes. If it is a new experience she may not know what is best, so you will have to experiment. Make this a highly enjoyable opportunity for both of you.

By now, she will be highly excited and will probably want you to make love to her.

Making love last longer

There are times in a sexual relationship when "quickie" sex can be exciting, and times when extended sexual intercourse is required.

Sensuous, prolonged intercourse can not only express an emotional commitment, it can also be far more physically satisfying than a quickie as both partners use all their love and skills to bring each other slowly to the peak of arousal.

Prolonged lovemaking is not an end in itself. The key is to share your thoughts and reactions and to be sensitive to your partner's needs and feelings.

Arousal can start long before sexual intercourse begins. It can be triggered by sensual kisses and caresses – and also by a wide range of other stimuli. Daydreaming about your lover or a fantasy figure, hearing a certain song, smelling an evocative scent, tasting a particular food or drink – can all put you in the mood for love.

If you want to prolong lovemaking, the best way is to extend not only the experience itself, but both the lead-up and follow-on to lovemaking.

Both men and women experience the same set of responses to sexual arousal.

The first stage is excitement. It can last from three minutes to many hours, and can be brought on by physical or emotional stimuli – kissing, touching or being touched by, or even just thinking about the object of your desires. The man's penis and nipples, and the woman's clitoris, breasts, nipples and labia, will engorge with blood.

In the second stage, or plateau, a flush spreads across their bodies and the engorged parts further swell and darken in colour. Once plateau is reached, orgasm usually follows after a half to three minutes. This is then followed by resolution, when tissue returns to its normal size and colour.

In women, orgasm can be followed by a return to the plateau phase and multiple orgasms, while men often need a period of at least twenty minutes to a day to recover before attempting further intercourse.

Several lovemaking positions help you maintain intercourse for long periods. All of them rely on giving the woman control of movement. Generally, the aim is to slow down the male, because while a woman can experience several orgasms and still enjoy intercourse, once the man has "come" that stage of lovemaking for him is over for a while.

If the man seems to be entering the plateau phase the woman can withdraw his penis from her vagina and stop him ejaculating by placing her thumb on his frenulum (the skin that holds his foreskin to his penis), with her index and middle finger on the other side of the penis, and gently squeezing.

FALLING IN LOVE

An enormous amount of information about a person has to be taken in before we develop the total trust needed to pursue true body intimacy. Courtship can be broken down into twelve steps, taking us from the first glimpse of the other person right the way through to the full mating act:

1 *The first and most crucial stage is simply looking. At first glance, we grade a person by size, shape, age, status or mood and the person is then subconsciously labelled.*

2 *"…and then our eyes met". For some of us, the meeting of our eyes is the most exciting stage for, in the other person's eyes, we can judge the response to our obvious interest.*

3 *The final non-physical stage is talking. Although the first few words may be on a trivial basis only, they give the first real indication of who we are.*

4 *First physical contact may be disguised as an act of support, protection or even guidance, or it may take place quickly and formally such as an introductory handshake. Once we are happy with holding hands, the relationship is declared openly.*

5 *As part of the courtship sequence, putting an arm around a woman's shoulders indicates a great advance from the days of tentative touching.*

6 *Hugging is a slight advance on the previous stage, but the difference is important. Men are reluctant to put their arms around each other, no matter how friendly they are, so the gesture becomes more overtly amorous.*

7 *Although a kiss on the cheek is a recognized and accepted social exchange, mouth-to-mouth kissing is a very intimate act that can lead to considerable sexual arousal.*

8 *Intimate kissing may be followed with a loving and lingering exploration of the face, neck, hair and hands – personal areas usually "out of bounds". For the first time we may use our hands to stimulate our partners sexually. Body contact and intimacy increase. We constantly test our trust in each other, trying optimistically to see how far we can go. The woman may allow the man to caress her breasts.*

9 *The most intimate form of pre-genital contact is when the woman allows the man to kiss and suck her breasts.*

10 *The next stage of intimate genital exploration and stimulation may continue for quite a long time before we are happy to have full sexual intercourse.*

11 *Moving from one stage to another has strengthened the bond of attachment, and the act of intercourse is the most intimate seal of friendship and love.*

12 *The maintenance of full emotional and physical intimacy between couples relies on a periodic return to all stages.*

Although partners have achieved the intimacy of lovemaking, they will still want, and need, to gaze into each other's eyes, talk or walk arm in arm along the street.

Side by side is the perfect position between the man on top and the woman on top. It keeps rhythm constant and saves wrenched muscles when you change position.

Alternatively the man may lie on his back with the woman astride either upright or lying full length on him, her legs outside or inside his. By pressing a hand on the small of her back in this position he stimulates the clitoris by compressing his penis between their bodies and allowing her freedom to move. He can caress her breasts and stroke her back and buttocks while she moves.

Another possibility is the "lap of luxury". Here, the man sits on a bed with his legs stretched out. His partner lowers herself into his lap, stretches her legs over his and, providing both partners are ready, takes his penis into her vagina.

She can wrap her legs around his back, or relax with her legs stretched out on either side of him.

Both can sit back, supporting themselves on their hands, or she can cling around his neck. He can also sit in her lap, with his legs over hers or wrapped around her back.

In a further variation, he can double his legs under so he is in a kneeling position, and she can lie back.

Afterplay

Given that intercourse is a very intimate experience, involving caring and sharing behaviour, it is hardly surprising that many couples feel exceptionally close after sex. But, equally, it is a fairy-tale fantasy to expect the average couple who have made love hundreds or perhaps thousands of times to be "lovey-dovey" every time after sex.

Because it arouses us and is a promise of what is to come, foreplay is bound to be more important and valued by the average couple than afterplay. As with so many things in life, the preparation and anticipation is often as good or even the best part. There will never be the same excitement and drive to

Choose a position where you are close enough to lean forward and kiss or caress your partner.

indulge in afterplay as there is to enjoy foreplay, and this is especially likely to be true for men who, on average, build up and resolve their sexual excitement more quickly than women.

Many women, however, whether consistently or inconsistently, don't reach orgasm during lovemaking. Some find themselves left high and dry when their partner has finished, because they feel it is somehow aggressive or wrong to tell their partner exactly what they like, where they like it and for how long.

Although some women have found various means to deal with their resulting frustration, if they were to tell their partner at the very moment of frustration, he would probably be only too eager to bring them to orgasm orally or manually – he might well be turned on by the prospect. Far from making the man feel vulnerable by admitting that his penis alone does not make her climax, a woman can add another dimension to sex by inviting her partner into her most intimate sexual life.

Many a man finds that in stimulating his partner he becomes re-aroused himself, and before he knows it he is making love again. In fact by some women, the first bout of lovemaking will often be regarded as a form of foreplay. They let their man make love to them quickly, possibly even roughly, and then start real foreplay with a view to having an orgasm both before and during sex.

This can be a particularly good way of coping with the man who comes too quickly. The couple make love so that the man is not so "trigger happy". He then spends time stimulating her and bringing her to orgasm while he is building up his next erection – which can often be harder and longer-lasting than before. This way of running things can work very well even for the man who does not come too quickly, especially at the start of the day when he is fresh and full of energy and vigour.

The golden rule for this type of restimulation is to do exactly what the woman most enjoys. This should be all the easier if the man has already come. He will have relieved his urgent need and can then concentrate entirely on the woman and her needs – and be totally unselfish in his lovemaking.

Every lovemaking experience should leave the couple satisfied, but not satiated. Ideally, we should all be so delighted with what we have experienced that we are looking forward to the next time with eager anticipation.

Sweet nothings and praising remarks are, in this context, a part of afterplay for this time – yet foreplay for the next time. It does not really matter if it is an hour later – or a week. It serves the same purpose.

We all take our partners for granted much of the time, but a few words of praise or genuine thanks for a lovely experience works wonders for a relationship, especially if one or the other feels low or sexually insecure.

Romance

Most of us understand romance to simply imply attentiveness, consideration and sensuality in a lover. It conjures up images of being in love when a relationship is new, fresh and exciting. The feelings it creates can be exquisitely insane or they may be agonizing and depressing.

In an ideal world, the climate would continue to be one where romantic lovemaking goes on all the time. For most of us, however, the practicalities of life mean that we cannot continue in that vein, but the effort made to restore some romance into our relationship from time to time will be amply awarded.

● **Practise the art of surprise.** *This need not be confined to gifts such as flowers or the occasional present – a meal at a restaurant, or just a specially cooked meal at home, can provide the right atmosphere for love. Candles, a favourite piece of music and a bottle of wine are a good idea for any pair of lovers and set the tone for the evening.*

● **Dress up from time to time.** *For a man, to see his partner dressed sexily is not just a turn-on, it is flattering as well. It does not have to be overtly sexy, but most men are susceptible to the idea that a woman has dressed specifically for him. For a woman, the fact that her man is making an effort to look good as well as praising her looks is a compliment.*

● **Act like lovers.** *Call one another on the telephone from time to time just to say "I love you". Show affection to each other in public. Even something as simple as taking your partner's hand can turn a walk into a romantic episode.*

● **Try to recapture the mood of your early courtship.** *This means finding more time to spend together. A short holiday away, even a day out or perhaps revisiting places that were particularly memorable can be a real tonic.*

● **Always remember birthdays and anniversaries.** *It is not so much the present that counts, but the fact that you remember. If possible, celebrate with a meal or an outing.*

● **Be more considerate.** *Try acting more selflessly: place a towel on the radiator before your partner has a bath, or make an unexpected morning cup of tea or coffee, for example.*

● **Share activities more.** *Domestic chores or shared hobbies and sports can be romantic in the right setting. Even painting and decorating can be a romantic experience between two lovers if the mood is right.*

● **Touch more.** *Holding hands or a touch on the shoulder does not need to have any sexual meaning and can often say "I love you" as fluently as words.*

● **Kiss and cuddle more.** *Do not be afraid to show each other affection – wherever you may be.*

● **Find new places to make love.** *Almost any room can be romantic for making love if the mood is right.*

A long warm bath together always acts as a wonderful prelude to lovemaking. And a romantic alternative to bathing together is for each partner to bathe the other, soaping them down gently, but leaving the most sensitive of their erogenous zones until last.

For the man who really wants to go to town, take lighted candles into the bathroom to provide sensual lighting. Prepare the room you intend to make love in beforehand, making sure that it is warm enough and perhaps leaving two glasses of wine by the bed.

Add fragrant oils to the bath as you run the water. Then take your partner into the bathroom and slowly undress her and wash her sensually all over, using plenty of lathery soap.

Most men love to be bathed too. Because your body will be such a turn-on for him, wear as little as possible – a pair of panties, and nothing else. Then undress him, pampering him like a baby. When he is lying in the bath, dangle your breasts over him for a moment, but do not let him touch them. Wash him all over; lather the soap over him, lingering erotically over his penis and his testicles, using soft, upward strokes.

The most romantic positions for making love are those that allow a couple to observe and communicate with each other.

Intimacy

Intimacy, like romance, can all too often go astray in a relationship.

To many men, in particular, intimacy is simply synonymous with sex. They have been taught to distrust or ignore the very emotions that make true intimacy possible, while many women have come to believe that their own emotional needs are much greater than those of their partners.

Fortunately, the type of alienation caused by these opposed attitudes appears to be on the decline. As society's stereotypes of male and female behaviour are becoming less rigid, both men and women are seeking to share their most intimate hopes, fears and dreams with their partners.

However, it is important to understand how and why a negative attitude towards intimacy develops in the first place, if we are going to achieve deeper and far more rewarding relationships.

Girls tend to be brought up to think of caring and intimacy as important and valued skills – but boys are generally taught to be more competitive and are judged on their attainment of goals. As a result, their emotional development is often likely to suffer.

This difference in childhood conditioning can mean that in an adult relationship between a man and a woman, it is the woman who does most of the "feeling", and who is much more aware of her own emotions than the man.

Clinical experiments show that difference of opinion as to what is "trivial" in a relationship can be the cause of so many rows and misunderstandings.

It is easy for a man who is embarrassed by his own emotions to dismiss "feelings" as unimportant – they may not seem very exciting or productive to him. Emotional needs often involve many grey areas. As a result, a lot of men cannot understand the value of emotions, because they cannot be measured.

According to the Hite Report, a major survey on sexual matters compiled in the 1960s and 1970s, many men saw sex not as an emotional matter, but as something they just "did".

Therefore, it is easy to see why many couples feel that their sex life could be improved. Whereas the man is trying to achieve physical goals in bed, the woman is looking for an emotional commitment from her partner.

When a woman says she wants a cuddle, that is often all she wants. To her partner, though, a cuddle can be seen as the first step in a trail which leads inevitably to intercourse.

Just wanting to be more open to feelings does not come naturally to many men – or indeed to all women. It is a skill that may have to be learned or regained. Intimacy is not easy to achieve, but the effort is worthwhile. It can lead to a deeper, more secure emotional relationship – and a vastly enhanced sex life.

Most of the suggestions here are for men, but women may need them too:

● **Try to understand yourself.** *Find time to be alone and work out how you arrived where you are in life. Think about your parents and their expectations of you and themselves. Look at* *your relationships with your brothers, sisters and childhood friends. How did your parents relate to one another, and are you simply repeating what they did? Do you really want to be like them?*

If you cannot find answers to these questions, try talking it over with your parents. If you also get on with your partner's parents, you could learn a great deal from talking to them too.

- **Talk with your partner.** *When you are ready, discuss your thoughts with your partner. He or she will be delighted that you are taking the trouble to discover the social and emotional background to your relationship. Be positive – do not attack each other's relatives, but try to find out why it is that you are unable to be as intimate as you or your partner would like. You are not necessarily trapped by your past – let your partner help to lead you out of it.*

- **Return to courtship.** *Remember how things were when you were trying to impress one another early on. Refrain from intercourse for a few weeks and regain the pleasures you used to experience from just being together, sending one another little notes, and phoning up to say that you love one another.*

- **Be prepared to take emotional risks.** *This is difficult for men, especially if it means revealing their vulnerable sides, because they are brought up to be "strong" – to know what to do both in and out of bed – and to lead the relationship.*

- **Share yourself with your partner.** *Talk about your fears and anxieties for the future, your job, the children, your sexual failings, and so on.*

● **Enjoy sex without intercourse.** *The next essential lesson is to separate sex from intimacy. The two may not go together, even in the best relationships. This means that the woman has to be more honest – particularly if she has been too inhibited to make her own sexual and emotional needs known. She cannot really blame her man for assuming that she wants intercourse when she cuddles up to him, if that is her usual signal.*

So the woman will have to learn to be more open and say "let's just cuddle up" or "let's make love", making it clear what she wants. Partners should never feel obliged to make love just because the other will take offense if they do not.

● **Develop a secret language.** *This way you will both know when physical closeness and intimacy can and should lead to intercourse. Teach one another the body language that gives the clues.*

● **Learn sensual massage.** *When you learn to give yourself fully and unconditionally to your partner during sensual massage, you will be laying the foundation for a degree of intimacy that you may never have thought possible.*

● **Give a good example:** *It is no good simply telling a man that being more intimate will be good for him – he has to see that it is worth it. Try taking the lead yourself. Cuddle up to him, and talk about your feelings. But if your man finds it difficult to express emotions, you should not overdo it yourself. Increasing intimacy brings an increase in caring, fewer rows, and a genuine desire to share life's pleasures and pains.*

CHAPTER 2

Pleasing your
Partner

Within any sexual relationship it is crucial that both partners concentrate not only on their own needs, but also on those of their partner. Finding new and different ways to please one another is the surest route to more fulfilled and exciting sex for both partners. Avoid getting into patterns of doing the same things, in the same order, every single time you make love. Keep the element of surprise, so that your partner never quite knows what to expect. And sometimes, you might decide that they deserve a special treat: a lovemaking session where you devote all your attention to giving them pleasure. Here are a few methods you might use.

Oral sex

Oral sex offers couples a blend of intimacy, trust, generosity and tenderness which is often very different from intercourse, yet can produce a high level of excitement and be deeply satisfying.

The kissing, licking and sucking of the female sex organs is called cunnilingus; similar mouth contact with the penis is called fellatio. Oral sex can be used as a complete sexual experience in itself with either or both partners being brought to orgasm; it can be the most practical way to make love, when contraception is unavailable, or after childbirth. More often, however, it is used as part of foreplay before genital intercourse takes place.

Oral sex has been practised for thousands of years. Cleopatra is said to have been a keen exponent and was called "Gaper" by the Greeks, and it is claimed that she fellated a hundred Roman soldiers in a single night.

Many people ask the question, is oral sex normal? Some find the thought of it distasteful, and men often feel it to be an

The simultaneous performing of fellatio and cunnilingus by two people to each other is known as soixante neuf, which is French for 69. The numerals represent two people lying curled together head to toe. It represents the supreme sexual sensation for some men, since they can give and receive pleasure simultaneously.

expression of homosexual tendencies. For healthy couples there is nothing perverted or unhygienic about oral sex. However, what any couple does in bed is what feels right for them both – not just one of them – at the same time.

For many women, cunnilingus is more exciting than intercourse. Lubrication is more readily provided by the mouth than the vagina and a man generally has more control over his mouth than his genitals.

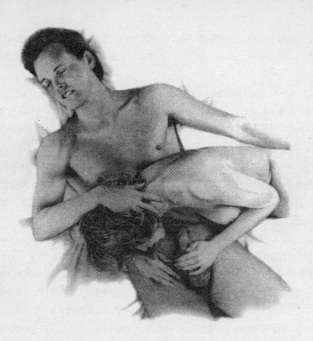

On certain occasions – such as after childbirth or when contraception is unavailable – oral sex can be the most practical way to make love. It produces a very different but equally high level of excitement and satisfaction.

The tongue, with its quick darting movements, is more tender than the skin of the fingers, and many women find that they have orgasms with oral stimulation even if they cannot do so in any other way.

For a man, fellatio is particularly exciting because it is so different from "conventional" intercourse. The lips, lined as they are with tissues similar to the vagina itself, feel like a new vagina. It also shows a high degree of intimacy and gives the man a chance to feel worshipped and play a passive role in bed, which he may welcome. At the same time, many women find that sucking a man's penis gives them intense sensations as well as him.

The only preparation necessary for oral sex is that both partners' sex organs be scrupulously clean. Then you can set about finding the positions that will give you both maximum pleasure.

A good position in which to fellate a man is for him to stand with his hands on his hips and his erect penis at your face level. You can then kneel before him, leaving your hands free to caress him and play with his testicles and anus.

Next, take his penis into the palm of your hand and, keeping your teeth out of the way, moisten the head with saliva. Then put the head of the penis into your mouth as far as is comfortable and move your head so that the penis goes in and out. The secret is to keep the teeth well out of the way at all times.

Once the man is sighing with pleasure, you can remove the penis from your mouth and run the tongue up and down the length of the organ and tease his testicles too. This drives most men wild, as does running and flicking the tongue over the frenulum, the little ridge of skin on the underside of the penis. After a few minutes' stimulation, stop and tease him by turning your attention elsewhere on his body – nibbling him, and kissing him all over.

Return to the penis and put it firmly in your mouth, squeezing the testicles gently at the same time if he likes it. Be guided by the man as to how much in-and-out movement he likes.

Swirl your tongue around the head of the penis so that you never lose contact with it. Do this clockwise and anti-clockwise. Dart your tongue into and out of the slit at the end of the penis and then continue swirling with the in-and-out movements. During all of this, make use of your hands too – ensure that you are giving your partner ecstatic sensations.

If you have decided not to take the semen into your mouth, as he hardens finally, take the penis out of your mouth and masturbate him so that he comes over your breasts. Do not try for vaginal penetration at this stage – it rarely works well if a man is just about to come.

Many couples do not take fellatio to the extent of ejaculation, but use it as a form of foreplay soon to be followed by intercourse.

The secret here is to get to know your man's unique signs of arrival at the pre-ejaculatory stage by watching for muscle tension, breathing changes, noises and any movements he makes as he is getting close to orgasm.

If necessary, squeeze the head of the penis between your finger and your thumb so as to cool him off for a while, until you are ready to be penetrated.

Pleasing women

Performing cunnilingus successfully is much more difficult than performing fellatio. Almost all men will become erect and come quickly with adequate oral sexual attention from a woman. For women things can be very different, mainly because individual women are so variable in their sexual needs and genital pleasures.

Almost all women enjoy oral sex that does not involve the genitals. They see it as romantic as it shows how much their man loves them. But when it comes to having their genitals kissed, licked and sucked, things can be rather different.

Some women see this as the most intimate thing a man can do to – and for – them and greatly value it as a sign of his total

If the man lies on his back with his partner sitting astride his head he can use his tongue to penetrate deep into her vagina. Many women find positions such as this one very arousing as they are free to move their body to enhance the sexual sensation.

love. Others think of their genitals as dirty and they cannot imagine anyone liking them, let alone wanting to kiss them.

At least some of these women can be persuaded to change their minds if, once they are aroused by clitoral or other stimulation, the man gently but firmly starts to kiss first around the vulval area and then the clitoris. Be careful not to tickle and make every effort to reproduce with your tongue what your partner usually does herself during masturbation and you will soon overcome her inhibitions.

Non-genital oral sex is a good starting point for a man looking to please his partner. Lie alongside her face to face. Kiss her face gently all over, not forgetting to suck her ear lobes, if she likes it. Kiss her mouth, lips and tongue and arouse her further by caressing her body with your hands. The beauty of almost all oral sex positions is that they leave the hands free to caress and arouse other parts of the woman's body.

Move down her body so that your head is on a level with her breasts. From here you can kiss her breasts, suck or blow on her nipples or put the whole of the breast into your mouth.

Run your tongue around her nipples and probe deeply with it over her breasts under the nipple and areola. Never bite, except very gently, and then not as she climaxes as you could do damage because she will be less sensitive to pain then. This will all be especially arousing to the breast-centred woman. It is a good position to use during a period or in pregnancy. Some women have an orgasm when this much time and care are taken to arouse the breasts.

Now move your mouth down onto her stomach. Lick and kiss her navel and run your mouth and lips all over her stomach, round and round in circles. Work down towards her vulva but, at this stage, do not touch it with either your hands or your mouth.

Lie in between your partner's feet, perhaps kneeling on the floor at the end of the bed. You can now kiss and suck her toes and feet. Some women so enjoy this that they nearly have a climax, even if the rest of the body is not touched. This is a good position for the woman who likes to caress her own breasts and/or clitoris while her partner caresses her feet orally.

Do not forget her hands. Get into any position you find comfortable and take her hand in yours or place it, palm upwards, on the bed. Run your tongue all over it and between the fingers and then suck her fingertips and kiss her palm, caressing it with your tongue.

Cunnilingus

Once aroused by non-genital oral contact, your partner will probably be very receptive to genital oral contact. This is the best time to try, but go gently. The best position is probably with your partner lying flat on her back with her legs apart. You should then lie in between her legs, so that you can easily lick, kiss and suck any part of her genitals. Place a pillow or two (depending on how saggy your bed is) under her hips. This will raise the vagina and bring it into a good position. This position is good for licking and kissing the clitoris but less so for putting the tongue in the vagina or caressing the perineum or anus.

A good variation is for the woman to lie in the same way, but for the man to turn round to face her feet. He now has his genitals over her face and she can suck and kiss his penis if that is what they both enjoy. If not, he can angle his body so that she does not have his genitals in her face.

By supporting himself on his elbows, he can kiss her vulva and clitoris very easily. The main precaution here is to be sure not to put too much weight on the woman's body. In this position the man can reach under his partner's thighs, pull them apart, and open the outer lips so as to give the best access for oral sex. The skilful man can even insert the fingers of one hand (or both) into the vagina while kissing the clitoris and vulval area. This is also an excellent position for the couple who like to use a dildo or vibrator in the woman's vagina while she is being caressed orally. The man can watch it going in and out and the woman's hands are free to caress him and she can suck his penis if she wants to.

Or the woman could lie with her hips on the edge of the bed and her feet flat on the floor. The man then kneels between her

A fun position for the really adventurous and supple couple. The woman lies with her legs in the air, taking most of her weight on her shoulders and gripping her partner's legs for support. He leans over, legs slightly bent, and kisses or licks her vulval area and her perineum.

thighs and kisses and rubs her vulva and clitoris. As she becomes more excited the woman can pull her thighs back to her chest, but still keeping them apart so that he has access to her open vulva. This is an exceptionally good position for the woman who likes her man to insert his tongue into her vagina.

Another possibility is for the man to lie flat on his back as the woman kneels over his chest and gives him her vulva to kiss. She can orally caress his penis.

The man may choose to kneel down in front of the woman who stands, feet wide apart. He can now lick, kiss and suck her vulva underneath. This can be fun if the woman is fully dressed, apart from her panties. He is then covered by her skirt.

Finally, for the adventurous couple, the man may lie down on his back on the bed or the floor with his knees drawn up. The woman now kneels over his face, legs wide apart, facing him with her vulva in his mouth. She then leans backwards onto his knees and relaxes with her head over his knees. The vulva is exceptionally wide open and the man can push his tongue into her vagina and caress her vulva and clitoris with his mouth.

Masturbation

Your body is a sensitive instrument, capable of giving you and your partner great pleasure. By exploring your feelings and responses yourself you can both gain an intimate knowledge of how to intensify that pleasure still further.

Unfortunately the term "masturbation" for most of us, is not only an embarrassing word but a taboo subject – something we never discuss, not even with our partner or our closest friends. Sadly masturbation is often seen as a second-rate

SHAPING SENSUALITY

Sexuality can be viewed as a seeking of pleasure. It is not just a matter of growth and of physiological differences between men and women. All our senses – touch, smell, taste, vision and hearing – are involved.

A newborn baby is sexually immature but is by no means asexual. The senses of touch, taste and smell are surprisingly developed. From the moment of birth, comfort is derived from feeding, being cuddled and reassuring sights and sounds. The baby's most immediate needs are for food, and so the earliest pleasures are mainly attached to the relief of hunger.

Suckling provides food, and reassures the infant that his cries will summon help and that his needs will be satisfied. If all goes well at this stage, the baby develops its first trusting relationship with another human being, laying the foundation-stone for the success of future relationships as sexual adults.

It has been found that babies who are not loved and cuddled by either parent are less sexually happy as adults.

Babies' needs

In one well-documented series of experiments carried out in the United States, rhesus monkeys were separated from their mothers at birth and were placed with surrogate "mothers" made of wire. These artificial mothers had teats which delivered milk and some were covered in soft, terry towelling material.

The research showed that when frightened, the monkeys turned to the towel-covered "mothers" for comfort, clearly preferring their softness against their skin. But more significantly, deprived of normal mother/baby stimulation, none of the monkeys was able to function sexually when it reached maturity.

Studies show that babies derive sexual pleasure from their bodies from very early on. A baby boy on discovering his penis will play with it, rubbing it gently, from about two months, and baby girls will also play with themselves from similarly early on.

These early explorations are normal and healthy, and they could be said to be essential. Sexual fulfilment as adults is all about pleasure, and it would be wrong to reprimand a small child for rubbing himself simply because it causes his parents embarrassment.

He will almost certainly grow out of it but will have gained knowledge and ease with his body which will be important to him later. In the majority of cases, children who are repressed by their parents have enormous problems when they are older and achieve sexual maturity.

Freudian theory

Sigmund Freud, the psychoanalyst, divided a child's development into three different stages – oral, anal and genital. He felt that children derived their first pleasures orally, through sucking, then became concerned with excretion, in the toilet-training phase, and finally progressed to the genital stage. He said that it is only when oral needs have been satisfied without hours of crying, and toilet-training effected with the minimum of pressure and anxiety that the sexually happy adult could be said to have been born.

substitute for sex. Of course it can be, but it is also an alternative to full intercourse as well as a useful learning tool, and it can be incorporated into your lovemaking to increase the pleasure and intimacy.

There are probably more old wives' tales about masturbation than any other area of sexual activity. Little boys are told that it will lead to blindness, hair on the palms of the hands, impotence – the list goes on for ever. Little girls are given the impression that to acknowledge their sexuality is somehow "not nice", that touching themselves "down there" will spoil them for their husbands or turn them into sex addicts.

It doesn't do anything of the kind, of course, but over the years these false claims have given masturbation an extremely poor press. Even today, most people secretly feel that there is something "wrong" about masturbation.

The fact is that almost all men and women masturbate from time to time. It is said that 90 per cent of men admit to masturbating and the other 10 per cent are liars. Some people – including about a third of all women – say that they cannot remember a time in their lives when they have not masturbated. Others date its beginnings from puberty, while yet others seem to start when they are in a permanent relationship. But most of us begin at a very young age.

Almost all babies play with their genitals, and most parents are aware that their toddlers sometimes masturbate, although not to adult orgasm.

It is often thought that masturbation is less common among females than among males, but this is partly because it is easier for male children to find their sex organs and thus discover that playing with them is fun. Female masturbation is also more difficult to define.

With men, masturbation involves direct stimulation of the penis and generally ends in ejaculation. But for women, it is more complex. Every woman has her own preferences and these may differ every time. Almost any part of the female body can be a source of arousal and orgasm, and different kinds of caressing on different areas can give an infinite range of sensations – sensual as well as sexual and comforting as well as exciting.

There are also social reasons why some women do not practice obvious masturbation, but stimulate themselves in less apparent ways. Our parents tend to be much more tolerant of small boys holding their penises than of small girls touching themselves. However, by finding these "no-hands" methods of stimulating themselves, girls can pretend they are not doing it.

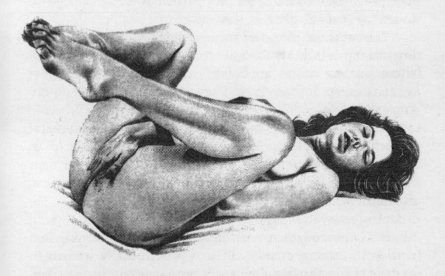

The considerate and loving man can learn how best to please his partner by watching how she uses her own hands to bring herself to orgasm.

Some little girls will masturbate while sitting on their heels or riding their bicycles. It can also be incorporated into permissible contact, such as washing in the bath or using the spray from the shower. In twenty years' clinical experience, one expert collected over one hundred examples of indirect ways in which women masturbate.

All of us would like to get more out of sex because of the pleasure it gives us, and to do so we have to know our own responses and what we like or do not like.

Pleasure is a combination of emotion and physical sensations, and this combination is different for each individual. The inhibitions we all feel about discussing what gives us sexual pleasure make it very difficult for us to say to our partner, "I don't like this, this does nothing for me", particularly if we can't go on to say, " . . . but I do like this, this sensation is wonderful".

It is much easier to steer your partner away from patterns of lovemaking which don't suit you if you can suggest an alternative to what they are doing "wrong". But don't forget that we can't expect anyone else to know what suits us if we do not know ourselves.

Touching our own bodies allows us to explore physical sensations in complete privacy and at our own speed. It helps us to become comfortable with our own bodies, to discover their immense capacity for sensual pleasure – a pleasure which we can then share with our lovers.

And as well as helping to learn about your own physical responses, masturbation is an important part of learning that your body belongs first of all to yourself. Many women in particular feel that their partners automatically have certain rights and feel very uncomfortable about saying yes or no to sex, which can put a great deal of pressure on the relationship.

Most men masturbate by stimulating the head of the penis with their fingers and moving their hand up and down in a pumping action.

Many men will pause at some stage to allow their arousal to build up, so that the pleasure is prolonged and the orgasm more intense. A variation on purely manual stimulation is to simulate sex by lying face down with the penis between the flat of the hand and the mattress and making thrusting movements.

The most usual way for women to masturbate is to lie on their backs and use one hand to stimulate the vulva. A few women will concentrate only on the vagina itself, inserting fingers or any roughly penis-shaped object, but most prefer clitoral stimulation. A common combination of movements might be to begin with light stroking of the pubis, with the fingers passing on either side of the clitoris on top of the outer lips. The pressure might then increase and the fingers close to squeeze the clitoris between them.

Direct clitoral stimulation can be made with a single finger, often the middle finger, which is used to press the clitoris against the pubic bone. The pressure could be a direct pulsing onto the bone or a rubbing movement which increases in speed.

But this is only part of the range of stimulation open to women; stroking the inner thighs, lower stomach, breasts and nipples can all be exciting. Some women find that pinching the nipples and then holding the pinch produces a slowly increasing surge of pleasure, which helps them achieve orgasm.

It is often thought that women masturbate by inserting dildos and vibrators into their vagina, and that the bigger they are, the better. In fact, most women find this uncomfortable rather than arousing. Vibrators and dildos are mostly used to stimulate the clitoris, the vaginal lips or nipples, and women often do not insert anything inside the vagina. If they do, it is likely to be something less rigid than the hard plastic of most vibrators.

They may also enjoy inserting something smaller into the anus and find that this intensifies their orgasm. Great care should always be taken, though, as the rectal lining is very delicate and it is easy to spread germs from the bowel to the vagina. Anything inserted should be clean and well lubricated.

Running water is very popular for clitoral stimulation. A jet of warm water from a showerhead, bidet or faucet directed over the clitoris is highly exciting for most women and can produce an intense orgasm.

Most women "mix and match" different kinds of stimulation on different parts of their body, depending on how they feel. Women can also have multiple orgasms during a single session, while men will usually stop masturbating after they have ejaculated.

As a shared activity masturbation can be one of the most exciting and stimulating ways a couple can learn about each other's needs and desires. By observing how your partner masturbates you can learn to bring them to orgasm in the ways they like best.

Set the scene, perhaps by taking a bath or shower together, then massage each other lovingly as you become aroused. Then, with the lights down low, ask your partner to masturbate, while you hold or caress them.

The man watching his partner should note the following:

● *her body and leg position*

When you both feel
confident about
giving each other
pleasure individually,
it's time to try it
together.

what she does with both her hands

where she puts her fingers to stimulate her vulva or clitoris

The type, size and pressure of her hand movements, as these vary considerably in most women from stage to stage in their arousal sequence

● *whether or not she puts fingers into her vagina*

if she stops stimulating herself and then restarts

what facial, breast, vulval, clitoral and skin changes occur

if she makes any noises or cries out during orgasm

what she actually does at the moment of climax

what changes occur as she calms down.

Setting the scene in the same way, the woman should observe her partner as he masturbates, noting:

the exact position of his hand

the location of his fingers on his penis

how much pressure he uses

the rate, extent and type of movement

● *the changes that occur in the penis, scrotum and testes*

● *other bodily changes, including his breathing rate, facial expression, muscle contractions, sweating and so on*

● *any other areas of the body he stimulates, for example his anus, the "root" of his penis or his testes*

● *the amount of pre-ejaculatory secretion*

● *the size and force of the initial spurt of semen and the number, speed and force of further spurts*

● *the stage at which he stops stimulating himself*

● *the changes that occur as he calms down.*

Once you are at ease with watching each other masturbate and have learned all you can, you can make the most of mutual masturbation. No one knows by magic, or even after simply watching, how to stimulate their partner to orgasm. Even the most experienced man will have more to learn about his partner, if only because the needs of women in this respect are so variable compared to those of men.

No two individuals masturbate in the same way. This means that the "teacher" must tell the "pupil" exactly what he or she likes best. So make sure that you give specific, practical instructions – not just woolly generalizations. Put your partner's hands and fingers where you want them, and do not be shy or afraid to say what does not feel good.

TELL-TALE KISSES

Just as you can tell a lot about a person by their style of dress, their home and the way they speak, so you can also learn a good deal about them by the way they kiss:

❤ *Closed-eyed kissers can be true romantics at heart, falling in love as often as other couples quarrel, despite knowing that the ending may be unhappy.*

❤ *Open-eyed kissers can be realists, but they are also fairly safe to fall in love with. Once they meet the partner of their dreams, they are likely to be eternally faithful.*

❤ *Kissers who begin with a short peck followed by another slightly longer one, before joining lips, hide a passionate and sensual nature behind that slow build-up. They are not the sort of people who commit themselves quickly, but once a decision is made, they stick to it.*

❤ *Lovers who kiss with their mouths closed may have closed minds as well. Closed lips signal a taker not a giver.*

❤ *Puckered-lipped kisses are very similar to closed-lipped. While the act of puckering seems to say come on, the reality of kissing with puckered lips reveals a definite rejection. These kissers have a tendency to want everything their own way in kissing and in life.*

❤ *The vacuum kiss occurs when two people open their mouths and, instead of caressing and exploring, suck inwards as though trying to draw air. Soon, the mouths adhere so* tightly together that there is pain instead of pleasure. Vacuum kissers are often quite violent personalities who like to rush their partners into lovemaking rather than let them decide for themselves. They may also have a jealous disposition.

❤ French kissers are gentle versions of vacuum kissers, letting their tongues explore at leisure and enjoy. They can make wonderful friends as well as lovers. Just as their deep kisses ensure that they can taste all their lovers' feelings, so they share all their friends' sufferings and joys too. They crave intimacy with another person to the extent that they sometimes leave themselves open to disappointment. They have no inhibitions about letting other people know what they want, and to this end can be surprisingly outspoken.

❤ Ear nibblers show something other than a knowledge of the body's erogenous zones. Ear nibbling can be a way for shy people to avoid direct confrontation. Their self-consciousness is evident in their unwillingness to put themselves forward until they are confident that they have something worthwhile to contribute.

❤ It is important, however, to differentiate between nibblers and biters, especially since a nibble can easily turn into a bite. Persistent love-bite kissers are human graffiti artists, leaving their mark wherever they go and on whoever they go with. A love-bite may be an owner's brand as much as a sign of passion.

After a certain amount of experience with one another, you will find that talk becomes unnecessary and communication will continue through hand movements, grunts, moans and other appreciative noises. Use these sessions to learn when it is time to stop talking and leave your partner to become abandoned to his or her individual erotic thoughts, fantasies and feelings.

Be aware of the whole body – many people enjoy having things done to them that do not involve their genitals. Many women, for example, like their breasts or nipples to be caressed or kissed and many men like to have their back stroked, their nipples stimulated or their buttocks squeezed. Simply concentrating on the penis or clitoris may not be enough and may actually desensitize your partner.

Once you have settled down into your chosen position you should aim to give your partner as much pleasure as possible. And bear in mind that most people like predictability in masturbation and this is especially true of women. Many women say that they achieve their best orgasms whenever their man does exactly what they like the best every time.

Breasts and sex

In the Western world women are probably more obsessed with their breasts than ever before. In an age when women are eroding men's traditional roles, breasts seem to be the one remaining sexual difference.

Since the 1940s Hollywood era of film stars, boys have grown up with the idea that big breasts are sexy. The combination of looks, plus a general belief that big-breasted women are more interested in sex, attracts men to such women.

However, it seems that society's ideal breast image is slowly changing. While the ideal woman, as portrayed by the modern media, tends to be slim and not very curvy, there is an increasing acceptance of women's different shapes and sizes, including their breasts.

But fashion, advertising and male conditioning all contrive to make women increasingly breast-conscious, and this leads some women to see the role of their breasts as exclusively sexual.

This means that when things go wrong (they find a lump, for example) they are too terrified to go to a doctor in case it means that their main sexual symbol will have to be removed. On average most women with a lump in their breasts wait six months before seeking medical help.

The size of a woman's breasts and nipples has no bearing on how responsive they are sexually. Some women have exquisitely sensitive nipples which when stimulated bring them to orgasm within seconds, while other women's nipples are almost totally unresponsive.

Generally, mouth stimulation (sucking and gentle licking) produces faster nipple erection than just stimulation with the fingers.

During sexual arousal, the first sign that anything is happening is that the nipples become erect. This comes about as the tiny, smooth muscles in them contract.

Touching by the woman herself, or by her partner, usually hastens erection but this is not essential. The nipples increase in length and diameter as the woman becomes more excited and blood collects in and around them. This mechanism is rather like that which causes a penis to become erect.

Once the nipples are erect, the patterns of veins on the breasts often become more marked and the breasts begin to swell. This swelling is most obvious in women who have not breastfed. Later on in this excitement phase, the areolae swell and, in light-skinned women, the breasts may become covered with a faint red flush or measle-like rash.

The next stage of sexual arousal is known as the plateau phase. During this, the breasts swell more and the areolae especially become swollen.

At orgasm itself, women experience all kinds of sensations, some of which are related to their breasts. Some women like their breasts or nipples to be held very hard or even squeezed as they have an orgasm. Because the intensity of the other changes to the body is so great, it is easy for a man to damage his partner's breasts or nipples as she comes because she is much less sensitive to pain.

It makes sense to draw a line between what a couple finds pleasant and stimulating and what seems to cause damage. This

During sex, the nipples swell and pleasure is heightened. The man should use his mouth to caress his partner's breasts. Go round the nipple with your tongue, gently sucking and nibbling.

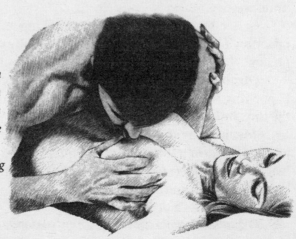

is particularly true of biting the breast or nipples during intercourse so care is called for.

Once orgasm is over, the first thing that happens is that the
areolae return to normal. This marks the onset of the final phase
of the sexual arousal cycle – the resolution phase. The change in
the areolae gives the impression that the nipples are becoming
erect again, but this is not so. They are simply more visible as the
surrounding areas begin to subside.

At this stage many women do not want their breasts
touched, because they are tender or so pleasantly "satisfied" that
further stimulation is positively unpleasant.

Almost all women say that they like their breasts to play
some part in their lovemaking. However, it is an unfortunate fact
that many men do not pay enough attention to their partners'
breasts.

There are a number of things that a man can do to his
partner's breasts to increase her pleasure – both in foreplay and
during intercourse.

● *Watch her as she masturbates. Take note of how she plays with
her breasts and at what stage. Does the pressure increase as she
approaches orgasm? What seems to stimulate her most?*

● *Be gentle. Use the palm of your hand to brush lightly over her
breasts. There are also a number of oils available – although
baby oil is as good as any – that can be gently massaged into
them. Go slowly around one breast at a time, leaving the nipples
until last.*

● *Be guided by what she likes. Her nipples may become so
sensitive that she finds direct stimulation painful.*

EMOTIONS

However much we try to hide our emotions, our voice, facial expressions, gestures and body posture all work together to reveal our true feelings.

Many of our expressions and gestures are natural responses and not part of a learning process and their meaning is universal across all human cultures. This is demonstrated by the fact that newborn babies and children born blind still exhibit them – with smiles, for example.

The smile is of unique importance to humans. Human babies, unlike other animals, need to "woo" their mothers to stay by their side and so the smile serves to bond mother and baby together. Later, our repertoire expands and we have smiles of greeting, sympathy and apology, plus the smile of happiness.

There are, however, some emotional expressions that are learned. Nodding, winking and shaking the head, for example, have different meanings in different cultures and so cannot be determined by instinct.

Negative emotions

The function of weeping tears is more mysterious. Tears are produced by lachrymal glands situated above the eye, and their normal function is to wash out grit and protect the eye from infection before draining out through the nose.

Increased activity in the sympathetic nervous system in response to pain, distress or unhappiness increases the flow of tears markedly, and when the drainage is overloaded, or blocked by facial contortion, they well up and roll down the face. Humans mostly use tears to gain attention and sympathy, especially when a silent signal of emotion is needed, although they may also be produced as a result of joy, laughter or sudden relief from tension.

Worry or anxiety are usually displayed by nervous movements such as blinking, fidgeting, scratching the head, biting nails and pacing up and down.

For some people, however, tension shows up in muscular rigidity with clenched jaw and staring eyes, as though they are trying to control or "hold back" their anxiety. Relaxation, naturally enough, is the opposite of these two tension patterns – the complete lack of muscle tension which amounts to preparation for doing nothing.

The words that people use are sometimes less significant than the manner of their delivery. Apart from body and facial gestures, the measurable characteristics of speech, such as volume, pitch, tone and speed, carry information about the emotional state and true attitudes of the speaker.

People who talk in loud voices are not necessarily dominant. They may have learned that they have to speak up or else nobody else will listen to them. A quiet, intense voice is often more threatening because it implies barely controlled rage.

Fear is usually expressed in variable pitch and volume and by an upward inflection at the end of sentences. A breathy, resonant tone sounds emotional and sexy, while thin sound is more formal and communicative, being relatively free of "noise".

Speed of delivery is also significant. Fast talkers usually come across as intelligent, well-informed, confident and energetic; although in some circumstances, the same people may appear nervous, especially if they stammer and make a lot of errors.

As an added
variation, you can try
using food or wine
and eating or
drinking them off
your partner's breasts.
Some women find
something intensely
erotic about having
their breasts bathed
in liquid.

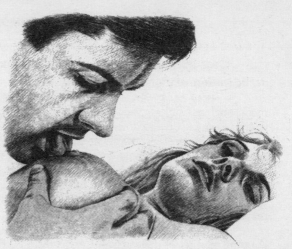

● *Be imaginative. Use other parts of her body to tease and excite her.*

● *Use your mouth together with your hands. Caress her elsewhere on her body, or caress the other breast as well. As an added variation you can try using food or wine and eating and drinking them off her breasts.*

● *Use your penis. Tease and excite her by touching her with your penis, but do not ejaculate unless that is what she wants. Use it to trace a path around each breast.*

There a few bigger turn-ons for a man than when his partner uses her body to tease and excite him. For the woman, this can be both exciting and flattering as she finds that she can use her breasts to bring her bring her partner to a pitch of arousal – perhaps even to orgasm.

The breasts can be used on their own, or in conjunction with the rest of a woman's body, to arouse her partner just about anywhere. Here the woman can take an active role and allow the man to lie back and enjoy what she is doing:

● *Trace a path with one, or both, of your breasts. Cover the whole length of his body, avoiding only his genitals at this stage. Use your nipples to trace a light fluttering path and alternate this with pressing your breasts flat against your body.*

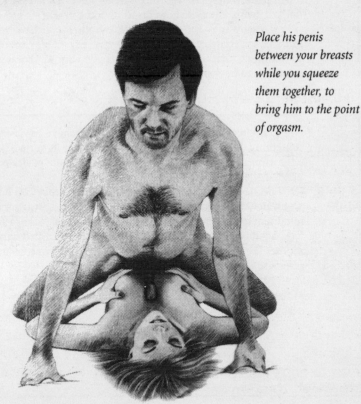

Place his penis between your breasts while you squeeze them together, to bring him to the point of orgasm.

TAKE THE INITIATIVE

In a well-balanced sexual relationship the question of who takes the initiative is rarely an issue.

Particularly in the sexually intense early days of a relationship, when desire levels run high, you are often so turned on by each other that neither ever has to make an obvious initiating move.

Later, when the relationship is more established a different pattern may emerge: one partner never initiates sex, or one partner is more likely to do so than the other.

Usually it is the one with the higher sex drive who initiates sex more often, but not always. Even today there is sometimes a tacit understanding between couples that it is a man's job to be the sexual aggressor.

Passivity

Often women have been brought up to believe that sex is something dirty, and they deny the strength of their own sexual feelings, preferring to believe that they only participate because their partner wants them to.

Some men are sexually passive because they too have ambivalent feelings about sex. Perhaps religious instruction told them it was wrong, so they bury their sexual feelings and feel bad about open displays of lust. Or they identified with a mother dominated by a brutish father and as a consequence associate sex with dominance.

Many men find it erotic when a woman takes the initiative in an obvious way – by telling him openly she desires him and wants to have sex, or simply by starting to arouse him in a way she knows he likes.

Some men, however, feel threatened by a woman who behaves like this. Sometimes it is because they fear that they will not be able to satisfy a frankly sexual and enthusiastic woman, or because they have picked up the notion that women who enjoy their sexuality aren't "nice".

Changing roles

When either partner always takes the initiative there is a danger that sex becomes unsatisfactory for both of you. The passive partner ends up in the position of turning down advances. He or she becomes suspicious of all displays of affection and never kissed or hugs spontaneously in case his or her partner "gets ideas". Denied affection as well as sex, the initiator feels angry and frustrated, and problems are likely to crop up.

If the dynamics of a sexual relationship are expected to suddenly switch, the passive partner, when asked to perform aggressively, may well freeze. It is the fear of not being able to fulfil the new role properly, fear of always having to act in this new way or shyness which can cause this. It isn't that the partner is incapable of changing roles, but that the sexual language isn't familiar.

One or both of you may feel that one partner is taking the initiative most or all of the time and that this is having a bad effect on your relationship. Try to talk about why this is happening. The shy and passive partner may need to be reassured that the other one would welcome a more active approach from them. Choose a time and place that is comfortable for you both and give it a try!

● *Turn him over. Do the same over his back, using your nipples to trace a path over and between his buttocks.*

● *Use your nipples to tease his eyes, mouth and ears. Tease him by not letting him take the nipple into his mouth before finally giving in. Remember you are in control and part of the turn-on for the man will be in seeing what you are doing. Keep your hands busy elsewhere if you want to. If he wants to touch your breasts as you do this, let him, but be sure that you stay in control.*

● *Tease his breasts with yours. Some men have extremely sensitive nipples, others do not. If your man does, try putting some saliva – his or your own – onto your breasts and rub them sensuously against his nipples.*

Lovemaking "extras"

Everyone likes to be sexually pampered from time to time. Yet probably the greatest single complaint that women have about men, sexually, is that their partners are not prepared to give enough time to them.

Women are much more variable in their approach to sex and what turns them on than men, and as sexual beings they are also far superior. Larger areas of their bodies are sexually responsive, and many types of stimulation can be arousing and bring them to one or more orgasms.

So, given the variable nature of a woman's sexuality, it is understandable that many men fail to explore their woman's particular sexual needs. A man tends to be sexually aroused quite simply and quickly – after he achieves an erection, he wants to move towards orgasm as swiftly as possible. But there are physiological reasons why this is not the case for a woman.

In her unaroused state the vagina remains tightly closed. Only after she has been caressed and cuddled and given an adequate amount of love play do the muscles of the vagina open and its walls start to pour out lubricating fluid. Only then does intercourse become easy and pleasant.

Pleasing a woman is not simply a matter of sexual technique. The man should understand and respond to what his partner wants, not because he feels that this is what is required, but because he is sensitive to her needs. He needs to be attentive, tender and loving, and he should ask what his partner wants and listen to her.

A vital step towards pleasing a woman is to take a look at yourself and how you treat her and try and improve on it. Then take every opportunity to show your love for her.

Forget preconceptions about what a man should or should not do. By putting her needs above your own you will not only please her but improve your own sex life as well.

See how you could improve on your personal appearance and behaviour and try behaving as you would if you had just started to go out with each other.

Probably the most common and most enjoyable form of manual stimulation for women is caressing the vulva.

Start at the tops of her thighs and work all around the vulva, gently stroking her lower tummy, her thighs and her perineum (the part between the anus and the genitals). Then slowly work closer towards the clitoris and inner part of the vulva itself. Run your fingers up and down the insides and outsides of the outer lips. Squeeze them gently between finger and thumb. Caress the areas on either side of the clitoris in the way she likes best.

Next, use your fingers to stretch her vaginal opening. Ensure that your fingers are well lubricated with her secretions or your saliva and insert first one, and then two fingertips into the vaginal opening. Run them around the opening, not going deeply inside at first. Massage the opening quite firmly and slowly, as she becomes excited. Insert more fingers until she says enough and then rotate your whole hand. She may well now want your fingers pushed deeply inside and held there or worked in and out as if they were a penis thrusting.

Once your fingers are inside her vagina, you can feel for the cervix and the G spot, both of which can give some women exquisite pleasure.

Women's genital sensations

In terms of what they enjoy having done to their cervix, women vary greatly, not least according to the time of their menstrual cycle. Some women find any form of cervical caress unpleasant or even painful while others are greatly aroused by it. It is up to each man to experiment with his partner, at different times of the month, to see what best suits her. But always be cautious and do not do anything that could hurt or damage the cervix.

Finding the G spot can be difficult at first. Let your partner lie face down with a pillow under her hips and, with your hand palm downwards, insert two fingers along the front wall of her vagina. About one third of the way down from the cervix to the vaginal opening is an area that she will most likely enjoy having stimulated. Stroke this and see what her reaction is. Keep on stroking and massaging this area until she says she has had enough or she climaxes. Not all women find this enjoyable or even arousing, so be guided, as always, by what she says.

In addition to kissing, licking and sucking the whole vulval area, some sort of food may be spread over it, then licked off. Cream is nice, as is yogurt or even a little honey. For extra fun – and only if you both agree – put a banana or confectionery bar gently into her vagina and eat it out of her, being sure to lick off all the remains of the food before going further with your lovemaking.

Other occasional lovemaking "extras" might include:

● *your partner on her stomach or back, while you rub your body against her bottom and vulva to arouse her*

● *your leg positioned between her thighs, rubbing her vulva*

● *sitting her on your lap and giving her a "horse ride" as you stimulate her bottom and vulva with your body*

"Extras" for men

There are few things that turn men on more than an inventive woman in bed. If the man is usually the one to initiate sex, it comes as a delight to have the woman take the initiative because it shows him that she has needs herself and that she is prepared to "use" his body to satisfy them. This can have a powerful effect on most men.

A man likes to have his penis caressed in the way that he does it when he masturbates, so it is essential that you watch him masturbate so that you will know exactly what he likes most.

When caressing or masturbating him, always be sure to reproduce the main things that you have learned, even if you add some refinements of your own.

Remember that it is not just the penis shaft that men enjoy having handled and caressed. Try rubbing the root of the penis firmly, perhaps while stimulating the rest of it in some other way. The area between the testicles and anus and the perineum are also very sensitive in some men and they might like to have it stimulated in several ways.

After pleasuring the penis, turn your attention to his testicles. Begin by cupping them in your hands and gently squeezing them. How much pressure a man enjoys can only be discovered by trial and error. He will probably enjoy starting off with gentle but firm pressure, and as he becomes more aroused he may want you to squeeze harder.

Many men enjoy some anal stimulation. Popular variations include running a finger around the anal area. Placing a finger tip just inside the anus can be highly arousing for some men and most others enjoy having their prostate glands stimulated.

Any form of anal activity means that the area should be well washed before you start. Even this can be fun if you have a shower together. You must ensure that your finger is well lubricated otherwise it will be uncomfortable and not in the least arousing.

What a loving and adventurous couple can do with the penis is almost limitless. Here are just some ideas that many couples may find arousing or simply fun.

Take a photograph of it in various states of erection. This is best done with a Polaroid camera because many, if not most, processing houses have a ban on erect penises. Some women enjoy decorating the man's penis with flowers or whipped cream.

Rings placed around the base of the penis have been in use for centuries. Almost all men obtain a much harder and bigger erection and using them makes the veins stand out greatly. All of these changes can be highly exciting to some women because they give a novel feel to an otherwise familiar penis.

The danger with any form of ring is that it can obstruct the return of blood from the penis so severely that it might not allow the penis to become flaccid again. Always use rings specially made for the purpose – they are available in adult stores and by mail order. Never use metal rings of any kind. If the worst comes to the worst, and it rarely does, a rubber or latex ring can be cut off by a doctor, but a metal ring creates real problems.

There are a number of points of caution to be aware of when trying to please your man:

Never blow down a man's penis. This could cause an embolism and force infectious organisms into the bladder and these could cause one of a variety of urinary infections.

Never put anything into the urinary passage. Some men, especially when highly aroused, want you to do this, but it is extremely unwise and can be dangerous.

Never kiss or touch a man's penis if you have cold sores around your lips as these could give him herpes. Likewise, never kiss or suck a penis if you know that it is infected with herpes or any other STD, or if a man has pain on urination or any kind of discharge from his penis.

Never bite the penis even in play. It is filled with blood and can bleed profusely, especially when erect.

CHAPTER 3

Understanding
Orgasm

The orgasm is a subject of clinical studies and heated discussions as well as a phenomenon surrounded by myths and rumours. A definite climax in lovemaking, the orgasm often has so much importance placed on it that those who do not achieve it, or do not bring their partner to orgasm during lovemaking, can feel that they have failed at sex altogether. While this feeling is a delusion causing unnecessary misery, it cannot be denied that the orgasm creates very powerful sensations.

One thing is certain: men and women experience orgasm quite differently. For men the sensations of orgasm are more closely centred on the genitals. Some describe a bursting and powerful energy in the penis, with a hot core of demanding pleasure. What is common in all descriptions given of orgasm is the climactic and explosive release of pent-up sexual emotions, the physiological changes and the subsequent sense of relief and calm. The surge of orgasm leads to a dramatic draining of the body.

A man's emotions after orgasm often reflect how he feels about his partner. For example, a loving relationship will allow him to feel happy and satisfied, while one-night stand sex is likely to leave him feeling depressed and empty.

The male orgasm is much more obvious and men are generally restricted to one orgasm at a time.

A man has no further interest in physical stimulation, unlike women who like to be held and cuddled for a while.

Women mostly describe an orgasm as something like an "explosive sneeze" which overwhelms them, physically and emotionally. The variations on this are vast, with some women describing exquisite genital sensations and others talking about whole-body experiences.

Women "come down" much more slowly after orgasm than men and they are less likely to feel depressed or sleepy.

Most women are capable of having several orgasms in quick succession (between one and three is the most common number), but many say that one is quite enough and they have no need for more.

The number of orgasms a woman has depends on many factors including her early sexual experiences, her level of inhibition, her emotional involvement with her lover, her partner's ability and willingness to continue stimulating her and, of course, her own desire to have more.

Pre-adolescent boys and some young men can have repeated orgasms, but few men can over the age of thirty. However, there is increasing evidence that multiple orgasms for older men could become the norm.

To learn to achieve better orgasms, it is necessary to understand exactly what happens during the sexual arousal leading up to them.

Sexual arousal

For a man, arousal usually starts in his mind. He is "turned on" by something erotic either in reality or fantasy. This mental change sends nerve impulses down his spinal cord to his genitals, closing off the outflow of blood from the penis. Blood continues to flow in, causing his penis to become stiff and erect and to darken in colour.

His breathing becomes faster, his pupils enlarge, his blood pressure rises, his heart rate quickens, his muscles tense, he sweats a little and he feels sexually excited. About 25 per cent of

ATTRACTING A PARTNER

Finding a partner often requires an investment of energy in going to the right places, wearing the right clothes, and acting in certain ways. Like everything else, we learn how to attract partners:

❤ **Dress sense:** *if you are comfortable with yourself you will find someone who appreciates your presentation, whether it is conformist or alternative. Dress to reflect your personality.*

❤ **Grooming:** *similar principles apply to hairstyle and make-up. Some people prefer a partner who wears noticeable make-up while others prefer the "natural" look. How much you wear is a matter of personal choice, both for you and them. Men should also pay considerable attention to their grooming as it is in their best interests to appear spruce and clean to a prospective partner.*

❤ **Body odours:** *some people find the aroma of fresh sweat exciting, but unfortunately, if we do not wash or change our clothes regularly the resulting odours may be unpleasant. Anti-perspirants and deodorants are a useful supplement to thorough and frequent washing.*

❤ **Fragrances:** *these are usually sweet smelling and pleasant, and arouse enjoyment for the wearer; they may also be very effective in stimulating interest from people around us. Some perfumes may contain animal* pheromones, such as musk and civet, which have been found to be attractive to humans.

- ❤ **Body image:** *proper diet and regular exercise may improve one's attractiveness to potential partners. Frequent and regular short sessions of exercise are a better long-term choice than dieting which can in the long term become dull, dangerous and obsessive.*

- ❤ **Personal habits:** *people have different pet hates, and it is important to be aware of yours and consider how others might see your "bad" habits. Excessive drinking in a potential partner may be a turn-off. Sloppy table manners may also be off-putting and nail-biting might irritate others. For some it may be the smell of stale garlic or tobacco on a person's breath.*

- ❤ **Warm signals:** *sending out lots of warm, positive signals is vital. Among the best known are smiling, nodding the head in approval, facing people and "opening up the body" so that it is accessible; this means removing any barriers formed by arms, knees and handbags.*

- ❤ **Conversation:** *in conversation it is best to be good-humoured, positive and optimistic. Try hard not to monopolize the conversation, listen to what the other person has to say and allow them ample opportunity to talk about themselves.*

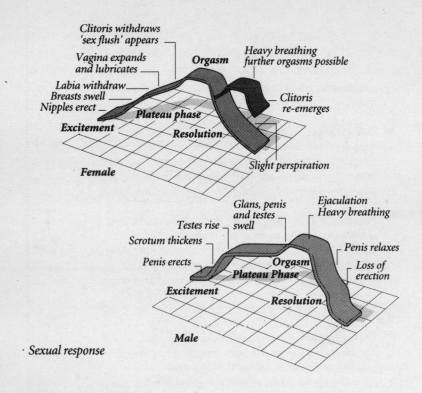

Clitoris withdraws
'sex flush' appears

Vagina expands
and lubricates

Orgasm

Heavy breathing
further orgasms possible

Labia withdraw
Breasts swell
Nipples erect

Plateau phase

Clitoris
re-emerges

Excitement

Resolution

Female

Slight perspiration

Glans, penis
and testes
swell

Testes rise

Ejaculation
Heavy breathing

Scrotum thickens

Penis erects

Orgasm
Plateau Phase

Penis relaxes

Loss of
erection

Excitement

Resolution

Male

Sexual response

men get a sex flush – a reddening of the skin which begins at the lower stomach and gradually spreads over thighs, chest, arms, shoulders, neck and face.

In this "excitement" phase, as well as his penis becoming erect, his scrotum, the pouch containing his testes, becomes tenser and thicker and the testes themselves are drawn up tightly against the body. Nipple swelling may occur – many men have very sensitive nipples and delicate caressing of the nipple or the whole chest area can be highly erotic. At this point the man can return to his normal pre-excitement phase within minutes.

Sudden non-sexual stimuli such as a change in temperature or any mental distraction can cause the man to lose his erection partially or entirely. But, having got this far, most men will go further by masturbating or by having sex.

Next comes the "plateau" phase, in which the penis swells even more. Its tip becomes purplish blue and the testes increase in size. It is less likely for a man to return to normal from this level. Once an orgasm is near and the man has passed the point of no return, there is nothing he can do to stop it – it takes him over. Women can be distracted from orgasm at this point, but for men it is inevitable.

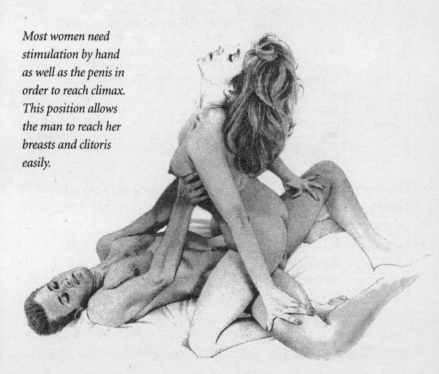

Most women need stimulation by hand as well as the penis in order to reach climax. This position allows the man to reach her breasts and clitoris easily.

WHAT TURNS MEN ON

Brought up to appreciate the female form, men set a high premium on a woman's appearance. But what exactly do they look for, and what turns them on?

❤ *Women wearing stockings has traditionally been one of the great male turn-ons. And lacy stockings which both conceal and reveal are considered by some men to be highly erotic.*

❤ *Long legs are, in themselves, powerful attractions to men. The transformation of a girl's legs into the shapely legs of a woman signifies that she has attained physical, and therefore sexual, maturity. High-heeled shoes accentuate the length and shape of the leg and also emphasize its allure.*

❤ *Women's buttocks also offer a powerful erotic signal to a man. More pronounced in women than in men, buttocks are the equivalent to sexual swellings of other species when they are "in season" except that in humans the swelling is a permanent feature.*

❤ *Breasts are the most obvious sexual turn-on for men. They may remind them of the warmth and security of their mothers' nurturing, or perhaps the fascination they hold is more straightforward than that. They are the most obvious body "label" of her sex and are sensitive, erogenous zones. Nipples rarely lie, becoming erect when the woman is aroused.*

❤ *If a man prefers to play the role of the "dominant father" in a relationship, he is more likely to be turned on by the little girl look of small breasts. If he prefers older, more mature women, he will probably go for larger breasts.*

❤ *The woman's characteristic narrow waist also highlights her breasts. Historically, bodices and corsets drew in the waist and accentuated the breasts. In Tudor times, the breasts were sometimes even left exposed over a tight restrictive bodice. Today, tight belts create a similar "hourglass" effect.*

❤ *A woman's shoulders, like her breasts, are an echo of the basic buttock shape, which, for our early ancestors, was the most erotic part of the body. Many men find exposed shoulders tantalizing which explains why off-the-shoulder dresses are popular for evening wear as sexual appetizers.*

❤ *The eyes are also powerful accessories to sexual attraction, for both men and women; the way the pupils dilate under the influence of strong, pleasant emotions, as well as the way we move our eyes, say to indicate interest. Men are turned on by women who appear to be turned on by them.*

❤ *For some men danger is a big turn-on. The idea of "sinful" sex, such as making love clandestinely in a public place where they might be discovered, fuels their desire.*

❤ *For others, the challenge of getting to know a woman can be exciting. Many men are intrigued by secrecy and are often tantalized by the woman who bares herself slowly, both literally and metaphorically. Expectancy and the ritual of courtship contribute enormously to sexual arousal.*

The head of the penis may darken in colour and a drop of fluid may form at the opening. This is not actually semen, but it may have some sperm in it. If you don't want to risk pregnancy or disease, take care not to allow the penis near the woman's vagina without contraceptive precautions such as a condom.

The next stage is the ejaculation itself. The intensity of sexual arousal is now so high that the man can't hold back. Surges of nerve impulses run back and forth from his nervous system to his genitals. The passages that run from the testicles to the penis contract to squirt semen out of the end of the penis. The ejaculated semen comes out under such pressure that it can travel for some distance away from the penis.

This is associated with a sensation of pleasure deep in the pelvis as the prostate gland discharges the fluid which carries the sperm. A series of four or five contractions follows with a gap of just under a second between each one.

Each contraction produces a smaller volume of semen until the tubes carrying the semen are empty. When the contractions stop, the man relaxes. His erect penis returns to its normal state and he feels relaxed and even sleepy. Many men will sweat immediately after ejaculation, but this is not directly related to the amount of physical effort expended during sex.

The amount of semen produced depends upon when the man last ejaculated and implies nothing about his virility. Each ejaculation, about a teaspoonful, contains millions of sperm. There is no way of judging the quality of semen by its appearance or volume, but the volume will decrease with each successive ejaculation until the prostate gland has a chance to produce more.

The time that passes between an ejaculation and the next erection can be up to several hours. This period, when the man's body is not sexually aroused, is known as the resolution period. The male cycle from excitement to ejaculation can be achieved very quickly, especially in teenagers and young men who can become aroused and ejaculate in a few minutes.

Female orgasm

In many ways the body changes that occur in a woman are very similar to a man's. But the whole cycle usually takes longer to get going, lasts longer and is capable of near-instant repetition.

Like men, women start off with the excitement phase. During this period, her nipples become erect, her breasts swell and the veins in them become more visible. The skin of her whole body usually becomes slightly dusky because of an increased blood flow and there may be a sex flush – a faint blush or rash over her stomach, chest and neck. This flush disappears at orgasm.

During the excitement phase the woman's genitals become engorged with blood. The inner lips of her vulva (the labia minora) and the clitoris swell and become darker in colour. As the clitoris is stimulated it becomes erect – like a miniature penis – but usually does so very slowly compared with the penis. Some women's clitorises swell to more than twice the size of the resting state, but others remain much the same size they were before stimulation began.

If stimulation continues, the plateau phase is attained. The shaft and the tip of the clitoris go back under the hood. This makes it seem that the clitoris has disappeared, but the tip and the shaft reappear if stimulation stops. After orgasm, only about ten to fifteen seconds are required for the clitoris to return to its resting position and size.

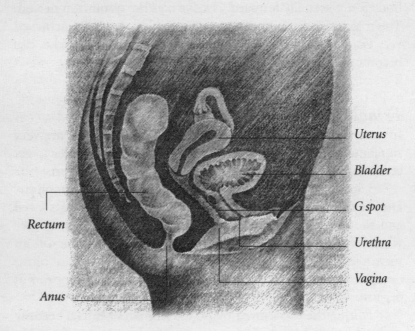

Uterus

Bladder

G spot

Urethra

Vagina

Rectum

Anus

The G spot

The outer lips, the labia majora, swell and pull back so as to open the vulva a little. The vaginal walls start to produce lubricating fluid and in some women this appears at the vaginal opening, making her physical arousal more obvious.

The woman feels moist inside and her sexual tension grows. She begins to feel the desire to be penetrated and internal changes take place to ready her for this. The vagina now relaxes and becomes enlarged at its top end. The womb is pulled upwards, making the vaginal cavity larger still and flattening out the internal folds. The vaginal walls near the opening swell with blood, reducing the size of this section by about a third.

Further breast-swelling occurs. The areolae around her nipples, swell and harden. Her pulse rate and breathing speed increase and her pupil size changes.

As she orgasms, she may arch her body. Her muscles tense up, her face may draw into a grimace and her vagina and uterus contract rhythmically, along with some pelvic muscles and the rectal sphincter. She may make some involuntary hip movements. Some women cry out, moan, gasp or bite their lips while others show little outward sign of orgasm. Once the contractions are over, she returns to the plateau phase and may be able to have another orgasm very soon after.

The G spot

Until the 1970s, it was thought that women were almost entirely aroused to climax by clitoral stimulation and that men could only have an orgasm if their penis was stimulated.

But there is a hidden area in both men and women that when stimulated correctly produces intense excitement and orgasm. For men this is the prostate gland; in women it is called the G spot. It was in the 1940s that the German obstetrician and gynecologist Ernest Gräfenberg described a "zone of erogenous feeling . . . located in the anterior (front) wall of the vagina". This area has become known as the G (for Gräfenberg) spot.

In the 1980s, American researchers Beverly Whipple and John Perry discovered that if this area is properly stimulated, the result can be an intensely satisfying orgasm, and that if these orgasms do occur, women will very often ejaculate a small amount of clear fluid. Analysis revealed that this fluid is similar in composition to the seminal fluid from the male prostate gland.

Such findings were initially thought to be unbelievable by those who insisted that the clitoris was the sole source of female pleasure. However, Whipple and Perry examined 400 women volunteers and every one was found to have a G spot, which seems to indicate that this hidden pleasure centre is not the exception, but the rule, among women.

The G spot appears to be a small cluster of nerve endings, glands, ducts and blood vessels around the urethra – the urinary passage running in front of the vaginal wall. It cannot normally be felt when it is unaroused, only becoming distinguishable as a specific area during deep vaginal stimulation.

When this happens, it begins to swell, sometimes very rapidly indeed, and a small mass with distinct edges stands out from the vaginal wall.

Because the fluid ejaculated during a G spot orgasm is very similar to the prostatic fluid (only without sperm), many scientists believe it to be a rudimentary version of the male prostate gland.

The G spot is not the easiest part of the female anatomy to find. The problem is that it has to be stimulated to be found, and found to be stimulated. It is a good idea for a woman to learn where her G spot is, if only to show herself that she does have one. She cannot do this lying down, since gravity tends to pull the internal organs away from the vaginal entrance. It is probably best for her to begin her search for the G spot while sitting on the lavatory. This is because deliberate stimulation of the G spot often causes an initial sensation that feels like a desire to urinate. If the woman makes sure that she has passed water first, but remains on the lavatory, she will gain an added sense of security.

Using her finger, she should apply a firm upward pressure to the front of the internal vaginal wall. It may help if she presses firmly down on the outside of her tummy with the other hand.

The G spot should now begin to swell and will feel like a small lump between the fingers inside and outside the vagina. Although, on average, it appears to be slightly smaller than a

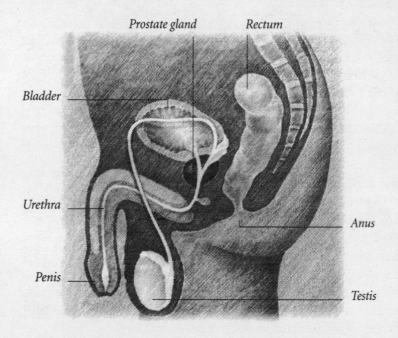

The prostate gland

WHAT TURNS WOMEN ON

While women are not unappreciative of classic male beauty, it takes more than just rugged good looks to excite them. Personality, reliability, sensitivity and a sense of humour may all play a part in turning women on.

One survey found that looks were thought to be important by only 23 per cent of women compared to 40 per cent of men. Faithfulness and personality were rated as more important than looks by most women.

The physical characteristics which women do seem to desire in men are quite different from those suggested by the stereotype of a masculine man. Sexual surprise, such as finding "feminine" characteristics in a man, for instance long eyelashes and soft hair on strong arms, excites many women more than rippling biceps and a strong jaw.

Not just a pretty face

Men who try to get on with women and tune into their conversation are also more likely to turn a woman on to them. Studies have shown that men who were successful at dating women were more fluent at saying the right thing and in joining in more quickly, and they agreed with the women more. They also smiled and nodded more than their less successful counterparts.

Because women tend not to see too many nude male bodies as they grow up, and because they are not assailed daily by a host of male pin-ups in their newspapers, they are not tuned into men's bodies as symbols of sexual desirability the way men are with women. Their unfamiliarity makes them uncomfortable with men's bodies in the abstract and therefore lessens their sexual responses to them.

Instead, women are more likely to react to a man's clothes and his "props". They might deduce from a man's sports bag, for example, that he is probably athletic, fairly healthy and fit, and possibly also an active lover. Or they might react to a man in tight jeans, responding not necessarily to the sexual symbolism of a tight crotch, but rather the nudge that the sight of the jeans gives them to make them start thinking about sex. Like the well-remembered voice or familiar turn of the head of a long-gone but never-forgotten lover, the jeans can act as memory prompters, encouraging a process of arousal which is as yet an early stage.

The attractions of power

Power and wealth have also traditionally been very important factors in turning women on. This may be because money and power are aphrodisiac in themselves, or an evolutionary throw-back to a woman's need for care and protection while she is bearing and rearing children.

In general, for a woman, attraction is mainly in her mind, so anything that pleases her, from a man's voice to his behaviour to his sense of humour, may be a turn-on. How he looks matters, but it certainly is not everything. If anything, many women find the crease lines around an older man's mouth and eyes more attractive than the less characterful face of a younger, perhaps less experienced, man.

penny piece, there is no real norm, and size does not seem to have anything to do with the sensation produced.

As the G spot continues to be stroked, pleasurable contractions begin to sweep through the uterus. Ultimately, a deep orgasm will be experienced that will feel totally different from one caused by clitoral stimulation. At this point, the woman may ejaculate a small amount of clear fluid from the urethra. Contrary to what she may feel, this is not urine.

Once a woman has become used to these sensations, she can continue to experiment while kneeling with her knees apart on the floor or bed.

Of course, a sympathetic partner can make the discovery of a woman's G spot far more intimate and enjoyable.

In this case, the woman should lie face down on the bed with her hips raised by one or two pillows. Her partner can then gently place two fingers inside her and begin to stroke the front of the vaginal wall.

By moving her pelvis back and forth, the woman can help locate the G spot and also discover the most enjoyable kind of stimulation. The main point to remember is that the initial sensations felt are not those of a desire to urinate.

Probably the two easiest positions in which a couple can achieve G spot stimulation are the "rear-entry" and woman-on-top methods.

Rear-entry lovemaking allows the man's erect penis to stimulate the G spot on the front wall of the vagina – particularly if the woman moves her hips back and forth, so that she can direct her lover's penis to the most pleasurable spot.

Woman-on-top positions afford direct stimulation of the G spot, and allow the woman to control the direction and depth of the penis. If the man lies on his back, with the woman

*Attaining a simultaneous orgasm usually means speeding up the woman's
response as well as slowing down the man. This position leaves the man with
both hands free – one can caress her clitoris while the other stimulates her body
elsewhere.*

straddling his erect penis, she can guide it to the place that
feels best.

   The man can help by moving his body and pressing the base
of his penis to make sure the head makes full contact. The result
can be a series of intense orgasms for both partners.

The prostate gland

Men also have a sort of G spot. Located around the urethra at the
neck of the bladder, it is called the prostate gland and, unlike the
female G spot, it has a well defined function. The prostate gland
helps produce the fluid that carries sperm into the vagina when a

couple are having intercourse. Many men have discovered that stimulation of the prostate gland prior to, or during, intercourse results in an orgasm of unparalleled intensity.

It is difficult for a man to reach his prostate gland himself, since to do so, he has to insert a finger – or thumb – into his rectum. But it is possible to reach it. The best position is if he lies on his back with his knees bent and drawn up towards his chest.

If he inserts a thumb into his anus, and presses against the front rectal wall, he should be able to feel his prostate – it is a firm mass about the size of a walnut.

As with the female G spot, however, the discovery of this hidden pleasure centre is usually more enjoyable if it is shared with a loving partner.

In this case the woman must ensure that her fingernails are not long and that her fingers are well lubricated with KY jelly or a similar lubricant.

She should then lie her partner down on the bed and slowly, gently insert a finger into his anus, giving him time to become accustomed to having the finger there. Feeling her way up the frontal rectal wall, she will find his prostate gland and can massage it firmly. Even if she does not touch her partner's penis it will probably become erect and he will have an orgasm.

Simultaneous orgasm

For many couples, the "ideal" form of lovemaking is one in which they both have an orgasm at the same time – anything else is considered to be poor in comparison. Certainly, when orgasms do come together in this way they can be very pleasant, but to make love with this goal always in mind is to store up a measure of disappointment and resentment for the future. In reality, for many couples, the very act of trying to come together prevents this from happening. The stress involved in trying to hold off his own orgasm can be very tiring for a man. It can interfere with his ejaculatory timing and so reduce the pleasure he gets from his orgasm. For the woman, things can be stressful if she hurries her own orgasm to coincide with his.

However, having said all this, most lovers would like love-making sessions to end in orgasm for both partners, preferably at the same time, and with care and sensitivity, simultaneous orgasm is well within the scope of most loving couples.

Obviously, with something as uniquely individual as a person's sexuality, there can be no hard and fast rules about how to produce simultaneous orgasms, but clinical experience does enable us to learn from others. For the majority of couples, the woman will have to speed up her orgasm, and the man hold back his. Of course getting the timing right may not be that simple; here are some tips that may help:

● *Oral sex beforehand is a great favourite. If a man brings a woman to near-climax orally, and then penetrates her, she might well come almost at once. The final stimulation of penile thrusting is enough to push a woman over the edge to orgasm.*

● *For the woman whose main area of sexual excitement is her G spot, rear-entry sex, especially the doggy position, can help to ensure that she is stimulated where it matters most.*

● *Try using a favourite fantasy. Some women can take themselves from being "pleasantly warm" to "boiling point" simply by using a particularly arousing fantasy.*

● *Foreplay is the answer to orgasms during intercourse for most women. This needs to be highly personalized to suit the individual woman.*

● *The couple should find a position in which the woman's clitoris can be stimulated easily and comfortably. One of the best positions in which to do this is for the man to lie at right angles to his partner's body and under her raised and parted thighs. This leaves both hands free so that one can caress her clitoris while the other pleasures her elsewhere on her body.*

Slowing down a man is rather more difficult than speeding up a woman and the couple who try may run the risk that the man

From kissing a partner's breasts, the man can move down her body, using his tongue to tease her clitoris.

gains so much control that he is eventually unable to have an orgasm even when he wants to.

This is a real danger when meddling with male arousal. However, assuming that the man simply comes sooner than he would like to on some occasions and so cannot wait for his partner to come, here are some things that may work:

● *Talk it over with your partner – she may well be able to help you. Perhaps she stimulates you too passionately or, during foreplay, brings you to the point of no return and then wonders why you come so quickly and she is not ready. The secret here is to balance your sexual paces.*

● *Use a sheath for a few weeks. This can so reduce sensitivity that it can break the cycle of too-quick arousal.*

● *Use a weak anaesthetic cream or ointment on the tip of the penis. This reduces its sensitivity.*

● *Contract your anus tightly at the end of each thrust.*

● *Focus your attention on something non-sexual to distract you temporarily from too-fast arousal.*

Taking control is an important factor in achieving simultaneous orgasm. If a man feels his own orgasm approaching without any sign of his partner's, he can either control the pace of intercourse by keeping his thrusting to a minimum while caressing his partner, or he can withdraw his penis and arouse her with his fingers, mouth or vibrator before entering her again. The lover who is in tune with his partner will know also when and how to change position.

Similarly, a woman who feels her own orgasm will take longer than her partner's can use his body to slow him down by keeping his arousal to a minimum while increasing her own. But, if her partner will take longer than her to come, she can increase his arousal by using her hands and then a woman-on-top position to control the pace.

Either way, remember that simultaneous orgasm is not the be-all and end-all of lovemaking. For some couples, the quality of their partner's orgasm is of greater importance than their own. It should be seen as a bonus, and lovers should concentrate on giving each other pleasure. Then the quality of orgasms for both partners will be increased and the lovemaking session will be what it should always be – a shared experience between two lovers.

Multiple orgasms

In the 1940s, the American sex researcher Kinsey found that one in seven women sometimes experienced multiple orgasms. Terman, another researcher, found the figures to be much the same. However, in the 1960s Masters and Johnson discovered that, given enough stimulation, most women were capable of having more than one orgasm. And they found that, in most cases, a woman was "capable of having a second, third, fourth or even fifth and sixth orgasm before she is finally satisfied." Many of the women were able to have five or six full orgasms within as many minutes.

A more recent survey of 106,000 American women of all ages showed that 67 per cent had multiple orgasms most of the time, with one in seven of all those over thirty-five saying that they had them every time they made love. Of those who had multiple orgasms, 66 per cent had between six and ten and 6 per cent had eleven or more.

Clearly, many more women have multiple orgasms than is generally realized, but the vast majority do not have them from intercourse alone. It is this that makes many men think that their partner is not multi-orgasmic when she is. Most women have multiple orgasms only when masturbating – probably because they can control the situation and maintain stimulation for far

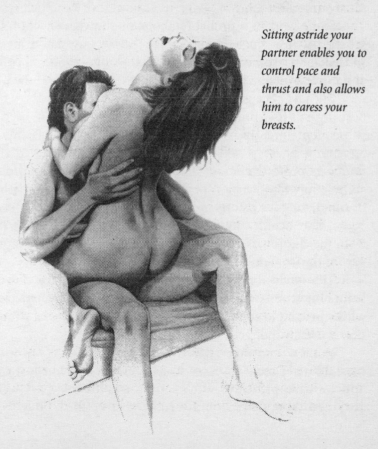

Sitting astride your partner enables you to control pace and thrust and also allows him to caress your breasts.

longer than is possible during intercourse. Masters and Johnson found that the largest numbers of orgasms occurred when women used vibrators.

For a woman on her own, the pleasure of multiple orgasms is purely selfish – and why should it not be – and many women claim that their second or third orgasm is much more intense than the first. And for a man, a multiple orgasmic woman is a great turn-on – although a truly insatiable one can be tedious to satisfy time after time.

Some women – probably about one in three – are totally satisfied with a single climax, in the same way that a man is. Indeed, many women say that stimulation after orgasm is painful and unpleasant and that it kills any further pleasure for them.

But just because direct clitoral stimulation produces their best orgasm first time, it does not mean it should be used for subsequent orgasms. Indeed, because the clitoris in the resolution phase is still erect and has now re-emerged from under its protective hood, it is still highly sensitive and direct stimulation may feel painful. The secret is to use other methods of stimulating the clitoris indirectly.

These include caressing the whole vulva area (keeping away from the clitoris), intercourse itself, and stimulating some other part of the woman's body altogether.

This is why it is so common for a woman who has climaxed before intercourse (by direct clitoral stimulation) to come again when the couple are having intercourse (when clitoral stimulation is usually indirect).

While a few women have multiple orgasms every time they masturbate or make love, most need the mood to be just right, and to have plenty of stimulation and foreplay as well as prolonged stimulation of the right area of their body. Some

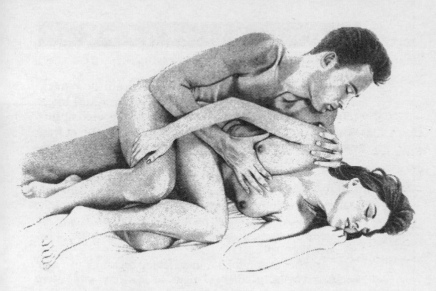

The intensity of both partners' orgasms can often be lost in the repetitiveness of long-term lovemaking. But they can also easily be regained. For example, the man can caress and stimulate the woman from behind.

women, on the other hand, are afraid to let themselves go totally, under the misapprehension that they might turn into nympho-maniacs and start chasing men.

For the woman who feels she might be multiple orgasmic and has contented herself with a single orgasm, there are a number of things she can do. Even if it does not work out, the following tips are pleasurable in themselves. All they require is the ability to relax and the attention of a loving partner.

● *Start experimenting on your own during masturbation. Next time you feel especially sexy, perhaps around your period time, get yourself very aroused and then when you have had an*

FAKING ORGASM

A lot of people would be surprised to learn how many women, unable to achieve an orgasm during sexual intercourse, deal with it – they fake it. According to a recent survey, as many as two out of five women fake orgasm at least sometimes, if not always. More shocking perhaps are figures that show how few men actually realize this.

There are several reasons why a woman might choose to remain silent about her lack of orgasm. The most common is that she wants to protect her man from feeling in any way inadequate. All too many men see a woman's failure to achieve orgasm as a direct criticism of themselves and their sexual performance.

Another reason for a woman faking orgasm is to avoid being seen by her partner as "frigid" or as a lousy lover. Men tend to use the word "frigid" as a way of putting a woman down for not being as keen on sex as he is. It is actually a meaningless word, only ever used as a destructive insult.

Some women resort to faking because they see it as an easy way of saving both time and trouble. A woman may feel that, in situations where she is having difficulty reaching orgasm, she and her partner will end up having sex for hours, with him desperately trying to make her climax. Almost inevitably this will result in frustration, disappointment and even anger on the part of both unhappy partners.

Why faking is futile

Here are ten good reasons why a woman should not fake orgasm:

♥ *Faking orgasm ultimately fools you more than anyone else.*

♥ *It prevents you from finding more mutually satisfying ways of making love with your partner.*

♥ *It gives your partner inaccurate messages and can even encourage him to continue using the wrong methods of stimulation in his efforts to bring you to orgasm.*

♥ *It merely compounds the problem you are having and prevents you from finding a solution to it.*

♥ *It may keep him happy in the short term but, sooner or later, you will end up feeling dissatisfied.*

♥ *It's a cowardly way out of facing and confronting a problem.*

♥ *It focuses your attention on his reactions, not on yours – which is what you need to concentrate on.*

♥ *It establishes a damaging pattern of behaviour.*

♥ *It focuses the attention of both you and your partner on your performance rather than your enjoyment of sex.*

Faking orgasm is a problem that needs to be solved and ultimately, the only way of doing this is to talk about it. This may be embarrassing, but it is better than pretending.

For the woman who wants to give her partner maximum pleasure, it is a good idea to watch how he masturbates.

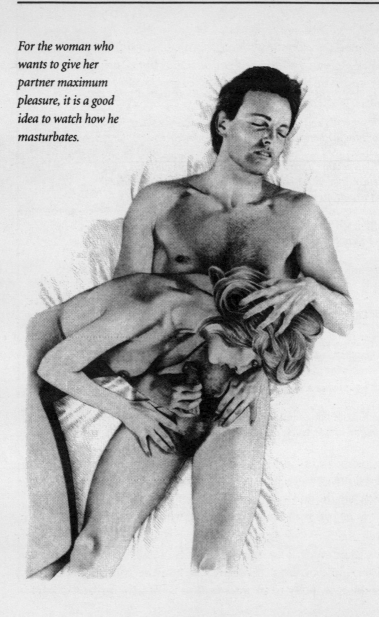

*orgasm, experiment with other ways of stimulating yourself
until you have another. If you usually climax using your fingers
to stimulate your clitoris, try a vibrator around the area until
you come again.*

● *When you are feeling very sexy, encourage your partner to
stimulate your clitoris – either with his tongue or his fingers – to
give you an intense and enjoyable first orgasm.*

● *Then, guided by what you have learned during masturbation,
tell him what you would most like next. Do not expect him to
be able to keep an erection for as long as you will need, and
encourage him to use a vibrator or dildo on or inside you.*

● *When you feel you have nearly had enough, let him make love
to you. At first, he may be so excited at your new-found orgasms
that he will come very quickly. As he becomes used to it,
however, he will be better able to control his speed to orgasm.*

● *If he does not want to go in for that much stimulation, ask him
to cuddle you, while you masturbate and have several climaxes
before inviting him inside you.*

Multiple orgasms in men are very rare. Young men in their teens
and early twenties may be able to ejaculate several times one after
the other, but few men over twenty can do so.

In a man the pleasurable sensations of orgasm come from
the seminal fluid hitting the urinary passage deep in the prostate
and expanding it. The male orgasm is usually at its most intense
after a couple of days' abstinence, when the volume of semen is
the most it is likely to be and explodes into the prostatic part of

the urethra, giving him intensely pleasurable sensations. If he comes again within a couple of hours, the sensations are usually much less intense because fluid has not had a chance to build up again. This is all the more true if he is stimulated again within minutes of an orgasm.

A few men experience "dry" orgasms – that is, orgasms without ejaculation. And some can have repeated orgasms, with all the physical and emotional signs, yet not ejaculate.

Improving your orgasms

Although the vast majority of lovemaking and foreplay techniques concentrate – quite rightly – on unselfishness as a prerequisite for good sex, there are times in most couples' lives when they want to concentrate on the quality of their own orgasms and not just those of their partner. This does not mean that selfless lovemaking has to go out of the window, but it does demand, occasionally, a slightly different approach to sex.

Perhaps the order in which a couple approaches sex might be reversed. For example, they could finish off with oral sex or try another position – or an existing one they like from a slightly different angle. The time and the place could be changed as well – lovemaking on the couch in the living room, or on a rug in front of the fire can really make a difference – even using the same technique.

In truth, because orgasm is as much a mental as a physical experience, it is only really the mental approach that has to change. If you find that the quality of your own orgasm has deteriorated, the same is probably true for your partner, and the first step is to sit down and talk about it. If a couple can say truthfully and without embarrassment, what they want – and what they would really like – the opportunities for experiment open up for both of them.

There are any number of techniques that a couple can use to improve the quality of their orgasms. But what follows is a series of ideas for a slightly different approach.

All the suggestions presume that you both spend time on a certain amount of foreplay. And if the ideas are already part of your sexual repertoire, this does not matter. You can always try them again or invent a slight variation that increases their novelty value.

Better orgasms for her

For a woman the first step along the journey to better orgasms is to recognize that her sexuality is something she herself possesses, not something that is done to her.

Using a vibrator is one of the most popular ways in which a woman can achieve a novel sort of orgasm – either by using it herself or with her partner working it for her. The main purpose is to use it on the clitoris and, by increasing the speed, to bring the woman to orgasm as powerfully as possible. But a vibrator can lend itself to more creative use. You simply have to instruct your partner how you want it done.

You can lie down on the bed facing upwards, or as an alternative, face downwards on the bed and place a couple of pillows under your stomach, as in a conventional rear-entry position.

Make sure that you are relaxed and tell your partner exactly what you want him to do. Be explicit so that there is no room for doubt. He should concentrate entirely on giving you the best orgasm possible – his own can always come later.

Assuming that you have chosen to lie face down, start off by parting your legs and raise your buttocks as high as possible. Get your partner to start the vibrator at its lowest setting and begin using it to delicately massage your perineum. As you become more aroused, tell him to move on to your vaginal lips but without touching your clitoris. There is no need to rush.

Then, when you feel that you are ready, get him to move on to your clitoris, increasing the speed setting a little. Do not let him move the vibrator around too much, just let it work almost on its own. Now, position yourself so that he can use his mouth and tongue on your clitoris instead and tell him to insert the vibrator into your vagina. Have him increase the speed setting and aim to use it as he would his penis, increasing the pressure and tempo all the time.

Encourage him to be as creative as he can and get him to keep the movements of his lips and tongue at the same tempo as the vibrator. Alternatively, he can keep the vibrator working on your clitoris with a slightly increased speed setting, insert a couple of fingers into your vagina and mimic the movements of his penis in this way.

He should be guided by your needs. If you want him to stop this at any stage and make love to you in this position, then tell him.

Another way in which you can achieve a feeling of abandonment is by using one of the woman-on-top positions – if you want his penis to hit your G spot as he thrusts, then facing him is best, so that you are able to caress your clitoris yourself. By so doing, you will control the point at which you have your orgasm and, if you have G spot-induced ones as well, you can ensure that your partner's penis stimulates this in the way that you move your body.

Lay your partner back on the bed – or floor if you prefer. When he is erect, take his penis and insert it into your vagina. Start moving slowly at first and stroke your clitoris at the same time. Caress your breasts as well if you prefer.

Take whatever approach you like – some women, for example, find this a particularly good position to use a vibrator on themselves as they "use" their partner's penis in this way. Shift your buttocks until your partner's penis is hitting your G spot and try to direct your pelvis so that it hits it each time he thrusts. Increase the pace at which you are stimulating your clitoris and lose yourself as your orgasm approaches.

Better orgasms for him

There are a number of ways in which a man can encourage his partner to give him better orgasms. Again, many of them will just involve a slightly different approach.

It may be that you like her to dress in a particular way. Perhaps you want to be more passive in your lovemaking and her to take the lead. Or there may be a favourite position that you would like to use, but perhaps somewhere different, like in another room.

But for many men, an orgasm where their G spot is stimulated can provide a very special sort of orgasm. For a unique experience, it is best done either when your partner is fellating you or during conventional intercourse.

She will need to have some KY jelly or oil handy if she is to put her finger into your anus. Lie down so that you are both comfortable and get her to start stroking your perineum very lightly. The key is timing – if it is done properly, then it may be one of the most explosive orgasms you have ever had.

As she strokes your perineum, get her to start licking the tip of your penis as she would if she were fellating you. Then, as she uses her mouth on your testicles and runs her tongue up and down the shaft of your penis, she should take your penis into her mouth and start to gently suck on it.

As the pace increases and you become more aroused, she can put her finger into your anus and find your prostate gland. You will probably need to adjust your position, bringing up your knees so that she can do this. When she finds it, she should then start to massage it, lightly, but insistently. As she brings you to orgasm with her mouth, you should find the dual sensations quite exquisite.

CHAPTER 4

Positions for
Lovemaking

F or enjoyable lovemaking every time it pays to experiment with different positions. Not only does it avoid predictability, it also creates scope for varying degrees of control for either partner over pace, and penetration and intimacy.

This chapter looks at all the classic positions and at more adventurous variations, so that there should be something for every couple, whatever their preference.

Woman on top

For the woman who likes to take the initiative and the man who enjoys watching his partner as they make love, woman-on-top positions cannot be beaten. And with deep penetration as an added bonus, they can increase the sexual pleasure for both partners in any loving relationship by adding new sensations to lovemaking.

Control is one of the first reasons women give when stating a preference for the woman-on-top position. Once the penis enters the vagina, the woman is in control of it in a way she cannot ever be when being penetrated in any other way.

The first basic woman-on-top position begins with the man lying flat on his back. The woman kneels astride his body, facing his head, and gently guides the penis inside herself. By moving her body up and down she can control both the speed and depth of penetration and her hands are free to caress him. He can handle her body and breasts and see his penis going into her.

From this position, the woman can lean forwards so that her breasts rest on her lover's chest or over his face. This reduces the range of her movement, but she can still raise and lower her hips over the penis while her partner is able to bury his face between her breasts and lick and suck her nipples.

It can be easy for the man's penis to slip out of the woman when she leans forward in this way. However, if she keeps her movements small and shallow, or simply presses herself firmly down on his penis and then circles her hips around the base instead of using sliding movements up and down the shaft, there should not be a problem.

The other basic position is for the woman to kneel astride the man's penis, but facing away from him. This offers deep penetration and allows him to caress her back, the lower region of her body and her anus. He can watch his penis going in and out of her, especially if she leans forward, and she can stimulate her clitoris with one hand.

Facing away from the man can be as sensuous as facing him, as in this position the woman can caress his testicles and inner thighs. The more athletic woman can swivel around from a facing position on his erect penis. This can be a whole new pleasure for both.

The woman can try swivelling sideways as well, swinging both legs to one side of the man's body. This position gives particularly deep penetration.

Many men find it highly erotic to watch themselves entering the woman, and of course this position offers the perfect view. It is also good for stimulating the female G spot, which is on the front wall of the vagina.

In either of the basic woman-on-top positions – woman facing man, woman facing away – there are delightful variations. The woman can kneel, squat or sit with her legs out straight. If she wants the sensation of more contact, she can lie stretched out on top of the man and feel him along the full length of her body.

A slight turn to one side or the other can create quite different sensations – a good position for those who like deep penetration.

She can also sit sideways on her lover's penis and bring his leg up between hers and towards his chest. This is a particularly good position for couples who enjoy the sensation of deep penetration.

As always when making love, take care to watch or listen to your lover's reactions. This way you will quickly find out what pleases each of you and how you can best work to increase each other's pleasure, arousal and satisfaction.

If the man does not want to come too quickly, woman-on-top positions are good for practising delayed ejaculation – especially useful for men who sometimes suffer from premature ejaculation.

A man's erection and ejaculation reflexes are slowed down when he is on his back and there is time to use the special "squeeze technique" of preventing ejaculation: if he feels he is coming too soon, he can signal to the woman who can take his penis out and squeeze the top of the glans firmly between her fingers until he begins to lose his erection. She can then re-arouse him and they can continue making love.

Woman-on-top positions are ideal during pregnancy and in situations where the man is recovering from serious illness or surgery.

Taking things a step further, there are a number of advanced woman-on-top positions which, although they do not allow her as much control, they do allow for penetration in new ways.

Bear in mind, however, that often such athletic positions do not produce benefits on a par with the effort and discomfort that they involve. Do not persevere if any position hurts or annoys your partner. Go back to one of your tried-and-tested ones and perhaps try one of these more unusual ones another day.

The woman who is hesitant or shy about taking the lead in lovemaking should first experiment with woman-on-top positions which allow her partner to hold her. If she sits astride her man, facing forward, for example, she can lean forward and he can cuddle, kiss and caress her as they make love.

Once she has become more used to these positions, she can try the more inventive and athletic woman-on-top positions. Many of these are difficult to maintain for long but they can produce new and different sensations:

The man lies flat on his back on the bed with his bottom on the edge and his legs supported on a chair. The woman stands astride his closed legs and inserts his penis into her vagina. She then

The man lies with his bottom near the edge of the bed and his legs supported on a chair. The woman stands astride him and lowers herself onto his penis. If she leans forward, he can caress her.

leans forward, facing away from him, to lie on his legs, while sup-porting most of her weight on her feet and forearms.

This is exceptionally good for the man who finds his partner's bottom stimulating to look at while making love. If the couple enjoy it, it is very easy to stimulate her anus and buttocks, and the man can, by simply looking down, watch as his penis penetrates her. (Note: a man must never put a finger that has been inside the woman's anus into her vagina as this can cause a transfer of bacteria that can produce a urinary infection.)

Movement is not all that good unless he pushes her bottom up and down with his hands. Anything else is very tiring for her if she does not have strong legs. She can kiss his feet and stroke her breasts across his lower legs to add pleasure to the whole position. The man is, of course, virtually pinned down and can do almost nothing in the way of thrusting. This can be good for the woman who wants a lot of bottom stimulation and her anus played with.

The man sits on a chair with his legs apart while the woman kneels on the seat of the chair. Her legs are either side of his pelvis, and she has her back to him and sits on his penis. She then leans forward to support herself on his knees with her hands. He holds her around the waist and can not only steady her in this rather unstable position but can also, to some extent, control penetration by pulling her onto his penis or pushing her further off it.

Movement is not very good and penetration is poor, but short jabbing motions are possible and some women greatly enjoy this. Once again the woman's bottom is very much on show and the man can closely watch his penis penetrating her.

The position is, however, rather tiring for the woman's arms. A way to get round this is for her to lean right forward to rest her hands on the floor between his feet. She can even rest her forehead on the floor on a pillow. The man's penis now enters her at a very different angle and the change can be exciting for the woman.

Obviously the woman cannot caress her clitoris, and neither can her man, so the woman is unlikely to experience a clitoral orgasm in this position.

The man lies on his back and pulls his legs right back onto his chest. The woman pulls his penis out and downwards between his legs and sits on it with her back to his legs. He can rest his legs

The man lies on his back and pulls his legs up to his chest. The woman then pulls his penis out from between his closed legs and lowers herself onto it.

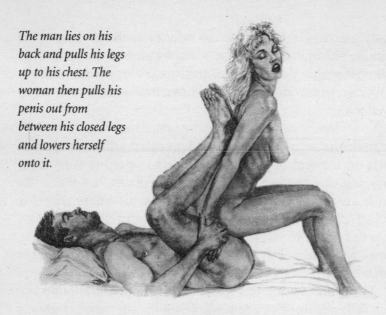

on her back to support both his legs and hers and she can support her weight by resting her hands on his thighs.

Very little movement is possible but she can, as in all these restricted movement positions, contract her pelvic muscles and wriggle her bottom about to stimulate them both.

Not many couples will be able to sustain this position for long because it places a strain on the man and many men find it uncomfortable or even painful.

Another woman-on-top position is particularly suitable for the pregnant woman. The man lies on his back on the bed and the woman kneels over his pelvis, facing away from him. She inserts his penis and sits on it. Now she leans right back and lies on his chest. In that position, he can caress her whole body and especially her breasts and can reach down to stimulate her clitoris.

The only tiring part about this position is that many women find that their legs and knees become strained, but this can be overcome slightly by lifting their knees off the bed a little.

Penetration is not deep but the penis is forced into the front wall of the vagina quite hard and this can be pleasant for the woman who likes her G spot stimulated during intercourse. The couple can kiss and her body is very open to caresses but she can do little herself to please her man. The penis slips out very easily in women whose vaginal opening is high up in the front of their pelvis.

This position is somewhat tiring but fun for a change during a lovemaking session. The man lies on his back on the edge of the bed with his feet and lower legs on a chair. The woman sits on his penis facing him and with her legs on either side of his chest. She leans back and supports herself with her hands on the arms of the chair.

Not much movement is possible like this and penetration is not especially good. The man can watch his penis entering her and he can lift up a little to increase penetration, but the fact that she is supporting her weight so much on her arms can be tiring. The man can reach in between her legs to stimulate her clitoris, but many women will need to be highly aroused in advance if they are to have an orgasm from this position because they will be unable to keep the weight on their arms for very long.

Man on top

For many couples, the most popular position in which to make love is the so-called "missionary position" in which the woman

RHYTHM IN LOVEMAKING

Throughout our lives, a combination of physical and psychological forces causes desire to ebb and flow within us in patterns as rhythmic as the tides. And in the act of love-making itself, true satisfaction is rarely achieved unless the lovers can tune into those subtly stimulating rhythms that make the nerves tingle and bring each other's bodies to a peak of excitement.

Locked into the cells of the body is a series of biological clocks that, under normal circumstances, governs the rhythmic pattern of people's daily lives: when we want to to sleep or wake, when we are most alert, most libidinous, or most physically under par, and of course, for the woman, there is the menstrual cycle.

Unfortunately, our own body "clocks" rarely coincide with those of our partner. What we have to try and do is to become more receptive to the way our rhythms affect us and those around us, especially those we love. Once we have a full understanding of the differences between individual rhtythms we can then set about achieving a balance by making sure we recognize them.

As a couple become used to each other, more worldly pressures cause them to drift back into the patterns of their own daily lives. This is the time to start listening to each other's "clocks" and to establish a rhythm for lovemaking.

Communicating rhythms

As with most sexual matters, everything hinges on communication. Talk to your lover to find out the times of day, week or month when they most enjoy sex. Make an effort to accommodate your partner by making love in the afternoon, for example, even if this is not your preference. Getting in step with the rhythm of your partner's feelings should begin well before you actually start making love.

Even at the caressing stage, rhythm counts for everything. Brusque, jerky movements can be a real turn-off, while gentle rhythmic pressing of skin against skin is very exciting. As you caress, be aware of the feedback transmitted from your lover's body.

By the intercourse stage you should both be ready for lovemaking in which both bodies move in perfect harmony and experience intense pleasure, instinctively aware of what stage of arousal your partner is at and whether to adjust the rhythm accordingly.

Finally, remember that what constitutes a thrilling rhythm one day can easily be a turn-off the next. Sexual rhythms are not like computer programs. The overriding consideration is always to sense what your partner is feeling at the same time – and please them.

lies on her back with her legs open as she is penetrated by the man who lies on top of her. Many women consider this the most romantic position, almost certainly because the couple are always face to face. Every expression can be noticed, they are free to kiss and each partner can see that they are being loved – something that is not possible in some other positions, such as rear-entry ones.

The missionary position, being such a passive one for the woman, absolves her of the responsibility of making anything much happen. Some women can relax and enjoy lovemaking more if they do not take the dominant, active role. Equally, many men enjoy dominating their partner during intercourse and this is a position which allows them to do so.

Because the couple's faces are close together, they can easily kiss – not just lips but all over each other's faces and even breasts

The simplest missionary position is ideal for couples who want to make love gently. When deep penetration is painful – for example, after a woman has had a baby – then this is the ideal position to choose.

and necks. This helps create a loving and caring atmosphere. For the woman who is aroused by nipple stimulation, the man-on-top position allows the man to kiss her nipples.

By altering the angle of her thighs to her tummy, the woman can change the degree of penetration even if the man stays in exactly the same position. As she brings her knees nearer to her chest, the penis goes in deeper. The woman can find just the right angle to give her the best sensations – perhaps as her lover stimulates her cervix with the tip of his penis. A variation of this is for the woman to rock her pelvis backwards and forwards. If, at the same time, she "milks" her partner's penis by contracting and

The woman who wants to open herself up completely to her lover, can take him into her while her legs are over his shoulders.

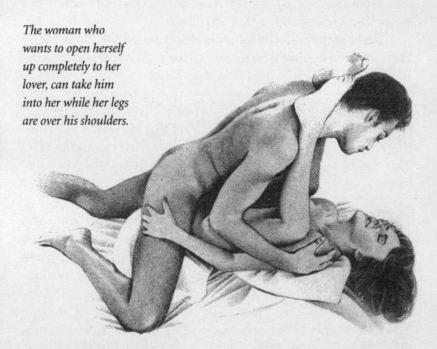

relaxing her pelvic muscles, this can be extremely exciting for him.

Another advantage of the man-on-top positions is that they are very good for couples who are trying to have a baby, because penetration can be very deep. If the woman holds onto her legs behind her knees and draws her thighs right back, sperm can be deposited deep in the vagina – at the neck of the womb. This provides the best chance for conception to occur.

If the woman stays lying down after sex, with a pillow under her hips, the semen stands the best possible chance of entering her cervix and the sperm will then be able to fertilise an egg.

The *Kama Sutra* and Chinese pillow books list many variations on the missionary position. Often the change is only very slight but can create quite different sensations:

The missionary position with one of the woman's legs pulled back to her chest is a pleasant variation that skews the woman's pelvis and enables the man to stimulate her ovary on one side. This may be tender for some women, so the man should be careful.

The man kneels and raises the woman's buttocks onto the lower part of his thigh as he penetrates her. She crosses her ankles behind his back. This reduces the depth of penetration quite considerably but can be very exciting for the woman who enjoys having her vaginal opening teased and stimulated.

The man kneels between her open thighs, penetrates her, and then lifts her bottom from the bed so as to bring her as close as possible to his pelvis. This can produce superb sensations for both partners, but it is tiring for the woman to keep her back arched in this way for very long. This may be avoided by putting a couple of pillows under her bottom.

The woman lies over the edge of the bed or a low stool with her legs open. The man enters her and leans forwards on her body, taking most of his weight on his forearms or hands. This can be very tiring for the man because movement is restricted. It is, therefore, not a suitable position for the couple who enjoy, or need, deep thrusting during lovemaking.

The woman lies on her side and raises her upper leg. The man cuddles into the front of her body and penetrates her. She curls her upper leg over his body. Here again, the angle of entry of the penis can be to one side, stimulating unfamiliar parts of the woman's pelvic organs. Most couples find this a very loving and restful position, as the man does not have to support his weight. However, movement is restricted and the woman may have to contract her pelvic muscles to give her man pleasure.

A variation is for the woman to raise her upper leg so as to open up her pelvis further and "release" him from the clamping effect around the waist. This allows him considerable movement, even though they are both on their sides, and she can obtain new sensations as she angles her upper leg differently.

Taking it further

As is the case with more advanced woman-on-top positions, the advanced man-on-top positions require a degree of suppleness

*A tiring position for the woman. The man
kneels between her open thighs, penetrates her,
and then lifts her bottom from the bed, bringing
her as close as possible to his pelvis. In this
position, the woman has to arch her back,
so suppleness is required.*

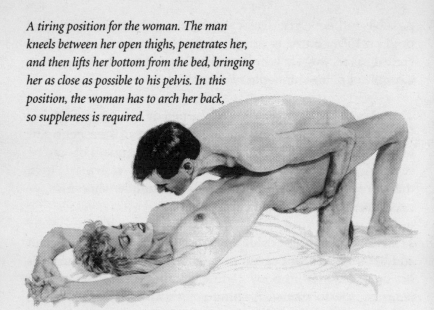

and stamina, but can provide both partners with an extra dimension to their lovemaking.

It can be helpful to embark on a simple exercise regime to loosen up some muscles. Your general health will benefit, as well as your love life.

The woman lies, face up, on the bed and draws her knees up to her chest. The man then enters her and she puts her ankles over both of his shoulders. The woman will find this position more comfortable if she places a pillow in the small of her back.

If the man pushes his partner's knees and kisses her while her ankles are still over his shoulders, he will be able to achieve exceptionally deep penetration.

This position calls for suppleness on the part of the woman.

A good exercise for this is for the woman to lie on her back, and slowly – over several sessions – try to get her feet further and further back over her body until she can touch the ground behind her head with her toes.

If the couple stay in this position for some time after sex, with the man on top taking the weight of his body with his hands, it provides the best possible chance of conception as semen bathes the cervix and none spills out of the vagina.

The man kneels down in front of the woman who has her hips raised very high. He supports her hips with both hands and penetrates her. This angles the penis horizontally, while the woman's vagina is nearly vertical. This allows the penis to stimulate the front wall of the vaginal opening. This can be highly exciting for the woman who enjoys having her G spot stimulated. By adjusting his partner's position, the man can get his penis tip into just the right place to do this.

Making love with the woman lying back in a large armchair can be very stimulating for the man. She lies with her hips very near the front of the chair. He kneels between her open legs, and can hold her legs wide apart while he penetrates her. She can easily reach down and caress her clitoris with one hand and her breasts or nipples with the other.

This is a very good position for learning about sex with a new partner, because it enables the woman to stimulate herself to produce the best sensations while she is being penetrated. It is quite awkward for the man to caress her clitoris, but it can be done.

Movement is easy in this position, and the man can thrust as deeply as the angle of the woman's vagina will permit.

OLDER LOVING

Myths put around by the young and our youth-obsessed culture suggest that getting older lessens the sex drive, but this simply is not the case. While the wild athleticism of young lovers is often neither possible nor indeed desirable for those over, say, sixty years old, there is absolutely no reason why if a couple still feels the urge the frequency of their lovemaking should decline. Indeed, recent research has shown that making love – specifically, having regular orgasms – is not only good fun, it's good for your health, no matter how old you are.

However, even those elderly people who have maintained a very healthy lifestyle will invariably experience at least a slight stiffening of the joints, and any minor health problems that they suffer from will unfortunately tend to get worse as the years go by.

Here are some ideas on how to continue to enjoy lovemaking as the ageing process sets in.

❤ *Avoid lovemaking that puts a strain on your back, such as "knee-tremblers" – up against a wall or standing up – or with the woman lying underneath on the very edge of the bed, with her back arched.*

❤ *The "missionary" position – face to face with the man on top – is great for intimacy and communication during sex, but may not be suitable in the case of the woman who is suffering from brittle bones or if the man is too heavy for her.*

❤ *Try the "spoons" position, with both partners curled up together, side by side, the woman "sitting" on the man's lap with his penis entering her vagina from behind. This can prevent thrusting being too rough, or knocking the cervix.*

💗 *For many, the years will have taken their toll and an element of vulnerability crept in. For example, a woman may have had a mastectomy and feel uncertain about her sexuality or attractiveness. In this and many other cases it is a good idea to concentrate on creating a gently erotic atmosphere through slowly building up the foreplay.*

💗 *Taking time to explore each other's bodies with fingertips, lips and tongues is an essential part of the older lover's armory.*

💗 *Try massaging each other gently with sweet-smelling oil, but avoid using it on the extremely sensitive genital area.*

Keeping lovemaking alive

When mobility is severely restricted full intercourse may well be out of the question. Your feelings and needs, however, will remain just as strong, and you will yearn for the release of a good orgasm and the closeness of your partner. The answer here could be to have oral sex and to masturbate each other.

There are many advantages in having sex in your later years. For women, anxieties about getting pregnant will be a thing of the past, and there will be no young children around to cramp your style. You and your partner will undoubtedly have much more time to yourselves, and can spend long hours in unadulterated sexual ecstasy.

Years of sexual – and life – experience can be put to excellent use at this stage in your life, and if you are still with the same life partner, by now you will know their every little like and dislike in bed.

Penetration is quite deep – but not so deep that the position cannot be used during pregnancy. If the man angles his penis correctly, he can stimulate her G spot, and his hands are free to caress all the front of her body.

The woman lies with her bottom close to the edge of a bed. The man lies on top of her – facing away from her with his knees either side of her chest. His weight is taken by his hands on the floor as he lies over the edge of the bed. His penis penetrates her in the reverse way to normal as she puts her feet on his shoulders.

Movement is somewhat restricted in this position and it is fairly tiring for the man's arms, especially if the woman's legs are heavy on his back.

Given that it puts no pressure at all on the woman's stomach, however, it can be a good position during the first sixteen weeks of pregnancy. The woman can caress her clitoris but the man cannot do much, because his hands are required to support his weight.

This is a position for occasional fun and variation and is ideal for the man who likes his anus played with during intercourse. There are only a few positions where this can be achieved.

For the really adventurous and athletic couple, the woman can lie as a bridge, her legs on the bed and her head and shoulders on a chair at the front of the bed. She opens her legs and the man straddles her hips and penetrates her facing away from her face.

This position is fairly uncomfortable, but if the woman arches her back and both partners move their pelvises they can achieve a stimulating sensation.

A variation of the "spoons" position, where the woman places one leg over her partner's thigh, is ideal for the female who enjoys a good deal of clitoral stimulation.

A more realistic version of this is for the woman to lie flat on her back on the bed with her legs apart. The man faces away from her and kneels with his legs either side of her chest. She draws up her legs, he penetrates her and rests his face down on the bed, possibly supporting himself on his elbows. She puts her feet on his back.

The woman lies flat on her back with her head on a pillow. She raises her legs in the air and parts them slightly. The man kneels with his knees on either side of her waist and penetrates her facing away from her with his legs either side of her hips. Again, he may well have to support himself on his forearms or hands. The woman can easily stimulate her clitoris and caress his anus.

The woman lies on a low table with her feet flat on the floor and wide apart. The man enters her. Penetration is shallow, but can be greatly enhanced if she raises her legs to put her ankles over his shoulders. He can hold her legs apart with her soles facing the ceiling as he penetrates her deeply and with good long thrusts. The height of the table has to be exactly right though. Trying to do this with bent knees is very tiring for a man.

Side-by-side positions

For couples who prize intimacy and close contact when they are making love, side-by side positions provide maximum scope for cuddling, caressing and kissing. These positions are more restful, particularly useful during pregnancy, and ideal for those who like their lovemaking to be accompanied by tender words of love.

The best-known side-by-side position is the "spoons". It is exceptionally good to use during pregnancy because the woman's stomach can lie flat on the bed.

The couple lie on their sides with the man cuddling the woman's back as she draws her knees up towards her stomach. He then tucks into her and penetrates her.

Penetration can be very good, especially if the woman angles her body down towards her feet and the man can, to a limited extent, make thrusting movements. He can reach around and stimulate her clitoris or she can open her legs and do so herself.

He can also reach around her and caress her breasts and stomach and, at the same time, kiss her neck and her back. The area of skin contact is extensive and this can be romantic and sensuous.

It is a very pleasant position for the couple who like to fall asleep together after sex – in fact it is quite possible to go to sleep with the penis still in the vagina.

A variation on this is for the woman, once penetrated, to roll over onto her back a little and to place one leg over the upper leg of the man. This opens up her vulva considerably and leaves her clitoris available for her or her partner to caress. She now has both hands free to caress herself, or her lover.

Movement is easier here and penetration can be quite deep, particularly if the woman raises her bottom off the bed a little. The woman cannot play a very active role, but her partner can caress her breasts and kiss her shoulders.

Her stomach is totally free, again making this position good for later on in pregnancy. Penetration can be good but not very deep, and any thrusting movement is somewhat restricted.

From the woman's point of view it is restful and she can stimulate herself and her partner's scrotum. In some women the man's penis stimulates the G spot in this position, giving extra sensations.

The couple lie on their sides facing one another. The woman draws up her legs to her chest and opens them widely. The man then enters her while the woman folds her legs around his back. She also cuddles him around the shoulders with her arms.

Penetration can be very good but movement is somewhat restricted. The couple can kiss very easily and passionately. There is a lot of skin contact and this can make the couple feel very much "at one" with each other. However, this position is not suitable for very overweight people or for pregnant women.

One of the best lovemaking positions of all is a side-entry one. The woman lies on her back and the man on his side at right angles to her body. The woman can then draw her thighs back towards her stomach while he enters her as he lies underneath her.

Penetration is deep and movement can be good, but not excellent. As another restful position it is particularly good during pregnancy or for the larger woman. Both partners can reach the woman's clitoris to stimulate it and the man can caress most parts of her body, including her breasts. The only real disadvantage is that they cannot kiss.

It is a good position for a "quickie" because it involves very little undressing. It is also good for conceiving, especially if the woman remains with her legs drawn back for a few minutes after intercourse. The woman can also reach the man's scrotum.

The anus of both partners is accessible for those who like anal stimulation, and it is also a good position for inexperienced women who have difficulty achieving orgasms during intercourse.

An ideal position for the woman who is making love for the first time after she has given birth, is for her to lie on her side, turning slightly on her front and supporting her top half with her forearms on the bed. The man cuddles into her back just as in the spoons positions, then puts his upper leg over her hips as he penetrates her.

It is a pleasant position for the man to be able to caress the woman's back with one hand but she can do very little. Penetration is not especially good because her legs are fairly straight, but he is allowed quite good movement.

By drawing her knees up to her stomach she can increase penetration, but the position then converts into the more restful and satisfactory "spoons".

Rear-entry lovemaking

Intercourse face to face is by far the most popular form of lovemaking, for a variety of reasons. For a couple who make love several times a week, however, making love in positions that involves the man penetrating the woman from the rear can be a refreshing change and can add a touch of variety to their sex lives which in turn adds new life to their relationship.

Whatever its physical and emotional advantages and disadvantages, it cannot be denied that rear-entry lovemaking is not very romantic. However, for many couples this is no drawback, as the woman will want to be taken with ardour on some

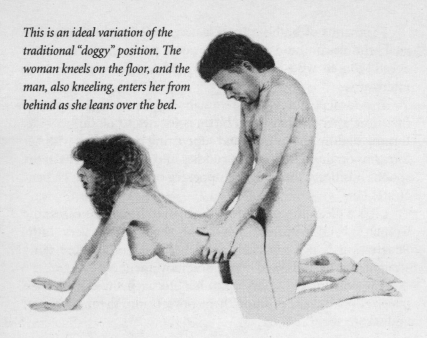

This is an ideal variation of the traditional "doggy" position. The woman kneels on the floor, and the man, also kneeling, enters her from behind as she leans over the bed.

occasions, while on others, she will want tender loving and romantic intercourse.

As human beings, we have a vast range of possibilities and this is to our advantage. It is fashionable today for women to talk about caring men in bed who spend ages with detailed and prolonged foreplay, but however pleasant it might be, it should not become a boring routine.

Many women, in therapy, say that they greatly enjoy being taken roughly. This proves to them that they are so desirable that their man cannot keep his hands off them, which is in itself sexually flattering. It also absolves them from having to put up with much foreplay which they may find contrived, boring or repetitive.

For the man who likes to see his woman's bottom and anus, rear-entry positions can be extremely stimulating. If both partners like it, the man can caress her bottom, stimulate her anus and so on. Because in many rear-entry positions, the woman's thighs are at an angle to her body (this is especially true of the classical "doggy" position) penetration is quite deep and can on occasion be very deep.

Rear-entry positions can be especially good for the woman who has a sensitive G spot. The man's penis can be arranged to hit the right spot or to massage gently, whichever the woman prefers. Even if the woman is not sensitive to G spot stimulation, she will experience very different sensations, many of which are highly arousing, if only because of the position's novelty to her.

A woman who is shy, who wants to fantasize about another man, or wants to be sexually satisfied but would rather not be reminded of her partner for some reason, may find rear-entry a good way round her problem. By facing away from the man she can enjoy her partner's penis and caresses in a somewhat detached way.

Rear-entry positions range from the simple "doggy" position to some highly adventurous positions that will please more athletic lovers. But whatever variation you choose to try, make sure it suits both of you.

Probably the best-known and most widely used is the "doggy" position: the woman kneels on the bed or the floor and her partner kneels behind her and enters her. She can angle her pelvis in several different ways according to how far she leans forward and how she supports herself.

Each position gives new sensations to both partners. The woman can, for example, keep her body horizontal by resting on her hands and knees. She can rest on her elbows, or even lie with her arms back along her body, or put them under her forehead as her breasts support her upper body.

Penetration is extremely good, especially if the woman lies with her chest on the bed. The man has a wide range of possible movements and the woman can be taken very forcefully, which many enjoy. A few women find that air becomes pushed into the vagina in some of these positions. This need not necessarily be a problem, but if the penis traps air and pushes it up into the top of the vagina it can cause pain. When the woman turns over the air may be expelled with an embarrassing noise, but most couples either ignore this or are able to make a joke of it.

A modification of the "doggy" position is for the woman to kneel on a low stool or table (covered with something that cushions her knees). The man stands behind her between her open legs and enters her.

For the more athletic, another good rear-entry position is for the woman to bend over with her legs wide apart and rest her hands on the floor in front of her. Her bottom and vulva are now exposed and the man can, by bending his knees a little, enter her from behind.

Movement and penetration are good (at least for the man) but the woman's movements are somewhat restricted, beyond being able to wiggle her hips from side to side to enhance the pleasure. She can, however, as in all rear-entry positions, contract her pelvic muscles to make it more stimulating for them both.

The man lies on the bed with his knees together and the woman kneels over his hips facing away from him. She takes her weight on her hands placed either side of his legs. She controls the amount of movement in this rear-entry, woman-on-top position. This position is particularly enjoyable for the bottom-centred man as he can see his partner's bottom and anus and caress them, while his lover takes the lead.

Another position suitable for the woman with strong arms is one in which she leans over the bed, supporting her entire weight on her arms, and the man lifts her open legs off the ground and stands between them as he enters her from behind. Although penetration can be quite deep, movement is fairly limited in this position.

This position involves considerable athletic prowess, and is not suitable for everyone. The woman has to be very supple and the man extremely gentle.

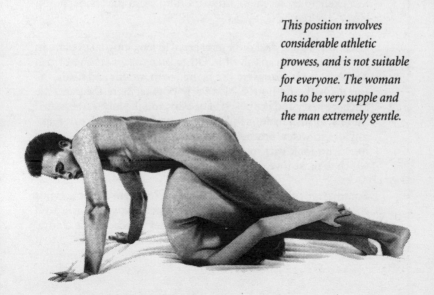

SEX TODAY

The findings of sex surveys make fascinating reading although they should, perhaps, not be taken too seriously given that the participants are self-selected and not chosen at random.

Here are just a few lovemaking statistics to consider:

Frequency: from the age of twenty-five to fifty-five and beyond, in Western Europe the frequency with which couples had intercourse gradually declined from two to three times a week to only once a week on average.

These figures probably overemphasized the fall-off in the frequency with which some older couples make love. Because people in the higher age groups tend to change their sexual partners less often than younger men and women, their sex lives are less likely to be receiving an extra fillip from the "honeymoon effect" as a result.

Location: a great deal of heterosexual lovemaking takes place in bed, but by no means all of it. Other preferences among British people of both sexes were the living room, woods and fields, the car, the bath and hotels. Also fairly popular were the park, the kitchen, water and the beach. The park and the kitchen appealed more to British males, while women preferred the idea of making love in water. Brothels were mentioned by 5 per cent of the men who took part in the survey as being enjoyable places in which to make love.

Foreplay: men's lack of interest in foreplay seems to be a major complaint of both American and European women. Most who were questioned about this said that they needed more clitoral stimulation but they would prefer their partners to build up to it slowly.

Positions: of the couples who took part in a US survey on positions, three-quarters liked their sex lying down. The missionary position, with the man lying on top was by far the most popular – half of those questioned said they made love this way, even though stimulation of the clitoris is more difficult in this position. Just over a quarter said they had intercourse with the woman on top, and one in twelve preferred to make love lying side by side.

The remaining quarter of those couples questioned had had intercourse "doggy-style" (one in twelve), standing up (two in every hundred), or in some other unspecified position (one in twenty).

Oral Sex: according to one European study, 88 per cent of the women who replied said that they had tried oral sex, and, on the whole, they seem to have enjoyed it. American women were less adventurous when it came to oral sex with only one in eight saying that they regularly participated in it, although a further seven per cent admitted that they had tried it.

Masturbation: in Western Europe, two-thirds of the unmarried women and more than half the wives questioned by sex researchers said that they masturbated.

Over 50 per cent of those who masturbated did so several times a month. Single women living alone masturbated slightly more often than women living with their husbands or partners.

More than 90 per cent of the women participating in a United States survey said that they masturbated, but more than a third claimed that they did so only in the absence of their sexual partners.

Deep penetration

Men have an almost primitive urge to thrust deeply as they ejaculate and for many – if not most – men this deep thrusting is regarded as the best part of intercourse. Most women, however, prefer shallower penetration.

This is an area of give and take in a sexual relationship. The loving woman who may not particularly enjoy deep thrusting can, from time to time when she is exceptionally aroused, allow her man to penetrate deeply, even if it hurts for a few seconds. This can be a tremendous turn-on for the man who perceives that filling his woman so completely is a sign that he is in charge of lovemaking. At both the conscious and unconscious level, this is a game that some couples enjoy.

Deep penetration can be very passionate and exciting, especially as the woman has to press her thighs back against her stomach to let her partner penetrate deeply. This "opening up" of the whole of her pelvis to her man makes him feel especially wanted. And some women similarly claim that they want their man to "fill them up".

Very deep penetration can provide entirely new sensations. The aroused vagina widens greatly at the top end and this means that deep penetration, rather than offering more stimulation to the head of the penis, actually stimulates it less. This gives a new dimension to the feel of the vagina for both the man and the woman.

Deep penetration can also be useful for the man who has trouble with coming too soon. If his partner is aroused, her vagina will have expanded at the top end and so will offer less stimulation to a "trigger-happy" penis. So, ironically, deep penetration can help him to make love longer, even though for the "average" man not experiencing these kinds of problems, deep penetration will make him come sooner.

For a couple who are having difficulty in conceiving, deep penetration could be the answer. If they make love every other day around ovulation time and the man penetrates his partner very deeply, conception may take place.

For some women, very deep penetration brings their partner's pubic bone into contact with the clitoris, causing intense excitement from the repeated friction. For many women, though, the pressure of the man's pelvis comes in entirely the wrong place and can even be unpleasant. There is only one way to find out – experiment.

The cervix is the lowest part of the uterus and projects down into the top of the vagina. Deep penetration positions enable a woman to enjoy her man's penis stimulating her cervix, and this can be pleasant for the man too. Some men say that hitting the cervix with their penis is one of the best parts of intercourse. Deep penetration in rear-entry positions is also highly arousing for those women who have a sensitive G spot.

Some women greatly enjoy being on top of their man and then positioning their body so that they can direct the penis tip to stimulate the front wall of the vagina. Many men find this exciting.

During the middle three months of pregnancy, when the vagina is widening and lengthening, some couples find that normal intercourse positions feel unsatisfyingly "sloppy" or "loose" for the penis. This is the time when deep penetration can be very exciting.

In the last month of pregnancy it is probably not sensible to use deep penetration, although it can be a very pleasant way of starting off labour if you are overdue. The absorption of muscle-contracting prostaglandins from the semen helps to contract the uterus.

Usually, deep penetration is highly arousing and the majority of couples greatly enjoy it. However, some do not. Those who find it uncomfortable should use other positions, which do not put pressure on sensitive areas. If either partner experiences real pain on deep penetration they should consult a doctor.

Advanced lovemaking

Advanced positions should be taken for what they are – periodic excursions into differing sensations for both partners. But what should not be ignored is that they provide a couple with novel and exciting ways to enjoy each other, along with opportunities to have fun.

Positions other than the well-known ones often look as if they have a bizarre or contortionist quality about them and, certainly, some require a degree of fitness, suppleness and athleticism which not all lovers possess. Yet almost every position can be adapted by an inventive couple to fit their own needs.

To begin with, you need look no further than your own home. Ordinary household props have a special place in the repertoire of the advanced lover. Various items of furniture and other bits and pieces, for example, are always available and within easy reach and can be used in ways that would probably astonish the manufacturers!

Chairs, either on their own or placed strategically near the bed, are probably the most versatile lovemaking prop of all. You can

If the woman has strong enough arms, it's well worth trying to master "Autumn Leaves", which is one of the few positions where you can make love on the move.

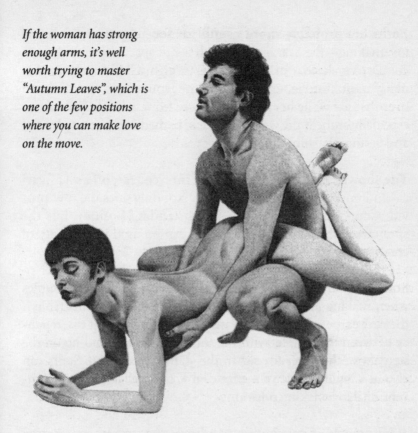

sit on them, use them for support, and you and your lover can even stand on them to get into novel positions. Placed next to the bed, a chair can provide support in a variety of positions for your feet, legs, bottom, back or head.

Tables are indispensable props, especially for rear-entry sex with the woman leaning over one as her partner enters her from behind.

Baths are probably more useful for foreplay than for actual lovemaking – the average-sized tub is not spacious enough for a couple to make love in. Like a table, though, a bath can be particularly useful for rear-entry sex: all the woman has to do is bend over the side while her lover enters her from behind. This can be especially erotic if the woman has just bathed in oil-scented water and is smooth, shining and slippery.

The shower, for both foreplay and intercourse, offers a practical and novel place for making love. Not only does the wall provide support for the woman for a standing position but the spray from the shower head nozzle can be used in a variety of creative ways.

Stairs are rarely used to their full advantage by most couples when making love. Their main virtue (it's more comfortable if they are carpeted) is that they make up for any height discrepancy between the couple, with the shorter partner standing on the step above the other for sex in the standing position. Stairs can also be a highly erotic venue for oral sex, as well as for more conventional lovemaking positions.

A hammock, if you happen to have one, or are considering buying one, offers unique lovemaking possibilities to any couple. When they are suspended in mid-air together, a couple can turn even the most basic position into a marvellous flight of sexual fantasy.

The bed in conjunction with the floor has a unique value in opening up possibilities for "split-level" positions, both for conventional intercourse and oral sex.

From the "Back of Beyond" can make a woman feel joyfully abandoned, and although it is not a position that can be held for any length of time, it is well worth the effort as there is no other position that affords entry in the same way.

Standing up

Standing positions have a unique charm all of their own, but are best attempted when both partners are feeling energetic or when they want "quickie" sex. Although most standing positions can be used as intercourse positions in their own right, it is often better to culminate with a floor or bed position, when and if the couple wish to achieve orgasm more comfortably. Even couples who have a marked height difference can still achieve satisfactory sex standing up. Stairs will allow their bodies to be in line where it most matters, as will a pile of telephone directories or other large books.

The standing position most people are probably most familiar with is the front-entry one with the man standing in front of the woman while her back is supported against the wall.

An interesting variation is for the man, after he has entered his lover from the front, to lift her up, place his hands underneath her buttocks and bounce her up and down on his penis. The couple can either do this against a wall or, if the man is strong enough, he can carry the woman around the room, still keeping the momentum going.

For the couple who want to try some really adventurous positions for "quickies" standing up, or some advanced positions using simply a chair as a prop, two of each are described here. Be careful though – some of them demand a high degree of suppleness. If you take up a position and either of you feels any discomfort, stop and try a simpler one.

In the "Autumn Leaves" position the woman goes on all fours and the man lifts her up to penetrate her. She supports herself on her hands while he takes the rest of her body weight by placing his hands on the top of her thighs. The woman can clasp her legs around the man's waist or place her heels on his back.

This wheelbarrow-like position really is one of the few where it is possible to make love, and have orgasms, while moving around the room. Unique sensations can be achieved from it as the normal thrusting movements from the man are replaced by sensations which derive totally from moving around. The main drawback to this position is that if the woman moves too quickly, the man's penis can slip out of her, so it is probably best left to the man to control the speed at which they move.

Of all the "advanced" positions "From the Back of Beyond" demands the most strength and athleticism, particularly from the woman. If she is exceptionally strong, however, such a position enables both partners to experience the flavour of what feels like a really new position.

The woman starts off by doing a handstand with the man standing in front of her waiting to catch her. Because she will be taking her weight on her arms, a good alternative for those whose arms are not strong enough is to start off with a headstand so that the woman can support her body weight on her head as well as her arms.

Whichever method is chosen, the man catches the woman and then brings her body right over so that she is literally offering her vulva to him.

He then transfers his hands to her buttocks so that he can support her from there and direct her vulva towards him and then enter her. If he drops into a kneeling position, the woman can bring her legs right down and he can penetrate her from there.

The man controls the tempo by using the woman's body, bringing it alternately towards him and away from him with a sensual rhythmic motion. If the woman has exceptional balance, the man can support her under her buttocks and use his other

PERSONAL MORALITY

Living in the West today, most of us more or less agree about what is morally right or wrong – and certainly on the more clear-cut issues, such as stealing or killing. When we come to the lesser "sins" of lying, cheating and envy, most people adopt a more flexible view – they adjust their moral standpoint to meet the circumstances.

But there is a whole area of behaviour which is concerned with relationships and sexuality, where a wide number of moral positions exist side by side in society. This aspect of morality has taken on such an importance in the past, that people were often judged as "immoral" when this referred only to their sexual behaviour, and not to their actions as a whole.

The nineteenth century saw a great upturn in professed moral standards. Marriage and the family were highly prized and illegitimacy was condemned. Many notions, such as the persecution of homosexuals, continued well into the middle of the twentieth century, and some of these ideas still persist today.

Changing attitudes

This all changed in the permissive climate of the sixties, as new and more effective methods of contraception – the Pill and the IUD or coil for example – were made available to women. Homosexuality became more acceptable, as did divorce.

While many women felt liberated there were those that took the view that the permissiveness of the sixties meant that sex had become overrated.

By the early 1980s there were movements in the USA and Britain to re-establish Victorian values. Pressure groups have concentrated on trying to prevent young people from becoming sexually active. They have also tried to exclude sex education from schools – saying that it is the parents' responsibility to educate their children in these matters as and when they feel it is right and proper to do so.

Morality today

Young people today are open to countless influences when building up their own moral code. Obviously, the attitude and behaviour of parents is very important in the formation of a child's moral viewpoint. But as children become teenagers, other adults, apart from their parents, as well as friends and acquaintances from their peer group also begin to exert a greater influence. Added to this are the sexual messages these children receive from films, television and magazines.

Younger people today are probably more aware of the moral responsibilities open to them, although many of them may be ignorant of the effect their choice may have both on themselves and on others. And some young people in Western society have moral views quite different from the majority because of their religions or ethnic backgrounds. Roman Catholics, for instance, are more strongly opposed to contraception and abortion than other Christians or non-believers.

Finding a moral standpoint

Your feelings about morality evolve through your interrelations both with people of your own and those of the opposite sex. Many people do not bother to decide what moral positions to take until they are faced with a situation. In trying to work out our own moral principles, we can only try to understand the relevant arguments and arrive at our own conclusions through personal experience.

hand to stimulate her clitoris. If the man drops to his knees, he will then be in a position where he can perform oral sex on his partner.

For the woman, the principal sensation will be one of abandonment as she offers herself up to her partner. But, however enjoyable, this position is not recommended for any length of time as blood can rush to the woman's head.

Aptly named, the "Ride-a-Cock Horse" position is quite simple for the man and should not be too strenuous for the woman provided she is capable of taking some weight on her arms. The man sits on the chair and his partner goes on all fours in front of him. He then gently pulls her towards him and lifts her legs while she supports herself on her hands. The man then wraps her legs around his waist as he guides his penis inside her. Using his hands on her buttocks, he controls her movements as his own tend to be restricted.

The "Squat Thrust" position also requires the couple to use a chair and they should take care, particularly as orgasm approaches. This is because the woman is balanced on the chair and too much thrusting from the man, or pelvic movement from the woman, during the abandonment of climax could result in the chair toppling over, which could have dangerous, even disastrous results.

The woman should first stand on the chair and then get into a squatting position while supporting herself on the back of the chair. Provided her partner is supporting her at this stage (he could use one leg to secure the chair in position) she should be perfectly safe. The man then places his hands on her waist or the tops of her thighs and gently enters her. He should then be able to thrust quite gently and she should be able to respond by moving her buttocks sensually from side to side.

This position, in which the man uses his hands to support the buttocks, allows him full penetration, but slightly less scope for movement.

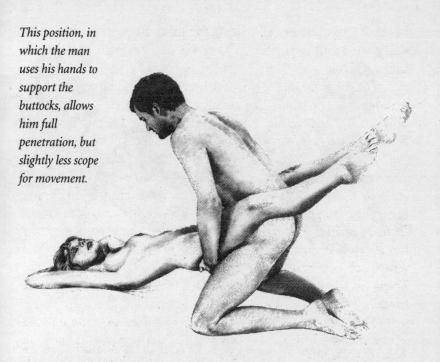

At the moment of orgasm, the man should make a determined effort to control his thrusting to enable his lover to get the most from the unique sensations this position offers.

There are countless more adventurous positions for couples to experiment with. Here are just a few:

● *The frog: this adds a new dimension to the simplest woman-on-top positions. The woman rests the soles of her feet on the top of the man's feet. This will make the woman splay her legs, and the man and the woman will have direct and complete contact all the way down the front of their legs.*

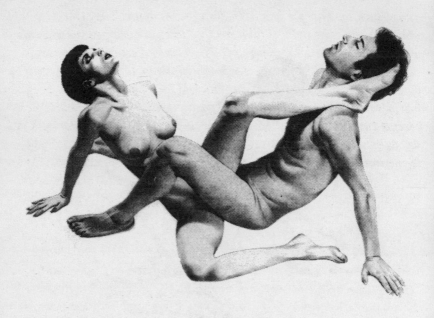

The X position requires the couple to face each other and the woman position her legs – one on the man's shoulder, the other between his legs – to form what looks like the letter X.

● *The X position: from the straight kneeling-on-top position, the woman can manoeuvre one leg so that it is under the man's thigh, then bring her other leg over that same side and rest it on his shoulder. Still sitting on him, she can then lean back so that his penis applies the maximum pressure on the front of the vagina. This position prolongs intercourse.*

● *À la négresse: the French often call rear-entry position coitus à la négresse. Rear-entry positions were considered bestial, and* much too base for "civilized" Europeans to use. They were thought to be only suitable for the "inferior" heathen races, being seen as submissive as far as the woman was concerned, and it may be that à la négresse has something to do with the advantage white plantation owners took of their female slaves in the past. In fact, the à la négresse position requires the female to be active and does not mean she has been put in a "humiliating" position. The woman starts by lying face down with her hands clasped behind her neck and with her buttocks up in the air. When the man enters her, she hooks her legs round his and uses them to pull him onto her. Using her legs in this way means that the apparently submissive woman can actually control the pace and depth of lovemaking.

● Cuissade positions: the cuissade positions are similar, except that the man takes the woman half from the rear. Usually the woman lies on her back and the man lies beside her, then threads his leg under one of hers and over the other, effectively turning her pelvis. From here, he can enter her from the rear, while propping himself up on his elbow so that they can still look at each other. The cuissade positions allow the man's penis to enter the vagina at some very stimulating angles. Or, if he remains lying on his side, this is a very leisurely position for both partners – although none the less stimulating for that.

● The Viennese Oyster: this position can only be performed by an extremely supple woman. She must be able to cross her feet behind the back of her head. She assumes this position lying on her back. The man then lies full length on top of her and squeezes her feet. Apart from the stimulation of the soles of the feet, this position allows a unique rocking pelvic movement.

All these positions take some practice to get right, but they are well worth the effort, offering as they do delicious alternatives to the more conventional ways of making love.

Sex and movement

According to the gentry of Victorian times, "ladies do not move". A lady was supposed to be sexless, and would not be so crude as to move her body during intercourse – just in case she appeared to be enjoying herself.

Unfortunately, this harmful concept still exists in many relationships. Some women, even now, lie beneath their partner with their legs open and remain motionless throughout intercourse, afraid to take a more active role.

Men need to experience penile movement during intercourse, or they will not be able to reach orgasm. They enjoy thrusting movements of various speeds and depths, but tend to thrust deeply as they reach orgasm. For a man to obtain the most pleasure during sexual intercourse, he will usually try to produce movements which are close to those he uses during masturbation. This will differ from man to man. For instance, some like long, slow movement, whereas others like short, jerky movement.

Women have a wider range of movements. Thrusting is popular, but a woman on top can thrust herself onto the penis (varying depth of penetration to suit her or her man), or rotate her pelvis so the penis is swept around the top of the vagina.

A woman can also contract the vaginal opening of her deep pelvic muscles. If she contracts her muscles as the penis moves in, and releases the pressure as it moves out, her man may quickly be brought to orgasm.

Some women have learned to control their pelvic muscles so that they can produce an orgasm in a motionless penis by "milking" it with these muscles. This is highly stimulating for both the man and woman.

A woman who has a sensitive G spot can angle her body when she is on top, to get her man's penis tip right on the spot, and move until climax.

The amount of movement each partner is capable of in lovemaking depends very much on the position adopted. Some positions allow each partner to move freely, while others limit movement, but at the same time allow for deeper penetration by the man.

Positions that allow full stroke movement are those in which:

● *The woman kneels on a bed or low stool or lies over the edge of something higher (a table) and the man enters her from behind.*

● *The woman lies back in a deep chair with her legs apart. The man kneels in front and penetrates her.*

● *The woman lies on her back with her knees up and her feet flat on the bed. The man supports his weight on his hands and penetrates her from above.*

● *In the same position, the woman can put her ankles over the man's shoulders.*

● *The woman lies on her tummy with her hips on a pillow. The man approaches her from behind and, supporting himself on his hands, penetrates her.*

Positions that allow full penetration but little movement, are those in which:

● *The man sits in a simple chair. The woman faces away from him (or towards him) and sits on his penis.*

● *The woman lies back in a deep armchair, raises her legs and puts her ankles on the shoulders of her partner who kneels on front to penetrate her.*

● *The woman lies down flat on her back with her legs apart. The man is face down on top of her with his weight mainly on his knees and elbows.*

● *The woman lies on her side facing away from the man who lies behind her, moulding into her body contours.*

Positions which allow the woman a good range of movement are those where:

● *The woman sits astride her man's penis, facing him while he is seated.*

● *The man lies flat on his back and the woman sits astride him facing towards or away from him. She can rest on her knees or have her feet flat on the bed.*

● *The man kneels on the floor and then leans back to take his weight on his hands behind him. The woman squats on his penis facing him.*

As well as varying their positions for lovemaking, a couple can also vary the thrusting movement they use. By varying thrusting movements during lovemaking the man can greatly increase his partner's pleasure. For maximum penetration and friction, he can also thrust to right and left.

CHAPTER 5

Imaginative
Lovemaking

*I*n many areas of life predictability is greatly valued. When it comes to sex, however, most couples find that it pays to experiment with more imaginative and creative techniques every once in a while. Breaking established routines can add excitement to life and stolen moments can be exhilarating. Spontaneous sex can prove that couples still find each other attractive, and are not simply responding to being turned on at prescribed times. The whole relationship can become more open, more honest, more relaxed, with couples talking about sex in a way that they had not thought possible before.

The following are some suggested variations on themes you may like to try in order to add some spice to your lovemaking.

● *During deep sleep, a woman's body relaxes profoundly and her vagina opens widely. A careful partner can lick his partner's vulva and even insert several fingers into her vagina without waking her. Some women sleep so deeply that they can be penetrated from behind without stirring. A woman used to the feel of her lover's body may well enjoy this in a state of semi-consciousness. Similarly, a woman who knows her partner's likes and dislikes may be able to do magical things to him during the night.*

● *The shower or bath is a natural venue for sex. For one thing, you are already undressed. Wash together or, maybe, make love in the water. It does not have to be that "advanced" – simply soaping each other all over can create pleasant sensations.*

● *Sex in a swimming pool has great possibilities because of the relative weightlessness involved. Some of those seemingly impossible positions featured on Hindu temples suddenly become attainable because the woman is now light enough to prop up. The sea, if you are in an extremely private spot, is even better. The salt helps buoyancy and there is no chlorine as a potential irritant. Shoreline sex, however, does have its disadvantages as sand can be abrasive.*

● *Many people get turned on by looking at themselves, or each other, in mirrors. This creates an exciting voyeuristic element – but without actually having other people present. Members of either sex may be stimulated by seeing themselves masturbate or being tied up. However some lovers, it must be said, merely find mirrors obtrusive or distracting.*

● *Some couples are turned on by making love in a profusion of sweat after some energetic sport – squash, for example – and some women like the "manly" smell of fresh sweat. The problem in this instance, of course, unless you have your own court, is one of privacy.*

● *Why not make contraception a turn-on instead of a turn-off? Putting a sheath on a man, or inserting a diaphragm into a woman, can be a sexual adventure in itself. Almost anything, used imaginatively, can be incorporated into your love life and be made a part of loveplay.*

● *A blindfold, provided it is not tied too tight, can provide unique sensations in even the most tried and tested lovemaking techniques. This is because if we do not use our eyes, the remaining senses tend to be magnified to compensate.*

● *Sensual massage is a tried and tested means of arousal. But
there are variations that advanced lovers can find exciting and
stimulating.*

● *The use of feathers on either partner's body as a means of
arousal can be a tantalizing and highly erotic experience. Use
them as you would use your hands during a conventional
sensual massage, leaving the genitals until last. Ice has a*

*Light restraint, using loose
bonds, can be highly erotic.
Choose a position where
you can see each other,
take things gently and
always have a prearranged
release signal.*

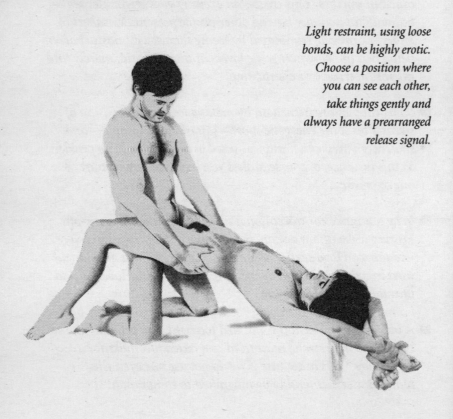

curiously shocking effect which some lovers find highly
stimulating. You should let it melt a little so that there are no
sharp corners – ice straight from the freezer could damage the
skin. Use it to trace a path all over your partner's body.

● *Many couples find bondage incredibly arousing. This is the*
gentle art of tying up your lover. The idea is not to make your
partner do something that they would not do unrestrained. It is
to enable one partner to tease the other until they almost beg to
be brought to orgasm, so greatly enhancing a couple's sex
repertoire. There are dangers, however. The couple should have
a prearranged signal that means "release me". Knots should
never be too tight, nothing should ever be tied around the neck,
and gags should also be quick-release. For couples who trust
each other, though, the dangers are minimal.

● *Spanking plays an important part in some couples' repertoire*
although men often seem to enjoy it more than women. For the
man to spank the woman, it is probably best done when she is
draped over his knee as he gently hits her buttocks. The man can
use his other hand, perhaps to stroke her clitoris or even insert
his finger inside her vulva. Used in conjunction with the finger
and thumb technique – inserting one or more fingers inside the
woman's vagina, perhaps stroking her G spot as he uses his
thumb on her clitoris – the extra dimension of hitting her raised
buttocks can be highly memorable for both partners. For the
man, having his buttocks spanked is more erotic if he raises
them. The intensity of sensations can be dramatically increased
for him by alternating between squeezing and parting his
buttocks and hitting them while masturbating him at the
same time.

SEXUAL DREAMS

Nearly everyone experiences sexual dreams at one time or another. The most obvious sexual dreams are those that contain sexual activity, or sexual feelings. In these the dreamer is involved in sex in some way or other – he or she may be vividly and actively involved in making love, or perhaps just doing something as apparently innocent as watching another person undress.

Most explicitly sexual dreams involve people who are known to the dreamer and may reveal something of the dreamer's feelings for that person. When the object of the dream is a partner, its meaning can be very clear, but when the object of the dream is an acquaintance, or even a member of the family, the meaning is often less so.

The psychology of dreams

The Austrian psychiatrist Sigmund Freud saw people as sexual beings from the moment of birth. This not only means that the sexual feelings expressed in dreams are really beyond our control, as are our dreams in general, but also that even very early impressions can become sexual in our dreams. What Freud and most psychologists today assert is that it is perfectly natural to respond sexually to those around us, even though we may have no sexual interest in them when we are awake, or it is socially unacceptable to acknowledge these feelings.

Many psychologists claim to have found clear meanings for common themes appearing in sexual dreams.

For example, dreams involving bisexual or hermaphrodite roles for the dreamer could indicate some problems with their feelings about their own masculinity or femininity.

Dreams involving intercourse are very interesting. If a male dreams of making love with an active or successful woman, the cause may be a wish that his partner play a less passive role during lovemaking and also in their life together. In this kind of dream psychologists claim the other woman is of little importance.

If intercourse in the dream is interrupted, inhibitions are indicated. The cause of the interruption may indicate something about the inhibitions.

Sometimes people dream about making love with their clothes on. This is not a sign of inhibitions, but in fact a sign of guilt.

Analyzing your dreams

Interpreting your own dreams may be easy if they are explicit, but you may find that they are well beyond your powers of analysis. Try referring to a book, but be careful. Ask yourself, "Does the book's explanation sound plausible – does it strike a chord?" Sometimes the interpretation may be right but you do not want to accept it.

However, at other times it really can be wrong or have no relevance to you personally. If it does not, simply ignore it. Psychologists admit that they are still just scratching the surface of the human psyche.

A man will often fantasize about women who will happily fellate him, perhaps making up for the lack of women who are willing to do it in reality.

● *Postillionage – inserting a finger in your partner's anus – can be highly erotic. The only danger is that bacteria lurk inside the anus so a man should never transfer his fingers from the anus to the vulva. Likewise, the woman should not use postillionage on her partner and then masturbate him. Position is all-important for this, so it is best if the recipient goes on all fours. For the man, this means that access to his prostate, or G spot, is possible*

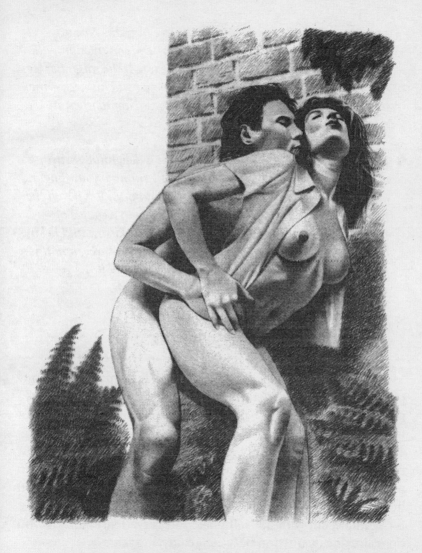

A sense of freedom and the sounds and smells of the open air make out-of-doors sex a popular fantasy for many people.

and the woman can use her finger to give him this type of
orgasm alone. For her, postillionage is best in conjunction with
intercourse – probably with the man on top. If she raises her legs
and clasps them around his waist – or better still his neck – the
man can choose his moment and, as orgasm approaches, insert
a finger into her anus.

● *For both men and women, the perineum is delightfully sensitive,*
and unique sensations can be provided by running your tongue
along the crevice between your partner's buttocks. It is best if the
receiver lies face down on the bed, perhaps with a couple of
pillows placed underneath their stomach. The kissing and licking
of the perineum can also be used along with masturbation. It is
probably best not to follow this with oral sex. And it is a good
idea for the giver to use a mouthwash afterwards.

Fantasy in sex

Most of us have sexual fantasies. They range from the common-
place to the exotic and bizarre, and they serve many purposes. An
invaluable aid to masturbation, fantasies can also be a source of
inspiration, relaxation and fun for both partners.

Whatever your fantasy, you can rest assured that it is almost
certainly shared by a large number of other people. Remember,
too, that your fantasy life need bear little relation to the way you
behave in real life. A fantasy involving domination or violence,
for example, does not in itself make you perverted, as long as you
do realize the distinction between reality and fantasy.

Dreams, both involuntary and contrived, are an outlet for
everyone. They enable us to express, in complete safety, private

desires that our "better" selves might never want to put into action.

Group sex is the most common element in male sexual fantasies. In one questionnaire, a third of men cited sex with two or more women as their favourite fantasy. Fewer women – about one in six – imagined themselves in a similar situation. Those who did, imagined themselves being made love to by numbers of attentive men or being watched while making love – often with their present or past partner rather than a faceless male.

When it comes to fantasizing about a pleasant place to make love, women tend to be a good deal more inventive than men. Many prefer to summon up erotic or unusual settings to add romance to their sex – islands, beaches, waterfalls, jungles, pools, Arabian palaces and so on. Men seem to prefer hospitals, airplane lavatories, buses, trains and other public places.

Rampantly sexual women who are ready and eager to please feature highly in male fantasies.

SUGAR DADDIES AND HONEY MOMMIES

The Sugar Daddy/mistress, Honey Mommy/gigolo relationship is fascinating to outsiders because it usually involves one partner bribing the other for sexual favours. Though the distinctions may at times seem fuzzy, we generally don't go as far as to describe this as prostitution. Indeed, most people who are involved in these relationships would be horrified to hear them described as such, perhaps preferring to call what they are involved in a "mutually beneficial" relationship. The "buyer" may be married or in a relationship with someone else, and so unavailable for a more "real" relationship, or they may be single and older or less attractive than the object of their desire.

Whatever the circumstances, these are relationships where there are incentives over and above – even instead of – simple attraction.

The incentives are not always financial. The buyer may be an influential person or a celebrity, and his or her paramour enjoys the sense of importance that the relationship brings them.

But however they choose to look at it, mistresses are being "bought". The central factor in the relationship is that one partner has money, power or social standing, and therefore dictates most of the terms of the relationship. The mistress or gigolo participates in the relationship because it suits them to do so.

Love is not an essential ingredient in such relationships. Neither partner feels that the lack of it devalues what they have, although often the buyer would prefer it if their lover wanted them for love as well as for the financial benefit or social standing. Eventually, this can turn into the reason for the collapse of the relationship.

What the mistress or gigolo is selling is sexual desirability. Without the hindrance of love they can sell to the highest bidder, particularly as money and power are the most important aphrodisiacs of all to them.

Can it last?

The down side for the mistress or gigolo is that when love and caring are absent, they can often be deserted without too much hesitation. Since they trade on sexual desirability, once it has gone they may find themselves without a settled relationship.

Men can maintain the role of gigolo for much longer and with successive partners because society unfairly dictates that while ageing women "lose their youthful good looks", men on the other hand grow "distinguished" and more attractive.

As time moves on, a mistress or gigolo can often decide that the idea of marriage looks attractive. This does not mean that they have finally fallen in love, it is usually a panic move – they might find themselves left on the shelf if they're not careful.

Living as the "other" person will suit some people, but not others. The ideal mistress or gigolo has to be able to look after him or herself while giving the appearance of only looking after their lover's needs and desires. It can be an exhausting double life in many respects.

Both men and women may imagine that their sexual roles are reversed. Indeed, many people of both sexes actually imagine being the opposite sex from time to time.

It is also common for heterosexual men and women to imagine making love to a person of their own sex, generally someone they know. This does not usually mean that the person is a repressed homosexual – it is simply the uncensored mind exploring or experimenting with a curious option, probing the unusual or unknown.

Exploring options is the nature of fantasy. Being happily married to someone of your own race, for instance, does not stop many men and women fantasizing about having sex with someone of a different race.

Fantasy also has the magical power of allowing us to recreate a past experience. Everyone has had good sex, bad sex and indifferent sex in their lives. Most men and women also have a few treasured memories of one or more perfect times when they made love. In the fantasy world we can recall that special experience at will.

Masturbation is the most common way of satisfying increased sexual urges which occur during the change from childhood to adolescence. But it is the sexual fantasies which accompany masturbation at this period – and in later life – which enrich the experience and prevent it from becoming purely mechanical.

Early on in a relationship, when we are still discovering a great deal about each other and revelling in the excitement of making love with a new partner, there may be no room – or need – for fantasies of any kind. But during a long term relationship, while affection and love may deepen, sexual excitement may very well fluctuate or diminish. Fantasy, however, can help brighten

*Some of the fun
of dressing up is
discovering what
is being worn
under seemingly
normal clothes.*

up the dull patches that most relationships go through from time
to time.

If partners can indulge in the occasional imaginary affair –
while accepting that it is just a fantasy – or perhaps even visual-
ize their own relationship in a different, more exciting context,
they may find that they look at their partner with renewed
enthusiasm.

Just as fantasies can inject a new lease of life into a relationship, they can help in all sorts of other ways too. A woman who is having difficulty in relaxing and enjoying sex, for instance, may benefit from imagining herself in a position of total power over her partner.

An inability to reach a climax may be based on fear of losing control over her body and her feelings. Fantasizing that she has control – of herself, her lover and the situation – may enable her to relax and enjoy her own emotions and sensations. Alternatively, she may be helped by imagining that her lover has total control over her.

Similarly, a man who has difficulties in getting or keeping an erection may be suffering from tension. Imagining that he has been magically whisked away from the dull routine and stresses of everyday life to an exciting, wonderful location may be enough to allow him to relax and make love successfully.

Many sexual fantasies are frequently spun by people who already have an active satisfying sex life. In one survey it was found that women who rated their husbands anywhere between "passable" and "excellent" as lovers were more likely to fantasize than those who considered their partners to be poor lovers. And wives who rated themselves as good lovers were more likely to use fantasy than those who rated themselves as poor lovers. So, a rich fantasy life seems to be a positive sign.

Clothes and fantasy

Clothes have an extraordinary ability to alter our sexual personality – at least superficially. We can dress for the part we want to act and, in doing so, also fire the imagination of our partners. This kind of dressing can also be catered for mildly in public but, in the privacy of our own homes, we can be as crazy or outrageous as we, and our partners, desire.

Men tend to place much heavier emphasis than women on the visual trappings of a fantasy. They often specify clothing for their imagined love partners – sexy underwear, black stockings or uniforms. Nurses, schoolgirls and French maids are all very popular fantasy lovers. Women are more likely to imagine their fantasy men as officers, in exotic clothes such as Roman togas or Arab robes, or in sophisticated evening dress. Materials such as leather, plastic or rubber are also popular with members of both sexes.

Many couples find that dressing for sex can be greatly enhanced if they give themselves a good run up to it. Some, for example, enjoy shopping together, especially for sexy things for the woman to wear. There is more choice, and sales assistants these days are much more helpful towards couples shopping for bedroom basics.

Dressing for sex need not only be an occasional event. Over the last few years women's and men's underwear has been designed to show both sexes off to the best advantage. Gone are the days when women wore knee-length bloomers and men wore long johns. Nor do you have to put up with only sensible white and gray. Nowadays, a lot of underwear is designed to expose and titillate.

Fantasies which involve some sort of uniform are common. In such fantasies, the individual can take on the role of someone or something they would secretly like to be.

Clothing is helpful when getting into the role and creates a feeling of safety – it's very obvious that you are in a sexual game. There are lots of different sorts of uniform. Some are very sexual and are made from leather, PVC or rubber. Others are uniforms

COMPULSIVE FLIRTS

Flirting is a game which most of us play from time to time when we want to signal sexual interest. However, the compulsive flirt does not limit him- or herself to someone to whom they feel a genuine attraction. They flirt indiscriminately in a desperate attempt to acquire sexual, social or professional power.

- ❤ **The vamp:** This is the most high-profile of the female flirts, immediately recognizable from the moment she makes her dramatic entrance in the room. The outfit she wears may not be fashionable or tasteful, but it creates an instant effect by showing cleavage, or being short and tight – she is clearly out to gain sexual power over men. The vamp loves parties, but only if she is the center of attention and will regard the evening as a failure if she is not. Her seductive body language is strong and unmistakable. Every man warrants her attention but it is difficult to gauge whether she really means what she says.

- ❤ **The stud:** This is the male version of the vamp, and equally easy to spot. The way he dresses may vary, but his swaggering air of self-confidence is always present. He is certain that many women are intrigued by a man who rates himself highly. The stud does not need tight or revealing clothes to make his object clear, but he must appear delighted with himself and his physique. His flirting technique depends on plenty of eye-to-eye contact, and a dazzled, appreciative up-and-down survey of the woman in front of him.

- ❤ **The tease:** This can be male or female. It is a sub-species of the vamp or stud in that they usually operate in a very similar way but rarely deliver. Teases most often fail because they are too frightened of their own success.

💜 **The flatterer:** He or she is usually in search of social rather than sexual power. Bathing their targets in a warm glow of personal satisfaction, their goal is to make every person like or admire them. The most successful flatterers are essentially subtle in technique, keeping the conversation on a general footing until they find out the soft spot or weakness of their target, then homing in with flirtatiously flattering comments.

💜 **The little girl lost:** In spite of the name, she can be of any age. She approaches men with a false air of naivete and exudes a kind of artless sexiness, very different from the deliberate and studied attraction of the vamp. The little girl lost may wear a dress that is constantly falling off her shoulder, and is likely to look bewildered and unsure at the same time while blushing in such a way that attracts attention.

💜 **The little boy lost:** He does not rely on silent flattery – his appeal is in making himself seem vulnerable and in need of mothering. He will ask a woman's advice on how to cook a certain dish, or he may tell a story about how he scorched his shirt when he ironed it, making it seem as though he is in desperate need of her assistance.

💜 **The manipulator:** He or she is a professional flirt, taking their habit to the arena of work. Women may use their sexuality to manipulate themselves into a position they want, deflect antagonism, or break the atmosphere if it is convenient. Men in power can compulsively flirt to control or humiliate subordinate women or, if successful at it, to try and hide the fact that they are often difficult people.

of eroticized power or powerlessness, such as policemen, maids, soldiers or governesses. Anything can be used in a sexual game if you are both really turned on. A couple may choose to play a game of "hospitals", for example, in which the crucial part of the fantasy is that the nurse has the power to control the patient, ensuring he is a "good" patient and does as he is told, otherwise he won't be treated nicely by his naughty nurse. Naturally, he can only handle the nurses in this hospital with permission.

The woman has the opportunity to be the sexual aggressor, which she may feel unable to act out in any other circumstances.

Exploring fantasy

An individual's fantasies can be a useful tool in understanding what is really going on in a relationship, as opposed to what simply appears to be happening.

For instance, if a woman appears to be sexually aggressive or highly uninhibited but has fantasies which seem to suggest the opposite, the revelation of those fantasies to a trained therapist can go some way towards shedding light on why it is that she behaves in the way she does, even though everyone around her, including her partner, may be convinced they know her sexual preferences.

Fantasy is a tool which may be used by all couples: you don't have to be professional to learn more about one another's sexuality. However, unlike talking to a professional about your secret fantasies, there can be pitfalls when it comes to sharing your intimate fantasies with your partner.

It is important to be sure of your motives when wanting to share your fantasies. The valid motives revolve around using the

Domination gives men and women an opportunity to enjoy erotic acts that they might otherwise feel awkward requesting.

information to understand each other and so enrich your sex life. When you want to discuss your fantasies, move gently and lovingly, not intrusively.

The best approach to fantasies involving specific individuals with whom both partners are acquainted is not to share them at all. Sharing a fantasy about a film star is, of course, completely different, because such a person is almost certainly unattainable and poses no direct threat to your relationship.

If you do decide to explore your fantasies together, the watchword must be caution. Start by talking over your least threatening ones. Choose the time and the setting to ensure that the atmosphere is very loving, sexy and reassuring, preferably when you are both aroused a little and already talking intimately. If your partner starts backing off, stop and put off the attempt for another time.

The manner in which you share your fantasies will, of course, be up to you and your partner, but almost any method that you find personally reassuring has the potential to greatly enhance and improve your sex life.

A more subtle way in which to find out about your partner's fantasies than actually discussing them is to watch closely what she or he finds sexy. Being vigilant all the time will usually yield good results. Watch for what turns your partner on in films, magazines, or TV.

If, for example, your partner always turns to the underwear pages of your favorite mail-order catalogue, how about using this as a sexual adventure by going through them with him and choosing an item or two that you both would like you to wear?

Another method that often works well is to write a sexy play or an outline for a sexy video, to be read by your partner.

Assuming that one or both partners has succeeded in getting to know more about the other's sexually intimate thoughts, what do they then do with this knowledge?

Making fantasies come true

Perhaps the best way to handle things is for the individual to say at the time of the revelation that they want the other to know about it but not necessarily to take it as a signal to do anything about it, at least for the time being, or until the individual says that this is what they want.

This need not be a cause for gloom. For example, in the case of a woman who has fantasies about anal sex but does not actually want to have anal sex, it is possible to make use of the information in a constructive way. Her partner could ensure that they make love in the rear-entry positions that encourage the woman to fantasize about anal sex.

Other fantasies, such as those involving bondage or group sex, can be dealt with in similar ways, perhaps using silk scarves and pretending to tie each other up, rather than going the whole

Domination doesn't have to be about whips and chains — woman on top is a dominant position, for her.

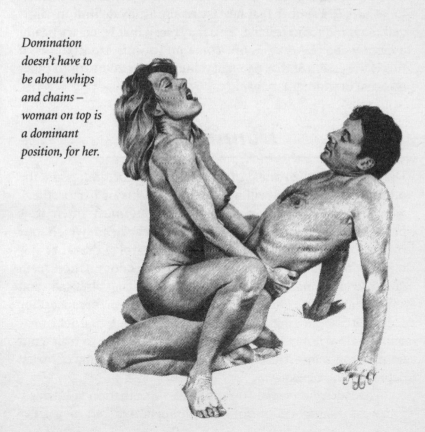

way and getting out the leather and chains. Positioning a full-length mirror so that you can see yourselves making love is a novel way of creating the illusion of more than one couple being in a room, and means you won't end up inviting friends around to realize your fantasies. Unless you know for a fact that you can handle group sex situations, and that your partner can too, they are usually best avoided.

If you do decide to act out your fantasy there is a lot of fun to be had. Remember that fantasy is, almost by definition, difficult to reproduce in real life. This may mean that when acting out a fantasy, the reality does not come up to your expectations. If this is the case, put that particular image away and turn to other material in your fantasy bank.

Domination

Domination – when one partner dominates proceedings and the other, passive partner willingly submits to his or her partner's whims – can sometimes be symbolic but most often it is physically acted out as a sexual performance in which one partner has total physical and emotional control of the other. It is this "control" factor which sometimes makes domination seem taboo. Understandably, people are scared of being physically and emotionally hurt, and domination scares them because they regard it as one step away from sadism and masochism – practices that imply pain. Another potential barrier to trying out domination is that it also carries a psychological stigma of sexual depravity and deviance.

Yet, despite social disapproval, domination is widely practiced – suppliers of domination apparatus and magazines

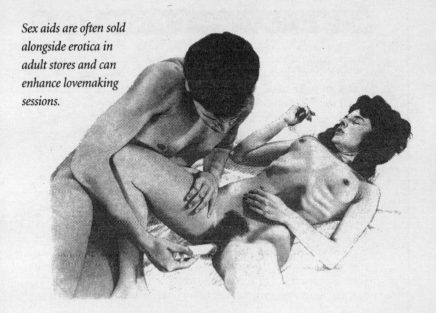

Sex aids are often sold alongside erotica in adult stores and can enhance lovemaking sessions.

claim that approximately 10 per cent of American households have some domination apparatus and indulge in practices that offer domination and submissive experiences.

Domination is fantasy. You can be who or what you want to be, giving in to a part of yourself that is ignored in everyday life. Many people who indulge in domination and bondage consider it the ultimate sexual experience: it heightens their level of arousal as power and submissiveness are great aphrodisiacs – and it frees them from the usual constraints of "natural" sexual order allowing the woman to be fully in charge. Domination is about trust – about trusting your partner so implicitly that not knowing what they'll do to you next or what you'll have to do to them is not intimidating, just incredibly exciting and erotic, a new and tantalizing adventure.

DANGEROUS OBSESSION

When you are very attracted to someone it is only natural to spend a lot of time thinking about them and conjuring up their image in your mind. You want to see them, talk to them, even smell them. Somehow you want them to surround you like a cloud. In a sense, you are obsessed.

But when does obsession become unhealthy or even criminal? When is that fine line crossed between the desire to be with a loved one and to take over their life completely?

People of the obsessive type tend to have very low self-esteem. Deep down they feel unloved and unattractive, and often have a history of failed relationships or no close relationships at all. Real-life intimacy scares them, so unconsciously they pick a focus for their attention in someone who will never put their devotion to the test, who will never see how inadequate they are, both socially and sexually. In a way, when such people turn on the object of their passion with hostility they are really turning on themselves out of their own passionate self-loathing.

Targets for the obsessed

Of course women can be just as obsessive as men. Celibate men such as Catholic priests are prime targets because they present a challenge while at the same time being completely out of the frame as far as the woman is concerned.

Another group of men who are adored and pestered from a distance are married men, usually professional and well-off pillars of the community. The female obsessive bombards him with letters and presents complete with provocative notes, knowing full well that his wife will see them, and hangs around his place of work and/or his home. Some will even take to phoning him and then putting the phone down.

Famous people are prime targets, for men in particular, because their schedule is well known and you can almost always get to see them, even if only from a crowd. Newspapers and television regularly show pictures of the "loved one", while there are often other public occasions at which they are present.

What lies behind this sort of fixation is a complicated mixture of things, but one of the main reasons for this extra-ordinary sort of lust is the very inaccessibility of the object of their desire. Yes, he may get to see them a lot, but he can never hope to do more than brush against them as they are rushed through the throng to their limousine.

Where does obsession lead?

It may begin as a sort of romantic ideal – just like the knights of old and their "courtly love" for a married lady. They contented themselves with writing love songs which the troubadours sang, and sighed over their hopeless love from a safe distance. But today's stalker, having chosen a hopeless "love", then starts to get fed up with her apparent lack of interest in him and wants more.

He thinks that if he goes to the trouble of writing and faxing letters every day, of sending bouquets of flowers and going to her every concert, match or whatever, then surely she can at least meet him and show her appreciation. It all starts to go sour very quickly, when it becomes obvious that his devotion is in vain. Soon his love gets tinged with hostility and his fantasies are about forcing her to listen, to give in to his will . . . gradually turning into the desire for violence, like rape and kidnapping.

In many cases it is possible to "snap out" of an obsession. If you, or someone you know, however is unable to do this, you owe it to yourself to seek help from a counsellor.

To include domination in your sex play, you should start by gently building up trust and confidence, and then, if you are both willing to, try moving on to "stronger" practices. Because domination can sometimes intimidate beginners, always make your bedroom, or wherever you want to have sex, a safe, clean, sensual, non-threatening environment: soft music, dim lights, candles and exotic smelling joss-sticks make for a comforting, erotic setting. It's your wild and wonderful fantasy playground.

Obviously you don't have to dress up to dominate but looking the part adds to the fun: stilettos, stockings, lingerie, basques, leather, rubber, uniforms, even masks and leads can make you feel more sexual, more dominant, more submissive, and definitely more horny. And using equipment can make domination a truly mind-blowing experience: satin and silk scarves can be used to tie each other up; vibrators and other sex toys can be used to arouse and stimulate each other (remember to clean sex toys thoroughly before sharing them) and when you're feeling brave enough, manacles and handcuffs can be used to render one of you helpless to the pleasures your partner will inflict on you.

Soft domination can be as simple as talking dirty to your partner. Ordering him to go down on you or telling her to strip and bend over can be exciting and stimulating especially if you both use crude language and harsh tones, and even more so if bad language and authoritative tones are out of character.

Basic domination can involve sex positions you are already familiar with. Any position that limits the control of one partner is a dominating one. The missionary position, with the woman on her back and the man on top, is dominant if he pins her arms down so she can't move or touch him. Many women love feeling the man's weight and strength on top of them and thoroughly

Pornography for men often portrays women in ways that other women find unacceptable.

enjoy being "taken". Woman-on-top positions, on the other hand, enable the woman to dominate. She can control the depth to which his penis enters her and she can also control the rhythm and speed.

Dressed up or down, domination is highly charged sexually: some people find it so erotic they spontaneously orgasm just by being tied up. Why not try it? The possibilities for domination acts are endless. The man can tie his partner to the bed post with a silk scarf, with her arms stretched so she can't move or touch him. In this prone position, he can straddle her face and order her to fellate him. She has no control and that's the joy of it – she's pleasuring him while turning herself on.

Or the woman can restrain the man by handcuffing him to the bedhead. She can strip in front of him, dance above him and tantalize him without letting him touch her. She could climb onto the bed, squat over him and lower herself onto his face. In this scenario, she is completely in control and can do whatever it is she wants to do to him.

The joys of domination sex are that anything goes (as long as you both genuinely enjoy it) and you can literally allow yourselves to lose control and just relish the sexual sensations. Remember that mutual consent is vital since commitment to sexual domination hinges on absolute trust. And absolute trust in any sexual sphere results in warm, loving sex.

Erotica

The proliferation of sexually explicit material today has resulted in increasing difficulty when it comes to differentiating between what is pornographic and what is erotic, between exploitation and education, between healthy sexual interest and mental disturbance. The very nature of the subject attracts controversy and everyone has their own ideas about it, so the more we discuss the subject, the better.

The word pornography literally means "the writing of prostitutes" and the word erotica is derived from the Greek god of love – Eros. Pornography has much more negative connotations, but under the title of erotica – because it usually suggests that the material in question has some "redeeming cultural value" – the pornography of ancient Greece and medieval China, even of the Victorian era, may go on display at your local museum or art gallery.

Works of art – paintings, literature, sculpture, plays and films – may well show people and situations which have the potential to sexually arouse, but are deemed acceptable because of their artistic status.

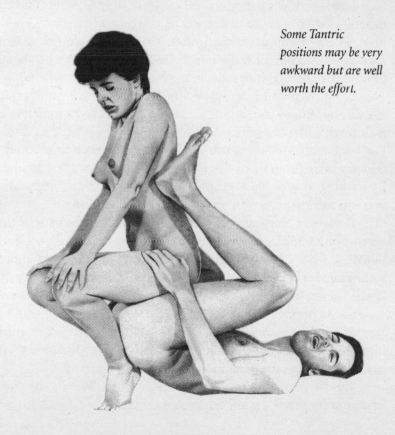

Some Tantric positions may be very awkward but are well worth the effort.

Similarly books and magazines whose main function is to educate you about your body and its sexual potential are very popular and, to most people, acceptable. Pornography, however, is more difficult to buy, and is subject to censure.

When it comes to pornography there are two categories – soft-core and hard-core. Soft-core generally shows naked bodies posing in atmospheric situations. It will often suggest sexual acts, but stops short of depicting them explicitly.

Hard-core pornography, illegal in many countries and in others, sold only at the discretion of the censorship laws, leaves little to the imagination and often worries people because it includes material which depicts the more extreme ares of sexual practice like flagellation, sado-masochism, bondage and rape.

If the idea of bringing pornographic literature into your love life appeals to you, it is of paramount importance to first talk it through with your partner. You might like to set aside a partic-ular time when you know you will be left alone. Each time you do this, try taking it in turns to produce a different story or picture. By looking at sexy photographs, drawings and erotic literature, you can work your way up the ladder of explicitness.

Beware of starting out using very explicit material straight away. For example, if a woman is very shy and finds sex and nudity deeply embarrassing, she is likely to feel even more intimidated if her partner ogles at girlie magazines – particularly if she thinks the bodies of the women in the photographs are superior to hers.

Men may also react badly to their partners taking an interest in pictures of other naked men, especially if they feel that their penis is small by comparison.

Take it slowly, and en route, you should gradually discover what it is that excites you both of you.

Concentrating on your partner and his or her sexual satisfaction heightens both partner's energies.

Few couples want to see sexy films in seedy cinemas, but now that explicit videos are on offer in most mainstream video stores, couples are able to enhance their love lives with raunchy films in the privacy of their own homes.

"Educational" films about sex and relationships are a very good introduction to sexually explicit material, and are particularly useful for less experienced people. They serve a dual purpose, both providing accurate information about sex and sexuality and stimulating the viewer, and they are free from the often sleazy connotations of pornography. Many couples, once they have watched the film through complete with informative voice-over, choose to watch the video with the sound down, perhaps with some favorite music playing as an accompaniment.

Filming each other with a video camera can be a fun and flattering way of documenting your sex life, and looking through revealing polaroids of one another can provide a valuable insight into a partner's desires.

However, always remember that exploring sexually explicit material is not something to rush into, and you and your partner will have to judge for yourselves whether or not your relationship would benefit from incorporating pornography and erotica into your sex life.

Tantrism

The cult of Tantra (or Tantric Yoga) goes back to around 5000 BC in India, where it developed as a part of the cult of the Hindu god Shiva and his consort, the goddess Shakti. Shiva was worshipped as the embodiment of ecstasy, and Shakti as pure energy. Hindus believe that Shakti gave form to the universe through uniting both sexually and spiritually with Shiva. To some Hindus, the creation of the world was the result of highly charged erotic love, and they believe that every creature on the earth is capable of experiencing beauty and ecstasy through the act of sexual union.

Unfortunately, Tantra got a bad reputation from the very beginning. Mainstream Hindus and Buddhists thought that Tantric masters were involved in all sorts of sinister practices from vampirism to necrophilia, and to this day many Eastern religions avoid the whole subject, finding it just as shocking as Christians and Jews in the West.

The word Tantra means "weaving", referring to the aim of the practice, which is to bring together and unite many different and even contradictory parts of your inner self. Another definition is "expansion" because Tantra sets out to make your soul expand with joy.

Tantra promises a rapid, direct path to God via sex. Unlike mainstream Hinduism and Buddhism, which teach that you have to overcome all physical desires and concerns to become truly enlightened, Tantra sees sexuality as essential for people to understand themselves and their place in the universe. In Tantrism, the couple are aiming for "cosmic copulation", and in order to reach this stage they will have to undergo intensive and lengthy training (albeit spiritually and sexually gratifying) over a period of many years.

The end result is supposed to be the release of the female Shakti energy, sometimes called the Kundalini. This energy rises from its normal place at the base of the spine, up through the invisible energy centers, the chakras, to the top of the head. Once there, it unites with the male energy, Shiva, and the couple feel intense bliss.

That's the theory, but in practice the ecstasy is somewhat more difficult to achieve than you might think. In stricter Tantric schools in India the *sadhaka*, or student, has to spend at least a year meditating and doing exercises to strengthen the muscles that will be needed for the actual sex itself.

The techniques for the fusion of mind and body can be taught but only by qualified and disciplined masters. Only when the teacher is satisfied that you have the mental and physical capabilities, will you be allowed to move on to the next stage: *maithuna*, or ritual sex.

This is nearly impossible for Westerners to imagine initially, as it involves the man keeping his penis erect and inside the woman for at least thirty-two minutes without any thrusting at all – and without giving in to the desire to ejaculate!

To most men the whole point of sex is to have an orgasm and release semen, but not so the Tantric male. In this kind of ritual sex the man is supposed to have an orgasm without letting a single drop of semen escape at the crucial moment.

The key to this astonishing feat is control of the muscles that cause erections. The man's partner can help by gently massaging his penis every day, but the real hard work is his alone. He has to be able to relax his erection completely, then will it to come back – at least four times. The best Tantrics can keep this up for four hours without any sign of exertion!

Everyday Tantrism

There are many Tantric exercises that are a lot easier, however, and they may be practiced by anyone who is willing to make a little effort. The ultimate aim is to unite more satisfactorily with your lover and to find yourself experiencing a deep sense of bliss and peace afterwards.

The simplest exercise is "Soul-Gazing". Based on the idea that the gaze of the beloved has a magical quality, it is said to "harmonize people's energy fields".

Lie down facing your partner and begin to synchronize your breathing. After a few moments you will begin to feel much more relaxed and more in tune with each other. Gaze gently and directly into your partner's eyes. Most people find this strange or off-putting to start with and find that they drop their gaze or start to giggle. But if you persist you will experience a very odd sense of drawing closer to your lover, almost as if you were joined to him or her by an elastic band.

Another simple Tantric technique is to watch each other masturbating after spending time stroking your own body with an increasing sense of erotic play. Imagine what it is like being his rapidly hardening penis, or being inside her vagina.

Tantra works best when it is taken slowly and involves the imagination as well as the body. Apart from the religious aspect of blissful union with God, it also results in greater respect for yourself and your partner.

CHAPTER 6

A
Time and Place
for
Loving

F or all couples, whether long-term partners or first-time lovers, the time, place, and conditions for loving can help to make or break a sexual encounter. Even the most ardent couple can have their passion dampened by an unnecessarily cold room, an uncomfortable mattress or the awareness of possible eavesdroppers such as children, parents or neighbors. All these factors should be taken into consideration as part of communication between partners. Often overlooked, this is a vital ingredient to the success of a relationship.

A room for loving

The vast majority of lovemaking still takes place in bedrooms, although many people make love in other places from time to time. Yet, few couples give any serious thought to the actual setting their bedroom provides, and then wonder why so many things seem to conspire against them to reduce their sexual pleasure.

With a little imagination, every aspect of a bedroom could be used to turn it into a sexual sanctuary.

In many – if not most – homes, the choice of which bedroom to occupy is fairly limited. It makes sense to choose the largest bedroom you can spare for yourselves as this gives you a lot more scope when it comes to sex.

If you have a choice – and many couples do, because they have not yet started a family, or their children are old enough to leave home – try to organize it so that your bedroom has an empty room next to it to act as a sound barrier.

Few people want to be overheard while they are in the middle of making love. Whether it is because of the sweet nothings they whisper, the giggles or the orgasmic cries, most couples prefer privacy, especially from children or house guests. Heavy carpeting and good quality, thick curtains both help absorb sound, but it might also be desirable to put sound-insulating boards on the walls that adjoin other people's bedrooms.

Talk to a builder if you have very thin walls that let all the sound through, or see if you can cover them with sound-proofing boards on a DIY basis – it is not a difficult job to undertake. Remember that a lot of sound travels up through the ceiling and across to other rooms. A simple solution to this problem is to insulate your ceiling.

If possible, it is both pleasant and practical to have some form of bathroom or shower as part of your bedroom set-up. An en-suite bathroom is ideal for bathing or showering together as part and parcel of a lovemaking session. It is best, however, for your en-suite bathroom to be completely separate from your bedroom if possible – for example, with a door that can be closed – as many people say that they like to prepare for sex privately rather than with their partner.

Few people enjoy lovemaking in very bright artificial light, so it is useful if you can dim the lights in your bedroom. And instead of using a central light, try replacing it with lamps either on the walls or by the bed. This kind of indirect lighting is much softer, and can be used to give a romantic effect.

If you cannot afford to do this, put a dimmer on your central ceiling light so that you can have a gentle glow or full light, according to your needs at the time. With good lighting and thick curtains you will be able to control the light level in your bedroom all year round. If you like natural daylight but do not want to be seen by people outside, some blinds are good for letting in light and keeping out spies at the same time.

How you decorate will obviously be a matter of personal taste. Try and keep the colours muted and restful, but otherwise be guided by your personal feelings. Warm colours are probably more conducive to feeling sexy.

In countries where it is often cold, it is essential to be able to heat up your bedroom quickly. Ideally, central heating is best for background warmth, but you may need additional heating to warm up the room quickly.

Electric heaters are good. A powerful convector or radiant heater is best for instant heat. Cure any draughty windows with draught excluders, or with simple double glazing if necessary.

An armless chair is an ideal support. The man sits while the woman gently lowers herself onto his erect penis.

Chairs can also allow the woman to adopt an ideal position for oral pleasure.

Furnishing your love nest

Bedroom furnishing is another matter to which careful thought must be given. When it comes to lovemaking, chairs can be a real asset. It is useful to have a simple, armless chair, because the man can sit on it and the woman can easily face him, legs apart, and sit on his penis. The permutations are endless and you can happily fill many an evening with hours of experimentation.

A low couch, bench, or chaise longue all take up much more space, but offer delights a bed does not. With a bench, the man can kneel in front of the woman who lies back, legs wide apart, for intercourse. Or she can kneel up on it and he can enter her from behind.

Some women like their man to lie flat on a low stool or chaise longue so that they can kneel comfortably in between his legs and fellate him.

Most couples find they need a lockable cupboard or drawer in their bedroom to keep prying fingers and eyes out of their private belongings.

The central piece of furniture in a couple's bedroom is their bed. Generally, most beds are poor, both for sleeping and for lovemaking. Here are some useful tips.

Without a doubt, the best bed for lovemaking is a double bed – and preferably as large a one as you can afford, taking the size of your bedroom into consideration. Some couples prefer to sleep alone because they have very different tastes in mattresses, temperatures and so on. Some individuals spread themselves all over the bed and are highly disruptive to sleep with. For such people single beds may well be the only answer.

However, from a sexual point of view a double bed is undoubtedly best. It allows more room for manoeuvre during intercourse, enables more adventurous positions to be taken up and means that after sex the couple can go to sleep together.

Ideally a bed should be at least six inches longer than its tallest occupant. So if either of you is very tall, you may have to consider buying a queen- or king-sized bed as they tend to be longer as well as wider. Having your feet poking out of the end of the bed can be cold and uncomfortable – a combination that is bound to be a bit of a passion killer.

Always choose a firm mattress, and go for the best you can afford. A good-quality mattress should last about ten years.

For lovemaking, the firmer the mattress the better – within reason. A saggy mattress means that the woman's pelvis sinks low into the bed and the angle of penetration of the man's penis is very different from that which occurs on the floor or a good supporting mattress.

There is little doubt that silk or satin sheets are the most sensual and sexy. They are, however, highly impractical as they are expensive to buy and to keep clean. Likewise, pure cotton sheets feel very comfortable but may need professional laundering, especially if they are big. They also need ironing.

Sheets and blankets have their advantages as some people like the sensation of being "tucked up tight" but duvets are far more practical when it comes to both sleeping and lovemaking. A duvet can easily be turned back or completely removed and placed on a chair so as to leave the entire bed clear and ready for sex. Similarly, once lovemaking is over, a duvet can be easily replaced.

If you can afford it, wall-to-wall carpeting is ideal for creating a cosy, sensual atmosphere.

When choosing curtains, go for the best quality fabric you can afford, to absorb sound and keep out the light.

Think about having some sensual or erotic pictures or prints on your walls. Erotic pictures help set the scene for sex and are more likely to give lasting pleasure than pornographic pictures. Perhaps a vivid scene that you enjoy fantasizing about would help turn you on and put you in the mood.

Some couples greatly enjoy having mirrors in which they can watch themselves making love. These may be on dressing tables, on wardrobe doors, on the wall – or even the ceiling.

The most readily available erotic material comes in the form of books and magazines. If you feel your sex life could be

BATTLE OF THE SEXES

The war between the sexes is a common theme of modern life.

The reason for differing views is both biological and social. In the early years of our evolution, roles were determined by the fact that women can bear children and men cannot. Once a woman had given birth, her food-gathering abilities were considerably reduced, and she became dependent upon her partner to provide food and protection for herself and her offspring. So, when it came to choosing a mate, she would look for a man who was strong, fearless and faithful.

Different attitudes...

But how do these factors affect our relationships today? At the start of a relationship both partners tend to look at it as new and exciting, the one that will make their life complete.

However, once settled in a relationship, men and women have different expectations: a man believes he can turn his attention back to his career and interests while for a woman, the relationship often remains paramount.

Men generally define themselves through their achievements. They gain their self-esteem through work, whereas women define themselves through their relationships. If a man is having trouble at work he will withdraw to try to solve the problem. A woman with the same problem will look for reassurance from her partner.

...different priorities...

Another bone of contention is that of interests or hobbies. Whereas men will continue to have interests outside the relationship, many women give these up in a long term relationship as they believe that the relationship is more important. They then resent their partner for not doing the same, believing he cannot love them as much.

Women often believe men are afraid of commitment because they don't want to be tied down, however men are frequently afraid of commitment because they fear rejection. So, although many men like to pretend their relationships are a bore, most of them secretly long for and appreciate a secure and loving home life.

Men and women lose their virginity from around the same age – early teens. Yet men do tend to have more casual partners than women, and this probably stems from the ancient evolutionary need to populate. Men do not necessarily need to be emotionally involved with a sexual partner, whereas women do and are therefore far more selective than men in their choice of mate.

. . . *different values*

And how do we differ in bed? Kissing tends to be far more important to women. It provides closeness and intimacy, and does not necessarily lead to sex. Men also like to kiss, however few men want to stop there.

Many men underestimate the importance of foreplay in lovemaking. For women, intercourse is only welcome when they feel ready and this can take a lot of stimulation in order to build up the levels of sex hormones.

Women want to hear that they are loved and cared for (it is a great turn-on for them), however, most men hate talking in bed.

The way in which men and women have been raised, conditioned and socialized, along with biological differences, can create any or all of these problems, and it is all too clear that we think of sex and relationships in very different ways. However, a clearer understanding of your partner and of the reasons why the differences between you exist, can help to improve your relationship in the future.

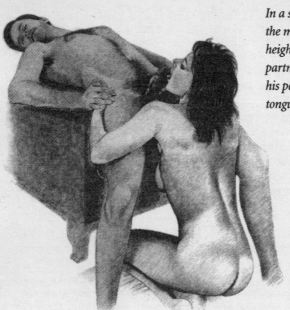

In a small armchair the man is at an ideal height for his kneeling partner to caress his penis with her tongue.

improved by reading erotic literature, find out what you both enjoy best and then always be sure to have suitable material in your private cupboard.

Some couples enjoy the smell of special room perfumes, or joss sticks. This is a fairly minority pursuit in the West, but in the Orient smells play an important part in lovemaking.

Certainly, the well-washed body of a man, and the fragrant scented body of a woman, can be real turn-ons for most people. But be careful not to so over-perfume yourself that your natural body odours are masked.

Finally, and perhaps most importantly, a lovers' bedroom should have a lock – every couple is entitled to their privacy.

Finding the time

After the initial excitement dies down, it is all too easy to relegate sex in a relationship to a lower position on the list of "things to do". Obviously, worries about money, work and sundry other facets of our lives can temporarily preoccupy us but, if domestic trivia impinge on our sex lives, it can cause problems for the relationship.

The first thing to do is to find the time to make love. While there is nothing implicitly wrong in making love before you go to sleep – and a bed is therefore the ideal location – if lovemaking just becomes another regular "job" to be done, prospects for a happy and fulfilling sex life may not always be that good.

If one or both of you are working every day, then making love during weekdays is more difficult than at weekends. Even so, it is surprising how much can be fitted into a busy routine if the desire to do so is there.

Many people feel at their sexiest in the morning, especially men, who often wake up with an erection. Add to this the relaxed feeling from sleeping well and the intimate contact of being together for a few hours, and you have conditions very conducive to making love.

Being woken gently by a loving partner with some sensual massage can be an exquisite experience for both men and women. If you are the first awake, begin gently and sensitively exploring your partner's body. Cuddle up close and kiss them gently. Stroke their face, neck and shoulders. Keep this up until they are at least half awake before moving onto the more erogenous zones of the body.

This is not a time to be selfish. Wait until they are fully aroused and wanting to make love before you try for full penetrative intercourse.

AROMATHERAPY

There can be few therapies more pleasant than aromatherapy, since it combines carefully chosen scents with soothing massage or long, lazy baths. Aromatherapy involves the use of essential oils by a qualified therapist who can treat a wide variety of physical, mental and emotional problems.

It is also a therapy you can practise at home on your own or with your partner to help you relax and reduce stress or simply to promote a feeling of well-being.

The origins of aromatherapy

Modern interest in aromatherapy dates from 1928, when French chemist Rene Gattefossé published a book on the subject and used the term for the first time. His curiosity had been aroused by his research work in the cosmetics industry, which revealed powerful antiseptic qualities in many essential oils.

Curiosity was further stimulated accidentally. While working in the laboratory he burned his hand badly, and without thinking, he immersed it in a bowl of lavender oil that stood near by. To his amazement the burn healed quickly and left no scar.

Further pioneering work in aromatherapy was carried out by another Frenchman, Dr Jean Valnet, who used aromatherapy in World War II to heal wounds. Later the French biochemist Marguerite Maury explored and developed other applications for essential oils, particularly in the field of massage.

The best way to find out more about aromatherapy is to consult a professional aromatherapist, preferably someone who has a recognized qualification in massage. Your first visit will probably last for about one and a half hours.

Aromatherapy at home

An alternative to seeing a professional aromatherapist is to use an essential oil, suitably diluted in massage or vegetable oil, to give either yourself or your partner a massage at home. Massage with oils is suitable for stressed, tense but otherwise healthy people. It can help you to relax and feel cared for – or it can be a good prelude to lovemaking. Caution is recommended if either of you has a medical condition, has been recently ill or had an accident.

Massage with oils does not have to involve the whole body. You can do it simply on your own face or hands, thighs or feet.

Another effective way to use essential oils is in a bath. Make sure the room is warm and that doors and windows are firmly closed so that the vapours cannot escape. Put about six to ten drops of the selected oil in your bath, swish the water gently so the oil forms a film on top, and immerse your body for about ten minutes, breathing deeply. A certain amount of oil should penetrate your skin and some should be inhaled.

If you want to inhale the vapours from essential oils more directly, you can put a few drops of the chosen oil in a basin of hot water. Lean over and inhale for several minutes. Rosemary is refreshing, eucalyptus and peppermint are good for head colds, camphor and eucalyptus for influenza, while cedarwood and benzoin can ease respiratory problems.

Sometimes only parts of you want special attention. If, for example, your feet are aching at the end of the day, soaking them for ten minutes in a bowl of hot water with a few drops of peppermint, lavender or rosemary oil should soon revive them.

Remember that essences can be extremely powerful and should not be applied undiluted to the skin.

On a warm day, a secluded conservatory can be an ideal venue for lovemaking – in this position, penetration is very deep and the couple can caress and kiss.

Another way of fitting in early morning sex is "quickies". These do not have to be confined to the bed, or even the bedroom, and can be undertaken while you are enjoying an early morning bath or shower. Oral sex is often one of the quickest ways to bring your partner to orgasm, and the knowledge that both your own and your partner's genitals are clean makes many people feel most at ease.

Making love during the day, when neither partner is tired, means that once you have climaxed you can spend time lying close before starting again – as with most things, the more time you have, the better.

For the truly loving couple there are absolutely no restrictions on when (or where) they make love. By experimenting and continually adding to your repertoire of lovemaking times and places, you can only strengthen and enrich your relationship.

Honeymoon sex

One very special time for lovemaking is, of course, the honeymoon, for long-term partners and new lovers alike.

These days, a large proportion of honeymooners have already had intercourse with each other, and possibly with several other partners too. For them a honeymoon can become a celebration of sensuality and sex.

For a number of couples, however, one or both may be a virgin on their wedding night. A couple may have been saving themselves – possibly for religious reasons – and the honeymoon sex will have assumed considerable importance in their lives.

The loss of her virginity is a major milestone in a woman's life, particularly if it has been put off until her wedding night. For her, it signifies the passing from childhood to womanhood and carries more emotions and unconscious overtones than is generally realized.

Yet physically, contrary to popular myth, most girls and young women find the first time no problem at all. A few may experience some pain as the man's penis stretches the hymen, and some go off sex for a time as a result. This usually comes

More than anything the wedding night is about romance, and kissing can serve either to arouse or relax.

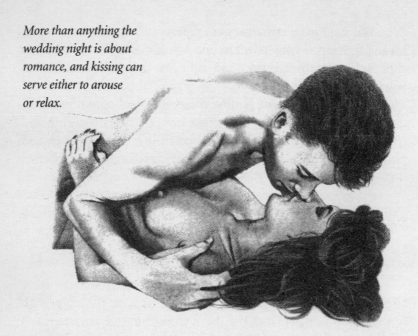

about as a result of poor foreplay, too little lubrication and general haste. Even if there is a small amount of discomfort it usually disappears after a few days and healing can be speeded up by taking hot baths. The vast majority of young women today have a stretched or perforated hymen even before first intercourse, because they have been using tampons, or have had fingers inserted into their vagina during masturbation and petting.

An inexperienced couple who want to prevent their wedding night from being marred by pain and bleeding can prepare the woman beforehand. She herself can insert fingers – one at first, then two – as she masturbates or when she is relaxed in a warm bath.

She can also encourage her man to stretch her vaginal opening with his fingers when petting. If during any of this, the hymen bleeds, there is no need to worry. The blood loss is very small and a sanitary towel or tampon will only rarely be needed. Usually a couple of tissues placed between the outer lips are all that is required.

Very often, the inexperienced couple gently discover each other's sexual responses and learn together about sex, with each other as teacher. It is helpful for them to read as much as they can about lovemaking and marriage, and to learn to share each other's worries so that they both feel confident and comfortable about sex.

For the couple who are tired after the excitement of the wedding day, the "spoons" position is one of the most relaxing.

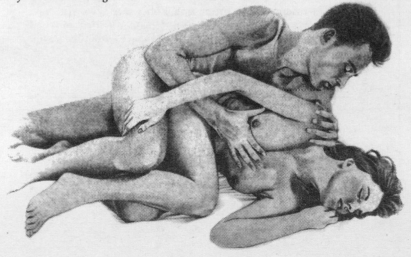

WHAT IS LOVE?

People will kill for it and die for it. They fought the Trojan Wars because of it. They will beg, borrow and steal for it. They will give up promising careers to keep it or live in poverty to earn it. Falling out of it can be one of the most painful experiences that we ever undergo and failed love can push a person to suicide.

Despite all of this, true love can be one of the most wonderful and powerful experiences of our lives.

So what exactly is this phenomenon we call love? What does the work of psychologists tell us about love? How does it come about and what does it do to our behaviour? What part does love play in our bonding to a partner and how does it affect long-term sexual satisfaction?

In a recent survey carried out on love, about 90 per cent of people interviewed claimed to have been in love at least once by the age of twenty and some 20 per cent to have been deeply in love three or more times by that age. Asked if they were in love at the moment, some 61 per cent of women answered "yes" compared to just 43 per cent of men.

The discrepancy is interesting. Either several women loved the same man, or loved and were not loved in return, or – as is most likely – men and women have different concepts of love.

How love develops

In a survey looking at infatuation as well as love, the findings were similar. Infatuation was defined as the situation where one partner feels much more strongly than the other one – indeed, the targets of their affections may not even know that they exist, like when someone is infatuated with a pop star. Love was defined as when a person's feelings are reciprocated by the partner and they both feel the same way about one another.

Love at first sight does undoubtedly occur, but if it is really love rather than infatuation, it normally develops, becoming more intense from that point.

Love involves behaviour, not just feelings, and as love develops, so both partners change their behaviour towards one another in subtle, and sometimes not-so-subtle, ways.

Eventually the couple has to work out the relationship and each will start to show concern over the partner's likely style as a parent or long-term mate.

Coming to terms with sex is not something that happens on top of love, or distinct from it. Coming to terms with sex is part of developing love.

Love and sex

Two psychologists, Scott Christopher and Rodney Cale, have investigated the links between love and sex. They found that couples who rapidly became sexually involved had more conflict in their relationship than couples whose sexual activity developed more slowly. Conflict is one area that we often overlook, and managing sexual and personal conflict is a very important part of a relationship.

Love is not just a feeling – it derives in part from our culture. Our cultural experience tells us about the things that we can or should be doing within our relationships. But being in love also involves us in decisions about managing our feelings and dealing with conflicts.

When we are in love it not only affects our hearts, but also causes huge changes in our everyday life-style.

A couple who are properly prepared – experienced or otherwise – will arrive at their wedding night eager for one another and not scared or apprehensive – because they are confident in one another's sexuality, whether or not they actually end up having intercourse.

This takes the pressure off the first night, which then becomes much like any other loving encounter they have. It also prevents either of them from seeing the wedding night as the be-all and end-all of their sexual lives – which it is not. It is simply one important day on their path through life together.

After the first night, and once you have the emotional and perhaps even the physical hurdles over, what then? Research shows that most couples make love very frequently on their honeymoon – more frequently than they ever do again.

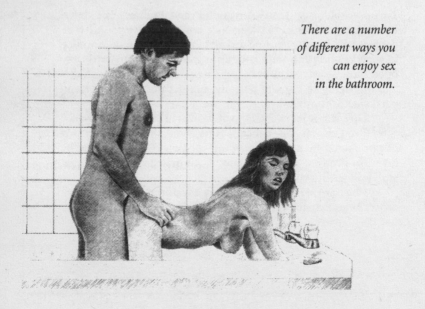

There are a number of different ways you can enjoy sex in the bathroom.

The only precaution here is to go gently. If you are not very experienced with one another sexually, do not go in for coital gymnastics – stick to simple, romantic lovemaking positions in these early days.

By all means try something other than the missionary position, but do not go trying complex, or unusual things which might put off a shy or inexperienced partner.

The ideal honeymoon for any couple should be a continuation of their courtship together, lovingly discovering one another's personalities – both in and out of the bedroom.

A watershed experience

On honeymoon or at home getting into a bath or shower together with your partner can be a tantalizing run-up to intercourse, or a soothing way to relax afterwards.

Water has long been considered to have cleansing, relaxing and healing properties, and these – together with its potential for sensuality – have always made it a powerful force when combined with sex. The feel of water on the skin can be invigorating or relaxing, depending on its temperature and how it is used.

Many people find that either sensation can enhance their enjoyment of a particular lovemaking episode. Applying soap and stroking your partner's body – or your own – can be a good excuse for intimate physical contact.

Bathing can also make a couple feel sexy, because it unites them in a comforting "back-to-the-womb" way, as they revel in the same watery environment. This is an occasion when the usually restricting design of a bath can work in the intimate

Don't fill your bath too full with water or you could cause flooding!

couple's favour. Close physical contact becomes essential with the intertwining of legs and the search for comfortable positions in which to caress or lather one another.

Intercourse under water is rather difficult to achieve even in a large bath, but the woman can kneel up and be entered from behind, or the man can lift up her pelvis as he kneels in the water and enter her as she lies back, supporting herself on her elbows underwater.

To make a real fuss of your partner in the bath, gently lather them in soap all over, and treat the experience as a type of watery, sensual massage.

Depending on the size of your bath, you can do this as you both kneel by the side or lie in it if it is big enough.

Use soap or shower gel to clean every part of their body, leaving the genitals until last, and then rinse your partner down. (You may prefer to use a very mild, unscented soap to avoid irritation around the delicate genital area.) Then turn sensual massage into a sexual caress, and bring him or her to orgasm.

The more adventurous can get their partner to support their weight on their elbows, and allow the lower part of the body to float to the surface. Their relative weightlessness will make this quite comfortable for them, while their partner brings them to orgasm with oral sex.

To finish off, allow them to lie back and wallow in the after-glow of orgasm and then – when they are ready – dry them down with a luxuriously soft towel, taking as long as necessary to turn

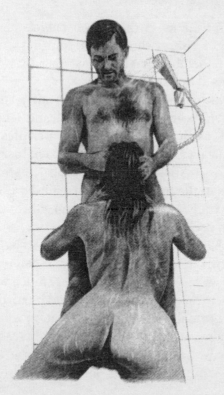

In the shower, the sensation of water on skin can enhance the pleasure of sex. For couples who feel that full penetrative sex may be a little risky in a shower, sensual caresses or oral sex can be equally enjoyable.

that into another long and lingering sensual experience that can be as erotic as you care to make it.

Showering together has many of the same attractions as bathing together but without the exciting sense of weightlessness that comes from being immersed in water.

Making love in a shower can be fun, but unless you have a particularly large shower area, it can be a little restricting and take a little imagination and physical dexterity. If the shower is at the end of the bath, the man can play the water over the woman's back as she leans forward and he enters her slowly and sensually from behind.

More athletic positions in the shower cubicle need some care. There is always a risk of slipping and injuring yourself or your partner. Also, remember that the shower-head is not strong and should not be used as a support.

A jacuzzi (a whirlpool-type bath which sprays jets of warm water against the skin) is an extremely relaxing and sensual way to refresh your body as air forced into the water creates bubbles which burst on contact with the skin, and help to release tension.

The sensual possibilities are almost endless. Intercourse is possible, just as it is in the bath, and you may find it is better as the flow and power of the water can provide an almost complete sexual experience in itself.

Waterbeds, fashionable in the 1970s, consist of a large water-filled bag which forms the mattress of the bed. It can be as rigid or as flexible as you wish – depending upon how much water you put into it. Lying on the mattress – which should be covered with a cloth sheet in the normal way – creates a sensation which some people like but which can make others feel slightly seasick! The bounce in these beds makes for interesting intercourse as the couple experience unusual rippling sensations. Also, as the couple move about the bed it seems to envelop their bodies, making for a unique experience.

An intimate encounter outdoors and in the water, whether by the sea, or in a swimming pool can also be a highly erotic and sensual experience, although what you can do in public is restricted by the laws of that country or state. You should make sure that you are completely alone if you want to make love out of doors.

Making love in a swimming pool can be extremely arousing. Simply being in the warm water with your lover is stimulating enough, but you will need your own pool, or at least be sure you have exclusive use of one, if you plan to take the matter to its logical conclusion.

In a swimming pool, the woman can float on her back in the water in the shallow end while the man walks backwards down the slope until his penis is floating horizontally on the surface of the water. Now penis and vagina are at the same level.

While supporting his partner under her buttocks and lower back, the man can penetrate her. She weighs almost nothing in this position, and can be easily positioned at many angles, making penetrations that are impossible on land comparatively simple to achieve.

For those who do not have a pool of their own, similar fun can be had at the seaside, but as beaches are public places, make sure you find somewhere deserted or you could find yourself in court on a charge of breaking local laws.

We all imagine that lying on the beach at the water's edge in a warm climate and making love to a handsome man or a beautiful woman will be a romantic as well as an arousing experience, but in reality the cocktail of waves, sand and sex is a little more sobering.

CREATIVE ARGUING

No two people are likely to agree about absolutely everything, whether it is personal habits or politics. If they have a healthy relationship, these differences are eventually going to show and should do so. If they do not, one or both are probably repressing their feelings, wishes or opinions. And no-one can live a fulfilling emotional life if they deny their feelings.

Confronting emotions

The most common causes of arguments between the majority of couples today are:

- ♥ Sex
- ♥ Each other's family
- ♥ Each other's friends
- ♥ Jealousy
- ♥ Excessive drinking
- ♥ Housework and related chores
- ♥ Money
- ♥ Work
- ♥ The bathroom
- ♥ Disciplining children
- ♥ Whether to have children

While any of these can spark off full-scale rows, if you and your partner are prepared to work at your relationship and are committed to each other, your arguments can be creative and positive – whether they are about how long one of you spends in the bathroom each morning or whether one of you keeps eyeing up the other's best friend.

If you can see an argument coming, ask yourself: Is it really worth having? Are you convinced that you are right? Are you saying what's really bothering you? Be positive – attack the issue and not the person. Keep to the point and try to avoid an argument in front of family and friends.

How to argue creatively

The key to creative arguing is trust. If you do not trust your partner, how can you be honest with him or her? In a bad relationship, rows only show up weaknesses. If your arguments leave the two of you as far apart as you were before, not only are they doing you no good, they will probably drive you away from each other.

In a truly creative argument, the following takes place:

1 *The initiator explains clearly, frankly and without abuse what is bothering him or her.*

2 *The "arguee" will listen, consider and answer carefully.*

3 *Without resorting to blame or attack, the two of you will try to work out why the disagreement has arisen.*

4 *Once you have come to understand the cause of the conflict, you will discuss to what extent it can be resolved*

5 *Having agreed to some possibility of compromise, each of you will offer a concession and accept one.*

6 *Each will feel sorry that the argument had to happen, ashamed at their own part in it and grateful that strengths, as well as weaknesses, have been pointed out.*

7 *Both should experience an overwhelming sense of relief that grievances have been aired and shared pleasure that the relationship is strong enough to profit by the argument.*

As each wave breaks over the lovers' bodies, it can cause considerable friction between penis and vagina. This friction can cause irritations. To avoid this, try getting into deeper water before starting to make love. If the shore-line is covered with boulders or pebbles, a sexual encounter at the water's edge is possible without much hazard although it may be extremely uncomfortable!

Communicating about sex

Just as important as finding a place and a time for sex, is a time to communicate. Couples can live together for years and never really talk intimately. Communication between partners is vital – and one of the best ingredients for a good sexual relationship.

Keep in mind that sex is a very private subject for most people – especially when it involves our own personal sexuality. Even within a close, truly loving relationship many people can still feel awkward about declaring their sexual needs, desires and anxieties.

How to communicate

The joy of a close personal and sexual relationship is that a couple can discuss and share their fears as well as their sexual desires. But all too often there is a lack of communication. A couple who can succeed in overcoming this communication gap will almost certainly find that the physical and emotional sides of lovemaking will improve as a result.

There are many reasons why communicating about sex is so difficult. A major problem is that we tend to make general assumptions about what men and women want and need, and on a personal level we assume the wants and needs of our partners. Not communicating about sex is at the heart of countless problems and arguments within long-term relationships.

It is a good idea to be quite disciplined when it comes to talking about sex. One answer is to make a special date with each other, a personal time when you will talk more intimately than usual. Try to set this fairly early on in the evening so that you are not both exhausted and likely to become irritable. It may be a good idea to go out as being on neutral territory can help enormously, but make sure you are not easily overheard.

Try not to talk about any sexual problems when you're both in bed and possibly feeling aroused. It is a vulnerable time and usually only results in frayed tempers and egos.

One of the problems when communicating about sex is that we often use different sexual terms. We usually assume we know what our partner means, even though we may never have actually asked.

One way to break down the barrier is to play a game with your partner. Make a list of all the words for sex and body parts you know – slang can be a great way to avoid embarrassment. Next to the different words, write how you feel about them. Perhaps some make you feel shy, giggly or just plain horny. Now swap your lists.

Another very useful communication tool is massage, strange though it may seem.

First, the very physical closeness that takes place is a solid foundation for any other form of communication about sex. Second, the "instructions" given by your partner during the massage are a more interesting way of becoming aware of each other's erogenous zones. Everyone is different and some of the areas can be a complete and pleasurable surprise. Third, taking the time to massage one another can help to reduce any stress which can often build up as relationships become more serious.

Much hostility in a relationship can arise over no-go areas. These can be areas that aren't about sex but spill into sexual communication. Fighting about subjects such as family, friends, religion or politics can lead to major conflicts and upheavals.

Be sure that you both know what the no-go areas are, and then work through them slowly and lovingly.

When you reach an area about which you repeatedly find you cannot agree, try to accept it. If your relationship is good, it will stand quite a lot of disagreement, provided you don't resort to ridicule and humiliation. When you set about discussing a sexual topic, always remember that your partner is probably also your best friend and that the most important thing of all is not to harm the friendship. At times this may mean holding your tongue.

How you approach your partner is the key to success. A loving friend may be the ideal person to sound off to, but if this becomes a habit, beware. Constant aggression can wear away the most solid of friendships and push the most tolerant partner into saying "I've had enough".

This may not necessarily mean that they will leave you, but they may withdraw their constant support. They could become remote and uncommunicative. The relationship will slide slowly and inevitably downhill.

Most people think: "I love him/her, therefore I would do A, B or C but not X, Y and Z." The usual assumption is that their partner has the same definitions of love, and almost certainly he or she will not.

Sitting down together and talking over the different gray areas should show you just how individual your own definition of love is and help analyze why you have this stereotyped notion. Communication means listening to all your partner's needs as well as voicing your own.

Partners who behave in a loving fashion as much as they possibly can will find that their relationship and sex life will be

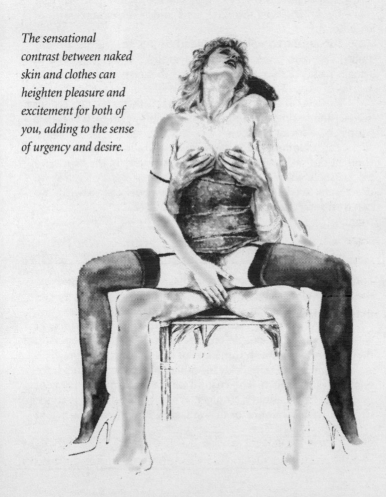

The sensational contrast between naked skin and clothes can heighten pleasure and excitement for both of you, adding to the sense of urgency and desire.

THE PSYCHOLOGY OF TRUST

Humans are social animals and depend on co-operation for their survival. They collaborate with others to pursue their goals and satisfy their needs. Trust is the measure of relationships, and is a skill everyone must learn. Psychologists say that learning to trust is the first and most important task of childhood.

Babies are completely dependent on the adults around them. The trust a baby has in its mother is absolute, and is usually justified. Even people who, in other respects, are untrustworthy can usually be relied on to look after their own babies.

However, if childhood trust is broken, the consequences are serious and lasting. Learning to trust people again then becomes a long and difficult process.

The emotion that first came naturally now has to be thought out rationally. The mind takes over from the heart and persuades us that trusting other people is necessary, even if we don't want to take the risk. But how do we discover whether we can trust someone or not?

Learning to trust

Looking for clues about someone's character begins with studying their face and its range of expressions. There are eighty muscles in the face, capable of an estimated 7000 facial expressions.

The eyes, in particular, are known to play an essential role in getting to know someone, in order to evaluate what sort of person they are, and to establish some sort of relationship.

Another traditional clue to someone's trustworthiness is the quality of their touch. The custom of shaking hands is a way of finding out more about a stranger. Whether this contact is confident or nervous, clammy or dry, quickly withdrawn or warm and firm, helps to round out the first impression. Subsequently, what people say and the way they speak gives us more to go on.

Cultural differences are also very important, as an American survey has shown: two large groups of people, one American, the other Japanese, were tested on how they gave and responded to compliments. The results showed that Americans complimented each other freely and frequently, whereas personal compliments were rare for the Japanese.

Receiving casual compliments from Americans left Japanese bemused and distrustful. Americans, in turn, found the Japanese reticent and impersonal, so trust was difficult to establish.

The irony of trust is that, although we need it to be able to function socially and personally, trusting others also makes us more vulnerable. We are thus more liable to feel betrayed when the person we thought we could trust lets us down in some way.

Trust and betrayal

When trust is betrayed, the last person you tend to blame is yourself. But it may be you who was wrong to trust that person, because they never accepted the trust that you placed in them. There is no reason why a person must reciprocate your feelings.

Many people who yearn for a deeply intimate relationship have a tendency to trust too much and too soon. By laying themselves open to their lover, they hope they will encourage a similar act of trust, and often find themselves hurt and disappointed.

The difficulty lies in judging when to trust someone so completely – and whether the relationship can reasonably be expected to become as meaningful as you want it to be. Learning how to make these judgements is very much a matter of trial and error, and may be mastered with experience.

able to withstand the criticism when it does occasionally happen to occur.

Being sexually in tune with your partner needs working at. You must invest time and effort or you will see no return.

Quickie sex

Having said that creating the right conditions for sex is an essential part of lovemaking, there must also be a place in every relationship for those unplanned moments.

The joys of "quickie" sex are often overlooked, even by experienced lovers. We all tend to become obsessed with technique, often forgetting the joy there is to be had in spontaneity. A moment of unbridled passion can bring you more than just intense and passionate pleasure. The urgency can rekindle old, forgotten feelings, and in no time you can be transported back to the early days of your relationship, or even the first hours of your sexual awakening.

With so much advice and freedom of speech on the subject of sex today, couples tend to see themselves as enlightened, which indeed they are compared to previous generations. But the knowledge gained is often at the cost of our more basic instincts, and our primeval powers of seduction.

The joys of "quickies"
Quickie sex often has a quality all its own. Within the confines of your loving relationship it is neither more nor less worthwhile or trivial than lovemaking which has been carefully considered.

Spontaneous sex shows a couple how much they are attracted to each other on a purely physical basis. Some women

If the woman is partly dressed while a man makes love to her, it can make her feel especially abandoned and sexy.

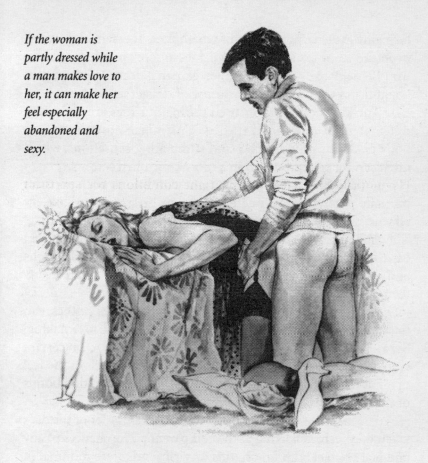

say that for them it is a better approach to sex than any other. As it is unplanned, they need simply allow themselves to be taken over by their man's ardour. In fact, some women only ever have orgasms when sex is sudden and out of their control, when they are taken forcefully by the man they love.

Spontaneous sex is often linked with the risk of being discovered in the act by other people. This risk of discovery can be highly exciting, as a degree of naughtiness is essential for some people to enjoy sex at its best. Quickies in semi-public places – in woods, fields or even your own garden – can build up this naughtiness with a stimulating sense of danger and urgency.

The kinds of positions used during quickies are often very different from those used in bed. Unfamiliar movements and body positions produce new and stimulating sensations, which often cannot be reproduced in a more controlled setting.

Quickies are usually carried out with one or both partners partially dressed, as you often have too little time to take off all your clothes. This in itself is highly arousing to many people. The sight of a woman who has simply raised her skirt and bent forward over the kitchen table to reveal her naked thighs and bottom can make even the most weary man ready for sex.

The addition of underwear, and in some cases clothes, can make a big difference to the style and the feel of lovemaking. Some people are turned on by the touch or look of certain clothes. The silkiness of a dress, the sight of high heels or the feel of a man's sweatshirt against bare skin can be an exciting bonus of quickie sex.

For many people, spontaneous sex is a reminder of the days when they were still living with their parents. The chances of any physical contact with boyfriends or girlfriends were minimal in those days, and most young couples became very adept at grabbing the opportunity when they could. While we appreciate the privacy that comes with leaving the parental home and having our own place, some of the spontaneity and excitement is always lost.

Quickies have other advantages as well. Not having prepared themselves for sex both partners are unwashed and therefore carry the smell of their sweat and other body fluids on their skin. This earthiness can actually prove to be a real turn-on, as the normal act of washing actually removes many of the naturally occurring chemical attractants. Many people, especially men, find their desire heightened by such natural scents.

For some, a quickie is the enactment of a sexual fantasy. Most people have fantasies of taking or being taken by a partner in various strange, unconventional or exotic locations. Quickie sex can achieve this with a little sense of adventure.

Given a choice, and time to think it over, many people would not readily agree to sex in such a place or in that particular way – they would always find some kind of excuse. When it is "forced" upon them, however, they often greatly enjoy it, and may even then build the event into future fantasies.

Some men are put off the idea of initiating a quickie themselves, because they cannot remember when their partner is having a period, but this problem is easily solved with a little forethought on the woman's part. After all, many women are most easily aroused during their period and it is a simple matter for the woman to remove her tampon or towel and be ready for sex in a couple of minutes. If the man still has qualms, then just avoid making love on the first heavy day or two or insert a diaphragm ahead of time. This will hold back the flow for a while and allow the couple to have a "quickie surprise".

It is often said that good sex depends on meticulous fore-play to arouse the woman so that her vagina is lubricated. But when she is in the mood for quick sex a woman's vagina can lubricate almost immediately. And some women are most turned on by quickie sex, because of the intense degree of passionate feeling involved.

Sex between true lovers takes many forms and serves many purposes. One of them is that it reinforces their secret bond and by doing so builds up their unique relationship.

In this context, quickies can be especially exciting in the middle of an event at which others are present. Why not take your partner outside the room at a dinner party or other social gathering and make love? You can develop your own private code for letting your partner know that you want them – now.

CHAPTER 7

Alternative Lovemaking

T here are inevitably times in any relationship when a more sensitive and careful approach to sex may be needed – whether due to pregnancy, recent child-birth or illness of either partner. However, sex need not be ruled out altogether, and if anything it can improve as a result of trying new and different techniques.

Sex in pregnancy

Contrary to popular opinion, pregnancy is far from a no-go period sexually. With the worries of contraception or trying for a baby removed, pregnancy can provide an opportunity for enjoying sex more than ever before.

It is helpful when discussing pregnancy to divide the nine months into three equal trimesters. These three three-month periods differ physiologically and are usually characterized by distinct patterns of sexual behaviour.

Research has found that there is a general fall in interest in the first three months, an increase in the second three months, and a dropping off as the third trimester progresses.

During pregnancy, both partners should be sensitive to each other's sexual needs. This might just mean cuddling, caressing, sensually massaging, or masturbating one another if either does not feel like intercourse. But by exploring each other's body and understanding the changing needs you both may have through the months, you will probably grow closer.

The greatest sexual advantage of pregnancy for many couples is that they do not have to use any form of contraception. Some say that this unhindered, free lovemaking opens up new doors to them. But this is often offset, at least to some extent, by the hormonal, physical and emotional changes that occur in a woman during the first twelve weeks of pregnancy.

During this stage, if any of these physical or psychological aspects are a concern, inventive couples can find other ways of showing their love and affection.

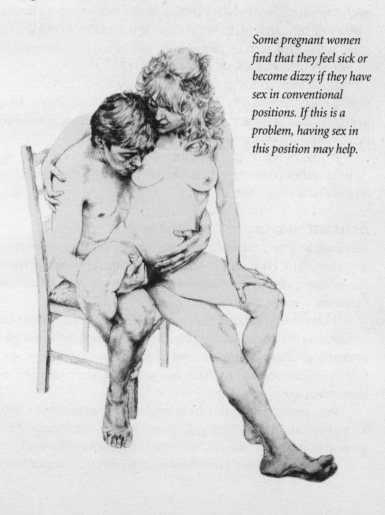

Some pregnant women find that they feel sick or become dizzy if they have sex in conventional positions. If this is a problem, having sex in this position may help.

Many people worry that the foetus may be particularly vulnerable, and could be harmed during orgasm. Although it is true that the uterus contracts very forcibly during orgasm, there is no scientific data to prove that this harms the foetus.

People also worry about sex provoking a miscarriage, but such fears are almost always unfounded. Unless the woman has a history of miscarriage, in which case it is sensible to refrain from intercourse and even orgasms from weeks ten to fourteen, there is nothing to worry about.

Quite early in his partner's pregnancy a man can start to feel that he has served his "usefulness" to her and is no longer necessary, but if he is made to feel loved and wanted, he should be able to cope with a period of abstention.

It makes sense to kiss and cuddle more, to discuss your feelings about parenthood and to get in touch with each other's emotional and physical needs.

Sensual massage in pregnancy

Learning how to massage your partner is a sensual experience at any time, but especially useful and pleasurable for a woman during pregnancy. Two important areas are the breasts and perineum.

There is no evidence that any treatment of the breasts helps in the success of breastfeeding, but it makes sense to give a woman's breast and nipples a lot of attention during foreplay so that she becomes used to them being sucked as a preparation for breastfeeding.

Perineal massage may help to avoid the necessity of having an episiotomy on delivery (cutting of the perineum on the grounds that the woman is "too small" to let the baby out).

The woman lies on the floor or bed with the soles of her feet touching. Her partner then uses his fingers, well lubricated with baby oil, to massage the perineum, best done three times a week from about twelve to fourteen weeks into the pregnancy.

From about sixteen weeks onwards you can extend the massage to include the vagina. The idea is for the man to insert two or three well-lubricated fingers into the vagina until the woman says that it is uncomfortable. With his fingers inside her vagina he massages the perineum, encouraging the woman to relax her pelvic muscles.

It is best to insert the fingers one above the other in the early days because this stretches the vulva opening less. As time progresses the man can insert the fingers in this position but then turn them through a right angle.

The woman may experience a tingling sensation like pins and needles. When it becomes too uncomfortable, she tells him and he keeps his fingers still in that position until, after a minute or two, the intense sensations pass. He can now massage her vagina and perineum from inside.

The second trimester

Generally, the middle three months – the second trimester – are the best and therefore the most active period sexually for both partners.

The woman, now usually through the worst of her physical symptoms, is probably beginning to feel fulfilled as a woman as the reality of the pregnancy makes itself felt, while the birth is far enough away not to be a real concern.

Some women experience more sexual drive and arousal at this point in their pregnancy than at any other time of their lives.

Most men enjoy their partner being pregnant from this stage on. Many of the changes – fuller, rounder figure, larger breasts, shiny hair, no periods, better vaginal lubrication, apparently permanently "aroused" genitals, better skin and so on – make women more attractive. A number of these changes mimic sexual arousal.

Rear-entry positions work well during pregnancy as they put very little pressure on the woman's abdomen, allowing her to enjoy sex in a relaxed and comfortable manner.

Just as their partner can be on top of the world during this time, so some men now also feel at their best, especially if their self-esteem had previously been poor. The tangible evidence of their masculinity helps such men to become more a ease with their sexuality. This enables them to relax more and to be a better partner. The second trimester is by far the most comfortable for making love. Early problems are over and the woman's bump is not yet big enough to get in the way.

All the usual lovemaking positions are possible, and many women feel that because they are producing extra vaginal secretions they are ready for sex at any time. Some women feel almost permanently sexy during these three months, with an increased need for orgasms which they claim do not leave them feeling satisfied as they normally would.

This may be because the time taken for a woman's sex organs to return to normal after an orgasm is greatly prolonged during pregnancy, possibly because the whole area is so engorged with blood as a result of the pregnancy itself.

The third trimester

For the majority of couples, the frequency of their lovemaking falls off during the last three months and only a few couples continue to make love right up to the birth. The main difficulties for those who do carry on are mostly centred on the woman's size and lack of flexibility.

The other big worry that some couples have is that if they make love and the woman has an orgasm near the delivery date she will go into premature labour. This can sometimes happen, but it is a rare occurrence unless the woman has a history of premature labours.

Here are some practical and popular options for sex during pregnancy:

● *The woman adopts an "all fours" position. The "doggy" position is exceptionally good.*

● *For a more restful approach, when the woman's tummy is very large, the "spoons" position works well. In this the woman lies on her side with her legs drawn up as far as her bump will allow. The man cuddles into her back and inserts his penis from behind.*

Squatting may take practice, but it allows the woman a greater degree of control.

● *Some pregnant women find they prefer being on top during sex. A woman's vagina enlarges considerably after about twelve weeks and this produces sensations that are very different for both the man and the woman.*

● *Many women like being upright, especially in the latter stages of pregnancy, because they have heartburn or feel dizzy when they lie flat. The woman sits on her partner's penis facing away from him as he sits in a chair, or alternatively, she sits facing him if the bump is not too big. Another possibility is for the woman to squat on her partner's penis as he lies on the bed or floor. This is also beneficial because it encourages her to become good at squatting – a very useful exercise in itself to open up the pelvis.*

● *Very late on in pregnancy it is a good idea to use positions that do not involve deep penetration. One position that works well is for the woman to lie back on the edge of a bed or large chair and put her feet flat on the floor. The man kneels on the floor between her legs and enters her.*

Sex after childbirth

Some women who have had no stitches after childbirth are back to normal sexual intercourse within a week or two, but they are the exception. Most women find that it is about six weeks before they feel ready to have sex again.

While waiting for intercourse to become comfortable again you can, of course, indulge in all kinds of other sexual pursuits if both of you are interested. Many women want to return to having orgasms almost immediately after birth. There is no harm

BROODINESS

What is it that makes so many women long for the same thing – a baby – and suffer the same relentless pangs when thwarted?

Psychologist and broadcaster John Nicholson thinks broodiness is not innate. "There are hormonal changes which happen, for very sound reasons, both during pregnancy and after giving birth, but there is no hormonal reason for a woman to want babies."

Nicholson feels uneasy, too, about the term "maternal instinct". The assumption that it exists is often because women have usually been responsible for childcare. But people who use this argument, he says, are guilty of an error of logic, believing that the way things are is the way that they ought to be. "What does exist," Nicholson suggests, "is a terrific social pressure to have children and also natural human curiosity, a reluctance not to experience everything there is to experience in life."

Infertility

As many as one in ten couples is believed to be infertile and for those desperately seeking a solution and a longed-for baby, broodiness is not a strong enough term. While no one asks women at antenatal clinics why they want babies, women with infertility problems are often asked that question.

In a study of infertile women, the women interviewed gave a wide range of reasons for wanting children. One had "always wanted children". Another woman imagined having a little girl for "something of me and my blood and my family history". Some women wanted to experience pregnancy and childbirth, while others wanted children to bring up.

Some discovered a particular relationship sparked off the desire for a baby as tangible proof of the relationship's importance, while others shunned adult attachment, wanting a child of their own, on their own.

There is evidence that sometimes an acute longing for a child can actually work against you having one. There are many cases of women who give up hope of having a baby after years of trying, only to find themselves pregnant as soon as they relax.

Most experts now accept a link between miscarriages and anxiety. As John Nicholson explains, "hormones, including stress hormones, can get into the placenta and affect unborn babies. It is quite plausible that anxiety may be a factor in ... infertility too."

The deadline decade

Many women today are painfully reminded of the biological clock ticking away through what John Nicholson dubs the "deadline decade": "For women who have put off having children to pursue their careers, the mid-thirties can be a time of great internal conflict." Sheila Kitzinger in *Birth Over Thirty* says women see thirty as a birthday crisis. "This is the time when they often ask, 'Who am I really?', 'What am I doing with my life?', 'Is this really what I want?', and 'Where do I go from here?'. More and more women in their thirties and forties decide to have either a first or another baby before it's too late."

More single women are having babies and keeping them. There is less stigma today attached to being an unmarried mother and, with the availability if AID (artificial insemination by donor), a single woman who wants a child can actually have one without a man around at all.

Others still long for a baby, building daydreams or subliminal visions in their sleep. For them broodiness is like a hunger, except that, for them it can never be assuaged.

Oral sex is not only satisfying for the woman but will encourage her uterus to return to its normal size quicker.

in this, and it could even be positively helpful, because orgasms encourage the uterus to return to its normal size more quickly.

Breastfeeding also makes a woman's sexual organs return to normal faster than they would otherwise. Indeed, many women who only breastfeed are able to get back to an active sex life within six weeks.

For a couple who are able and inclined to go straight back to sex after a baby, all well and good. But the story is often not so simple. Having a baby is the most disorganizing event in a couple's sexual life and it affects both partners profoundly, particularly if it is a first child.

There are a number of reasons why so many couples have trouble with sex after the birth of a baby:

● *Some women find that caring for their baby is so satisfying or so exhausting emotionally – and such a full-time job – that they simply do not have any emotional resources left to invest in their partner. As a result, he becomes ignored and sex falls by the wayside.*

● *Many women only feel attractive if they have a "perfect" body image. After a baby, when they may have a bulging tummy and some stretch marks, they feel sufficiently unlovable that they cannot imagine any man wanting to make love to them.*

Deep penetration can be painful for the woman. The missionary position allows the man the necessary control to make love more gently.

● *"Sex is for making babies and I've got a baby" is something that many women feel, whether consciously or subconsciously. These women go off sex for some time, feeling that it has achieved its purpose.*

● *Tiredness is the most commonly quoted reason for going off sex after a baby, and this is certainly a real factor. Physical exhaustion from the birth, compounded by night after night of broken sleep take their toll on new mothers.*

● *A few women are so preoccupied with the baby — its every noise, movement and smell — that they just do not have any energy*

The woman-on-top positions allow control of depth and penetration at this most delicate time.

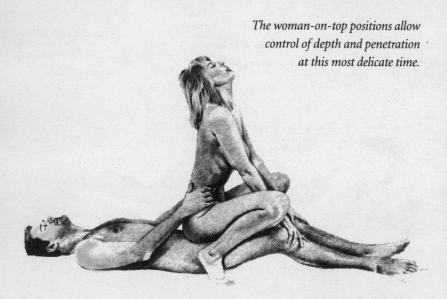

left to give to their partner. Such women often overreact to the
baby's behaviour and worry about any problem – no matter
how small.

● Fear of another pregnancy is a very common cause of going off
sex at this time. About a third of all pregnancies are unplanned.
It is hardly surprising, therefore, that after an unplanned – and
possibly unwanted – pregnancy a woman may be somewhat
worried about risking another.

● Post-natal depression affects a surprisingly large proportion of
women, although the majority suffer only mild "baby blues" in
the first few days. True depression is a powerful force against sex
at any time, in both men and women.

● Some women are not happy with motherhood, and resent their
new lifestyle, the loss of their job and possibly their partner's
attitude to them. Sex then becomes the thing that has landed
them in this situation.

● Pain on premature resumption of sex can cause bad
associations for the woman and put her off sex. If she has had a
Caesarean birth, a bad tear or painful episiotomy, anything
which puts pressure on the wound will hurt. Her partner should
try to be understanding about this and woo her back to the idea
of sex gradually.

● Equally, the woman should try to remember that her partner
still has sexual needs, and find alternative ways to fill them.

FATHERHOOD

Years ago people believed that babies were women's work and that men should have very little to do with that side of life. These days, things are different and fathers play a much bigger part in bringing up their children. For some fathers, however, making the decision to be more involved is not so easy, since in many ways society is still built on a stereotyped pattern.

The news that a baby is on the way usually evokes a mixture of joy and slight anxiety. Mothers certainly feel this way, but what has often been ignored is that fathers feel the same.

Indeed, fathers can at times feel even more worried than their partners about what is going on. Mothers become the center of attention, swept up in a whirlwind of visits to the doctor and the hospital, where they are given advice and information on what is happening to them physically.

But men are not automatically absorbed into the same supportive network and they can feel very left out of the whole process. It is rare, for example, for a father to get the time off work to go along to antenatal appointments with his partner. So, in general, he has to rely on her to provide information about everything to do with the pregnancy.

A man's role during pregnancy

Another problem for men is coping with the physical effects that pregnancy has on their partners. In the early months many women suffer from nausea and fatigue; while others are faced with these and a variety of other niggling physical problems throughout pregnancy.

Although quite a few women enjoy their pregnancies, many feel less pleased about what is happening to their bodies. They also have moments of anxiety about what lies in store – what will the birth be like, and how painful will it be? Will the baby be all right? What sort of mother will they make, and will they be able to cope? It is hardly surprising, therefore, that some women are prey to changeable moods and may feel irritable from time to time.

Sex is another area that often suffers during pregnancy. Good communication is, as always, the key to good sex, and this applies during pregnancy, perhaps more than ever.

With all these anxieties, many couples actually find themselves drifting apart when they should be drawing closer together. The important thing is for fathers to be as involved as they can from the start.

The reality of fatherhood

One of the most positive ways a man can make a commitment to parenthood is by being at the birth of his child. Most men are deeply moved by the experience and their partners often feel that they could not have done it without them.

However, the decision should not be made lightly. There are some couples for whom the presence of the father is not essential, and may even be harmful, and no man should ever be forced to attend a birth if he does not want to. Hospitals now actively encourage fathers to be present. It is generally believed that if a woman has a companion she trusts with her during labour, she is likely to have a shorter, more problem-free birth.

Sharing the experience of birth can give a father a terrific start to parenthood, but it is also very important for a man to be around in the early weeks after the birth as much as possible. It will take his partner a while to fully recover from the birth, and for the first weeks she will certainly need someone to help in general and with the baby. She may also want a shield from all the visitors who are eager to see the baby.

Having the hands kissed and the fingers sucked slowly is a supremely sensual act.

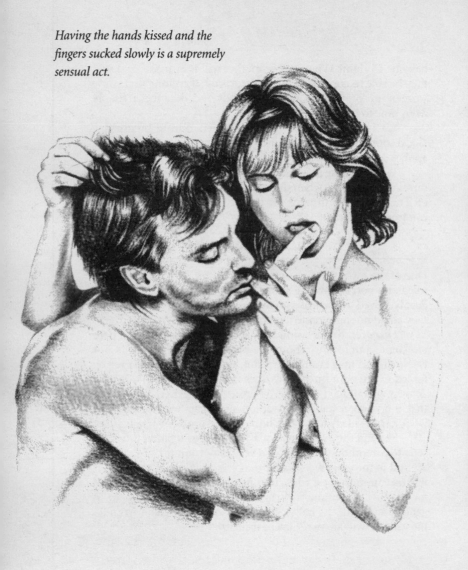

Sex without intercourse

For many loving couples, making love without having intercourse plays an important role in their daily lives. There are many fun ways for a couple to enrich their time together.

Touch can be a valuable tool in any loving relationship. A couple can even make love all day by touching a lot, yet expecting no genital activity to follow.

A cuddle while you are washing up can turn a boring chore into a part of lovemaking. Such things broaden the scope of what two people can do without any genital touching.

Sensual massage can also play a similar role in lovemaking. The one rule is that the partner receiving the massage remains completely passive.

The massage is better if the genitals are left alone, since it is not intended to be a prelude to intercourse, although sometimes intercourse will follow naturally.

An extension of this non-genital kind of lovemaking is to start involving the genitals in one way or another. At the simplest and often highly arousing level, one partner can stroke or gently fondle the genitals of the other. This is not taken as far as sexual arousal but is one step up from kissing and cuddling.

It may lead to masturbation, oral sex and other forms of non-intercourse lovemaking that can be used when intercourse is forbidden or unwise for some reason.

Many couples indulge in these sorts of lovemaking as a matter of course, and those who play like this rarely have trouble knowing when and if the other wants sex. If one of them does not, there are no bad feelings: they are confident enough of themselves and their partner not to feel rejected.

A sensual holiday

Taking time out for a "sensual holiday" can greatly benefit a relationship. A sensual holiday can be an hour, a weekend or even longer, when you decide to throw out your old routines of love-making and start all over again.

As a relationship progresses many of us become sloppy and the amount and quality of intimacy can fall dramatically. A sensual holiday provides an excellent opportunity to rediscover this intimacy. It is a time for devoting yourself totally to each other and developing the sensations and a level of intimacy you may have lost. It is also an excellent time for romantic games.

Like everything else that is worthwhile it needs preparation and planning. This has the advantage of making it something that you can look forward to, and will also make you think about what would most please your partner.

Once you have had your sensual holiday, try to capitalize on what you have learned and gained, then make plans for your next soon afterwards so that you have something to look forward to and do not lose the momentum.

Many couples never really had a courtship – they have rushed headlong from a flirting interest in one another to bed, and then into a full-blown sexual scene. This is a pity because it shortcuts so many of the learning phases of the development of a male-female relationship. So for some people going back to the stage of early courtship may be a new and worthwhile experience.

Start by taking every opportunity to show your love for each other in non-sexual ways:

Give each other unexpected presents; show more interest in each other's hobbies; phone just to say "I love you"; leave each other little love notes and "date" each other as you did in the early days, taking care to be extra courteous, caring and sympathetic.

Using the fingers to stimulate the skin hairs rather than the skin is particularly pleasurable.

THE NEW BABY

The first few months of parenthood are marked by a great range of conflicting emotions, most of them new and some quite unexpected. Being prepared for change in all areas of a couple's life together can mean the difference between confidence and chaos in the early days.

For the mother and father, the birth is a testing ground of their love and trust, and it means rediscovering each other to some extent. Qualities such as tenderness and protectiveness, perhaps not seen before, emerge in the father, and for him the transition of his partner from companion and lover to mother can be a source of deep pride.

The triangle of mother, father and child has all the potential for increasing love, but it can also set up divisions and tensions in the early days. Just as the parents probably underestimate the strength of feeling they find they have for their baby – concern for safety and well-being opening up new depths of vulnerability in them – they may also be shaken by the intensity of negative feelings such as frustration and resentment.

From couple to family

Today, many couples enjoy a fairly long period of "freedom" – time for leisure and each other – before having a family. However much they think they are prepared, the new regime can be a shock. The routine which a baby needs can seem relentless and inescapable. The demands can easily come to dominate everything else at first and the couple's former spontaneity, even privacy, seems lost forever.

Both parents face upheavals in their lives with a new baby. The mother's feelings immediately after birth are notoriously unpredictable especially if she has experienced a long or arduous labour, or has to cope with the after-effects of drugs. If she does not love her baby instantly she may feel worried or guilty – almost always unnecessarily.

The idea of "instant bonding" of mother and baby has perhaps been over-emphasized, so that mothers can easily feel inadequate if they do not experience it. A response which falls short of immediate love is not unusual and certainly does not mean the mother lacks normal maternal feelings.

A period of "baby blues" is experienced by at least half of all new mothers, and many feel trapped and isolated.

The new father has to face major adjustments too, although they are all too often unrecognized. His life has irreversibly changed and adapting to it can be hard. He has not just acquired a baby, his partner has altered and has new priorities.

Supporting each other

By helping in simple, practical ways the father can prove his continuing love and support. Care of the baby can also be shared. If the baby is bottle-fed, it is obvious that the father can be as involved at feeding times as the mother. But there is also a role for him to play if his wife is breastfeeding. It can be a lonely and frustrating experience for a woman to spend a part of each night feeding her baby, and she may welcome a helping hand changing a diaper or being given a hot drink.

To a certain extent, it is only when a baby arrives that many men can really appreciate that their partner is in fact a complex mixture of mother and lover. She, in turn, will discover new facets of him as he grows into his new role of fatherhood. For many couples, these discoveries can deepen their relationship.

Some people may be so shy that, as much as they want to behave in less inhibited ways, they simply cannot. Here are a few tips to help such people along:

● *A glass or two of your favourite drink can be relaxing and may help to start things going. Alcohol lessens inhibitions and if this makes one partner less shy or more accepting of the other's loving advances, it might be worth a try.*

● *Almost any room in the house can be sexy if the mood is right, and there is always an alternative to the bedroom if you are both feeling sexy. If one partner has a fantasy about making love in a field or the back of the car, the other might co-operate to please their partner.*

● *Dress is a part of all social occasions whether they have any sexual purpose or not, and we all feel more attractive in certain types of clothes than others.*

● *Fun and games between couples often arise out of acting out various situations spontaneously. More formal games can involve the couple playing out any role which turns the other on. Again, dress can be an important part of this, as looking different can help you to behave differently.*

● *Many couples fail to make sufficient use of erotica to arouse themselves. This can take the form of sexy clothes, erotic books, or videos.*

Using sex aids

Many couples find that using sex aids and toys add a touch of excitement and variety to their sex life. Most are quite safe, as long as they are used for their intended purpose

The vast majority of aids need no more servicing than thorough washing and cleaning before and after use, and if used with imagination in a loving relationship they can give countless hours of sensual pleasure.

Good vibrations

By far the most popular sex toy of all is the vibrator. These are used mainly by women, but men also find them pleasurable. Other than washing them well after use you need only ensure that the batteries are in top condition. Poor battery power renders them almost useless and so mains-operated ones are much better – if more expensive.

If you are using a vibrator on your body – on your nipples for example – then lubrication will not be necessary. But some women do enjoy spreading oil on the part to be massaged with the vibrator beforehand. As with everything in sex, experiment to see what you prefer.

Be inventive and explore all over your body with the vibrator. You will be surprised at the areas that feel terrific when vibrated and massaged. Try different speeds of vibration. Some areas of the body are stimulated most when the vibration is coarse and others when it is fine. Most vibrators have adjustable speeds for this purpose.

Once you have experimented with the vibrator on various parts of your body, you can turn to your vulva. Start with the vibrator at a medium speed and rub it around the top of your thighs and then move it around the pubic area.

Next, stimulate the area between the vagina and anus. This part can be particularly sensitive on some women. Now open the lips of your vulva with the fingers of one hand and gently find where the vibrator gives the most arousal.

Most women find that stimulating the clitoris directly is too powerful and can actually be unpleasant, so start off by experimenting around the clitoral area. After a few minutes' experimenting, you will have a fairly good idea of what you most enjoy. If you begin to have really powerful sensations you might want to go straight on to have an orgasm. If you prefer not to at this stage, try the vibrator inside your vagina.

By now you will probably be highly aroused and so will be wet with natural secretions. If not, use a lubricant on the vibrator: a little saliva, KY jelly or a sexual lubricant.

Anal vibrations

Another option is to try playing with the vibrator around the anal region. Many women enjoy the sensations produced by vibrating this area and a few, especially those who enjoy anal sex, like the vibrator actually inside them.

Some men enjoy being stimulated with a vibrator, but they rarely get as much pleasure out of it as their partner. They may like certain parts of their body stimulated and a few like their genitals vibrated but it rarely causes orgasm as it does in women.

A man whose anus is highly sensitive can greatly enjoy both external and internal vibration and, as in women, the G spot or prostate gland can be stimulated to great effect with a vibrator. This can be best done if he is lying down with his legs pulled back and the vibrator inserted several inches and aimed at the front wall of the rectum.

Vibrators are most useful to women who are unable to have orgasms without powerful stimulation from a source other than their fingers. Use of a vibrator can actually teach them to have an orgasm and they can then transfer the ability to their own or their lover's fingers.

Many women are concerned that they will become addicted to the stimulation of a vibrator, but this rarely happens.

The dildo

Perhaps equally as popular as the vibrator is the dildo, a penis-shaped latex rubber object, especially made to be put into the vagina. These are useful when the man cannot achieve an erection because he has a nervous disorder that prevents it or he is impotent. Some dildoes have vibrator units built into them.

Apart from these men, the main users of dildoes are women who like something inside their vaginas as they masturbate.

A dildo is easy to use and unlike a real penis, has great stamina, so it is ideal for the woman who needs lots of thrusting to have an orgasm. Most women when they masturbate insert two fingers into their vagina so a dildo of this size is best. It can be held still, thrust in and out just inside the vaginal entrance, or thrust deeply in and out, as the woman likes.

More unusual dildoes have a squeezable bulb at the end which can be made to ejaculate milk or water as the woman climaxes. Double-ended dildoes are suitable for two women at once, while others can be inflated by squeezing a bulb so that their girth can fit the vagina of the user. This is useful for the woman whose vagina has become slack after having children.

Love eggs are used by many women as part of masturbation, but they are even more fun when inserted by their partner.

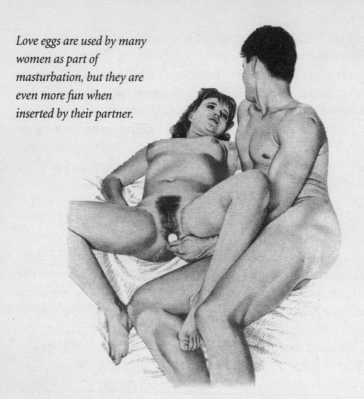

Other sex aids

Vibrators and dildoes may be the most popular sex aids, but there are many others – some obvious, some not – which can be fun to use. There are other vaginal stimulators such as love eggs (with or without vibrator units) and latex finger covers for the man or woman.

Almost any penis-shaped object can be pleasant to masturbate with but many are fraught with danger. Nothing breakable should ever be put into the vagina and it is sensible to stick to long cylindrical objects. A spherical object, like an orange, may be highly stimulating to push into the vagina at climax but can be difficult, or even impossible to remove without surgery. The vagina contracts down on such objects and, because they are so slippery and round, they are often hard to remove.

Textured and contoured sheaths come in a variety of shapes and sizes. They all give a slightly different vaginal sensation when used on a man's penis or a vibrator. However, most women get very little sexual pleasure from them.

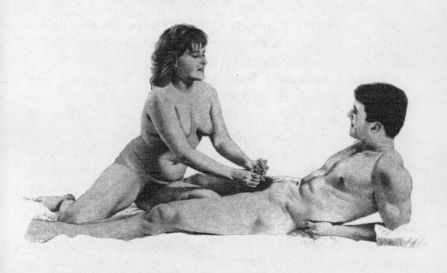

Sheaths with attachments at the teat add a little amusement and can also increase stimulation.

When used on a penis they must be donned in the same way as an ordinary contraceptive sheath – with their novelty element, it is easy to forget that precautions are still important. Some sheaths are washable and can be re-used, but make sure, or you could run the risk of an unwanted pregnancy.

Probably the most widely used of all sex "aids" is sexy underwear. Make the giving and receiving of gifts of sexy lingerie into a game. Take the opportunity to dress up in them as soon as you can so that your man knows that you like them. Do a striptease for him, or let him undress you.

Leave one piece of your underwear on when making love, such as the suspenders and stockings. You will both find this highly arousing.

Some couples like to pretend that the woman is a model for a catalogue, posing in her sexy lingerie for photos. She can strip this off as the session progresses.

If the man is away from home he can send some sexy underwear through the post to his partner. She can then wear them while he is away and write or phone to tell him all about them. This can be highly exciting for some men.

Penile rings are another exciting option for some couples. Any man who puts a ring around the base of his penis will have a bigger erection because the blood that would normally flow out of the penis back into the genital circulation becomes trapped in the penis, causing it to swell. Penile rings are useful, but must be chosen with care: if it is too small it will be very painful and if it is too large it will be ineffective.

Put the ring on well before penile stimulation starts, and once the man has ejaculated he should wait until the penis has subsided before trying to remove it: it could cause pain or injury Also, only ever use rings that are specially made for the purpose.

Penile stimulators can be effective for retaining an erection – especially if the woman takes control.

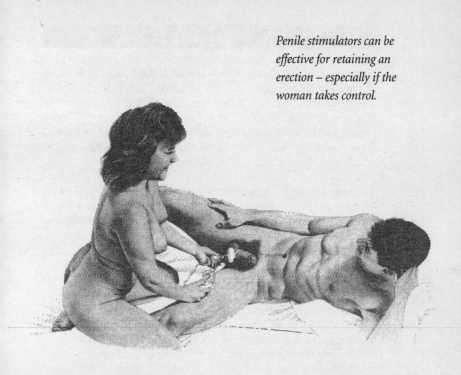

Many men find masturbation aids useful. Hollow latex tubes, with or without vibrator mechanisms, are straightforward to use. They need to be kept very clean, and well lubricated immediately prior to use. They are used by men who have no partner, and help give additional sensations to those obtained with hand stimulation alone. Sex dolls require similar care, especially the more expensive ones.

For those who enjoy anal stimulation there are a number of options. The simplest of these are attached to ordinary vibrators and are easy to use. As long as they are firmly attached, these

BIRTH ORDER

Sometimes known as the family "constellation", the birth order of your family is a game played out for as long as the players – the members of your family – are alive. Whether you are the firstborn, a middle child, the youngest or the only child is a crucial factor in forming your attitude nxot only to those you share your home with, but also to everyone in the world outside, which includes your future life partner.

The only child: To outsiders, being an only child is like having everything. But the only child knows it is also having to be everything. The sense of isolation and responsibility can last for-ever.

Problems surface as soon as the only child tries to make friends. They often discover that, although they are perfectly behaved with adults, they have no social skills whatever with children of their own age. Not only do they have no concept of sharing, they also constantly expect to be centre-stage.

Most only children have a problem with spontaneity, finding the idea of just taking off for the weekend with a tooth-brush in your pocket and nothing else romantic in principle, but totally alarming in practice. For them, life must be organized and scheduled, even though they may be naturally untidy and scatty.

But once they learn to lighten up and enjoy life, they are just as likely to be good lovers, parents and friends as anyone else. Only children will rarely take a relationship lightly and will devote time and effort to making it work – as long as they are given space.

The firstborn: For a while you are the only child, and have all the benefits and drawbacks that implies. But then the cosy three-some of you, Mom and Dad is shattered. In one sense the pressure is off you – there is a new child to fuss over – but in another the pressure is very much on as it is up to you to be the role model.

In your later relationships there will often be a tendency for you to lay down the law, to fuss, to feel responsible and to over-explain. Firstborns take relationships very seriously and rarely run away from them when they become tense. You have many strengths, including the ability to deal with a crisis and to be supportive and caring against all odds.

The middle child: Middle children often grow up feeling picked on by everyone, and they tend to give in, to become the confused and ineffective person others seem to think them. Somehow they are not expected to dazzle, and mediocrity is handed to them on a plate. Middles often carry an inferiority complex around them like a banner, and they tend to attract people who will abuse or neglect them.

The up-side, however, is that they do know all about the rough and tumble of life and the need to share, and are often very caring with a lot of love to give, and have the ability to be tolerant of others' foibles.

The "baby": Being the youngest in a family means that no matter how old you are, you will always be "the baby". The youngest tends to seek out someone to take revenge on their behalf, just as their older brother or sister used to come to the rescue for them.

They also have the ability to get their own way through a battery of tactics from tantrums to emotional blackmail. On a much more positive note, however, they can be enormously affectionate and appreciative. They are also great fun, thanks to their capacity for spontaneity. And their admiration and respect for other people's opinions is very attractive and endearing.

should work well. They are very narrow and can do no harm to the anus itself.

When inserting anything else into the anus, be sure that you stretch the anal sphincter slowly or it can be very painful. Special "butt plugs", wide latex aids that stretch the anus, are available for this purpose. These are safe provided they are not inserted deeply as they could get lost or cause damage.

If ever anything you do to your anus makes it bleed, it is probably best to stop and not do it again. Never put anything into the anus that is not made for it. The anal muscles can be very powerful and things can break off and become trapped inside.

Clitoral stimulators are attached to a ring that fits around the base of the penis – always be very gentle when using one as some women find them painful.

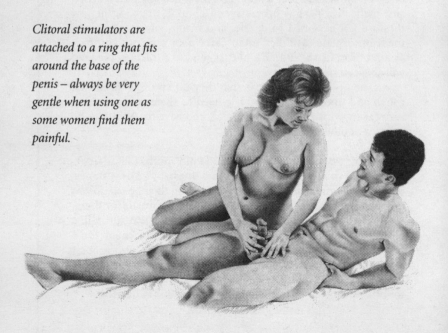

Safer sex

Since the mid-1980s, when AIDS (Acquired Immune Deficiency Syndrome) was first brought to the world's attention, safer sex has been the phrase on everyone's lips.

The reason we need to practise safer sex is to prevent the transmission of HIV (Human Immunodeficiency Virus), the virus which causes AIDS. If you and your partner are not infected with HIV and stay strictly monogamous, sex is safe, but if either of you have had previous sexual partners, it is wise to consider safer sex.

Safer sex is any sex which does not allow HIV-infected blood, semen or vaginal fluids to be passed from one partner to the other – through open wounds, through ulcers or sores in the mouth or through the inside of the vagina or anus. The infection cannot be passed on through saliva, sweat or tears.

Safer sex is a way of adapting your sex life to minimize the risk of giving or contracting HIV infection. It embraces the whole range of sexual activities, making the minimum changes necessary to make them safer. Not only does it make sex less risky, but it can actually improve your sex life. The key to safer sex in the age of AIDS is good communication. Discussing how to make sex safer with your partner can only make your lovemaking more satisfying and thrilling. The main issue remains the same – that of pleasure.

There are two main high-risk sexual activities. Unprotected vaginal sex is high risk because the virus can be passed by both men and women to their partners through semen and vaginal fluids. Unprotected anal sex is high risk because the lining of the rectum is especially thin and prone to tearing, so the virus has easy access to the bloodstream.

THE SENSITIVE PARTNER

One of the qualities most people look for in their partners is sensitivity. Its true meaning implies a caring, generous person with a sympathetic capacity to understand others and the mature ability to use this understanding for the good of the relationship. But "sensitive" can also be a euphemism to describe a person with a basic inability to cope with life and relationships, throwing all responsibility onto a stronger partner. It can also be used to describe people who have never been able to grow up.

The Peter Pan: The book *The Peter Pan Syndrome*, by Dr Dan Kilev, deals with men who could not or would not grow up. It suggests that Peter Pans are out of touch with their feelings and unable to express them or even consciously recognize them. They also feel a deep dislike of having to be subjected to anyone else's emotional problems. Many basic difficulties in relationships are features of the Peter Pan syndrome, including an inability to get on with their own fathers and male children, and a tendency to be under the thumb of their mothers.

The Cinderella: "The Cinderella Complex" was first documented by American author Colette Dowling in her book of the same name, subtitled "Women's Hidden Fear of Independence". Dowling's theories suggest that the Cinderella complex is created in part by society's pressure on women today. It is a result of traditional expectations of women – quiet, docile nurturers relying on a strong man – coming into conflict with feminist beliefs that women should be high achievers, independent of, and equal to, men in all walks of life. While ultimately creating the Cinderella role for themselves, they also grow to resent it. Frightened of independence, they also hate what dependence does to them and their relationship.

The wimp: The term "wimp" is often used to describe the genuinely sensitive man who rejects macho stereotypes. But a man who is kind, sensitive, and able to show feelings to the point of weeping is often very strong and mature. True wimps – male and female – avoid confrontation at any cost. They ingratiate themselves with bullies, and will make a complete about-turn if challenged on an opinion. An instinct for self-preservation makes the wimp the most insensitive of all people, as the damage they often do to people around them can be great yet they rarely care, so long as they are all right.

The phobic: Many phobics are hypersensitive and fearful, but their preoccupations with their own problems mean they are unable to give time and attention to anyone else. Phobias – irrational fears – can be crippling. Because they are irrational it is hard for the partner of a phobic fully to understand the problem.

The mourner: The mourner is really a discontented child who has never grown up. As an adult they only see the past – including past relationships – as good. This allows the mourner to deny responsibility for his or her present happiness, and that of their partner. A favourite phrase is "if only", but the ultimate problem that these people share is that whenever the "if only" comes to pass it is never good enough, so they are never satisfied.

The perfectionist: Perfectionists are very similar to mourners, except they usually look forward instead of backward. They too are never happy because nothing is ever right for them – but they fail to see that it is something within their own control which makes happiness impossible, whether it is lack of money, their partner, the area in which they live, or their friends.

Oral sex also has some risk factors attached. Cunnilingus carries a higher risk if the partner has bleeding gums, ulcers or sores in, or around, the mouth, and if the woman is having her period. Fellatio can carry a higher risk if the woman has cuts or sores in her mouth but a lesser risk if the man doesn't ejaculate in her mouth.

Practising safer sex provides the perfect opportunity to bring creativity into your sex life, to realize there is more to sex than penetration. Concentrate on getting to know and enjoy each other's bodies again. Shower together, or massage each other with sensual aromatherapy oils. Stroke each other's bodies, kiss, lick, suck and nibble whatever your mouth lands on. These sensual acts are all risk-free and incredibly stimulating.

When you are more aroused, get more intimate. Whisper your fantasies to each other, talk dirty, tell your partner what you'd like to do to them and what you wish they'd do to you. Dress up in sexy underwear and take polaroids of each other stripping off or naked. Or why not hire a camcorder and film yourselves caressing each other; film your partner or both of you together, masturbating? None of these activities entails any risk whatsoever.

Making safer sex fun

Safer sex doesn't mean humourless hours spent perfecting technique at the expense of fun, or having to put up with near-abstinence. All the time you usually spend worrying about getting pregnant or catching a disease can be spent on having a wonderful, more imaginative time together.

Why not experiment with the delights of sex toys? Dildoes, vibrators, even food, are all safe, and very exciting, although infections can be passed on through sex toys, so keep them clean, use condoms and do not exchange bodily fluids.

Fellatio can still be enjoyed as part of safer sex. Just make sure you don't take any unnecessary risks.

Role-playing and sex acts that are often perceived as dangerous, such as bondage, carry no risk if practised sensibly, and in a loving, non-threatening environment. Tying people up is very sexy and perfectly safe as long as both partners are clear about what is going on, and rules are made and obeyed.

Bondage can involve ropes, chains, hoods, gags, straps, leather and much more, or merely a silk scarf. You don't need a

Boy Scout knotting certificate, just some imagination and the ability to tie the simplest knots. The only precautions you need to take are common-sense ones: avoid tying things around the neck and take care not to cut off the circulation in the limbs or hands, avoid hurting each other and avoid cutting the skin.

If you are lusting for coital, anal or oral sex though, you can indulge safely. Just use a condom. Male and female condoms are an efficient barrier against pregnancy and all sexually transmitted diseases including HIV, and if used properly make penetration low risk. Remember, however, that condoms do split, so you must follow the instructions and check for the manufacturer's mark of approved standard as well as the sell-by date on the packaging. For anal sex which carries the highest risk of all because of the sensitive, delicate nature of the lining of the rectum, use an extra strong condom and lots of water-based lubricant, as oil-based ones dissolve the rubber. To make cunnilingus and analingus (licking the anus) even safer you can opt to use a dental dam, a latex sheet around five inches square which comes in a variety of different colours and flavours and can be placed over the vulva or anus for added protection. They prevent bodily fluids from getting into your partner's mouth.

Safer sex means more enjoyable sex because you are taking the worry out of it. You know that you are being responsible, protecting both yourself and your partner against infections. Learning to negotiate sexually, to describe exactly what thrill you want, and why you want it, is an imaginative and exciting way to expand your sexual repertoire. Both men and women relish the idea that their partner is a good lover and capable of taking charge with ease.

In fact, there are so many safer sex variations, the question isn't what activities to stop, it's which ones to begin!

HIV AND AIDS

HIV (Human Immunodeficiency Virus) infection is the most significant threat to public health at the end of the twentieth century. The epidemic is complex. Recent trends include a significant reduction in newly-diagnosed AIDS cases in homosexual men, an increasing number of cases in injecting drug users and a steady increase in the number of people who get infected during heterosexual intercourse.

Thousands of people in the West are infected and know this, but it is believed that many more carry the virus without being aware of this. The most rapid spread is being seen in heterosexual transmission.

AIDS can affect anyone who puts themselves at risk. It isn't dependent on sex, age, colour or sexuality. It is important that everyone knows the facts about HIV and AIDS, because only by knowing the facts can we protect ourselves.

HIV is a virus which attacks and damages the body's defence system, stopping it from effectively fighting infection. The virus lives in body fluids such as blood, semen and vaginal fluid. It is this virus which causes AIDS (Acquired Immune Deficiency Syndrome). A person has developed AIDS when they become affected by certain infections and cancers which occur in cases where the body's defense system has been weakened by HIV. However, this can occur some time after initial infection, and in the meantime it is impossible to tell whether someone is infected unless they have a test. It is believed that most people with HIV will eventually develop AIDS.

CHAPTER 8

Problem Solving

*E*ven in the most loving relationship there can be sexual problems. They may be long- or short-term, emotional or physical, but either way, there is no reason why, with goodwill on both sides, they cannot be solved either with or without the help of a specially trained counsellor.

When a man can't come

Many men have, at some time or another, found themselves in the situation where they cannot sustain an erection long enough to have sex, or indeed even manage to achieve one. Occasional impotence is part and parcel of male sexual life. If it occurs only infrequently, there is no need to worry. If it happens often it can wreak havoc in a couple's love life.

Impotence is a term that can be applied to masturbation as well as intercourse. Some men find that they are impotent in intercourse and mutual masturbation but can come perfectly well and enjoyably when masturbating alone. In therapy, some men who successfully masturbate lose their erection when asked to fantasize about intercourse with a woman, indicating that they are unconsciously avoiding sex.

There are a number of medical reasons why a man might experience difficulty in either achieving or maintaining an erection. These include the following:

● *Painful conditions of the penis which can make a man fear an erection.*

● *Diabetes which affects the nerve supply to the penis.*

● *Low levels of the male hormone testosterone.*

● *Medication or drugs prescribed by a doctor, especially those taken for raised blood pressure.*

● *Lumbar sympathectomy, kidney transplants and prostate problems.*

● *Smoking and/or eating a high-fat diet, which can constrict blood supply to the penis.*

● *Illegal drugs and alcohol.*

● *Ageing. This is the most common reason for a man being unable to come. Almost all men over the age of forty or so have more difficulty in becoming aroused and sustaining an erection.*

Added to, or possibly independent of, the above physical reasons, there may be psychological ones:

● *Worry about penis size, although to most women it does not matter.*

● *Stress such as moving house, a bereavement, redundancy, business worries, financial concerns and problems with children*

● *A fear of assertive women.*

● *Anxiety about causing pregnancy or catching STDs.*

● *Previous failures.*

● *A fear of injuring the woman.*

● *Latent homosexuality.*

● *Growing apart from their partner.*

The most important factor in overcoming impotence is an interested partner. A woman who is sympathetic to the problem and who wants to help her man to solve it can work wonders. The first step is to sit down and talk to try to get to the root of the

A woman's body is one of the most powerful weapons she has to encourage her partner back to virility.

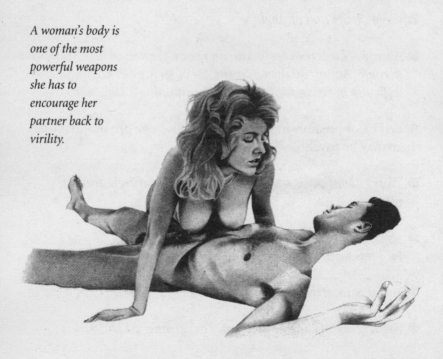

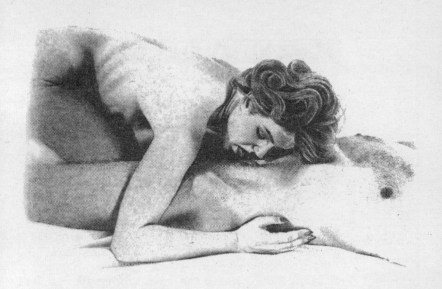

Licking her lover's chest without making sexual demands is one way to help a man overcome impotence.

problem. If the couple can talk frankly they are half-way to sorting it out. It is important at this stage for the woman to accept that this is her problem, too.

The next step is to stop attempting to have intercourse. It is amazing how alleviating the pressure to perform can help the man regain his confidence. Whilst the couple are abstaining, it greatly helps if the woman continues to reassure her lover that she understands the problem and is happy to forego intercourse for as long as is necessary.

During this period, a return to courtship behaviour is beneficial. Both partners should take every opportunity to show their love for each other short of intercourse. The emphasis

PLEASURING

Pleasuring, also known as sensate focus, encourages partners to concentrate on the feelings – both physical and emotional – that are produced when each gently caresses the other's body. It is widely used by many sex therapists as a method of combating a person's inability to respond sexually.

Stage 1

During this stage, you should not have any genital contact. That way there will be absolutely no pressure. You are not being asked to perform, only to experience. You cannot fail because you are not being asked to succeed. Both partners should be naked, and take turns at giving and receiving pleasure. The active partner should lubricate his or her hands with body lotion or oil, and gently stroke and massage their partner's entire body, apart from the genitals. Practise this three times a week for at least two weeks.

Stage 2

The emphasis at this stage is on receiving, rather than giving, pleasure. The passive partner should give his or her partner positive feedback on what he or she finds pleasurable. There is still a ban on intercourse and on genital touching. Both partners should again swap roles and change positions, letting each other know exactly what pleases them. At the end of a session they should talk to each other about what they liked most – practise stage 2 for at least two weeks.

Stage 3

This involves taking it in turns to arouse each other by touching the genitals. Once again, you should not have intercourse and should not bring each other to orgasm. If your partner becomes too aroused and orgasm seems imminent, change your caresses to another part of their body. In this way, you can bring your partner to the brink of orgasm several times in one session. At this stage both partners should explore and stimulate every part of each others genitals – the centres of their sexuality – guiding each other's hands and making their wishes clear.

Pleasuring is a sexual technique which enables partners to return to the long-lost sexual plateau of heavy petting and sexual courting. It's easy to become lazy when you have a long-term sexual partner. It's also easy to forget to continue communicating with each other, and this lack of communication has the unpleasant habit of emerging only when there is a problem. Pleasuring gives you the chance to reinvent or recharge your sex life.

should be on closeness, cuddling and massage. Maximize the power of touch. Stroke your partner's back, shoulders, limbs, buttocks and face – but stay clear of the genitals. Take it in turn to massage each other. Learn to relax together and put out of your mind any notion that these activities have any purpose whatsoever beyond the simple pleasure of touching your partner's body.

When the genitals are eventually brought into play, act like children, touching and exploring. Still continue to avoid having intercourse, but move towards mutual masturbation. Many couples, once they have been together for some time, tend to ignore or underestimate the pleasure that can be gained from this.

Reading erotic literature, browsing through "girlie" magazines or watching sexy videos can all help in arousal.

At this stage the man will still be extremely vulnerable, so it is essential that the woman is extremely careful to avoid any kind of dominating behaviour.

When the man has achieved an erection, the couple may still not be confident enough to attempt intercourse. In this situation oral sex is the next stage.

The woman should take her partner's penis in her mouth and use her tongue and lips to tease him. She should take as much of the penis in her mouth as feels comfortable and use regular, rhythmic movements up and down. She can use her own body to keep his excitement going. If her partner wants to come in her mouth she can let him, provided she is happy with this.

Once a man can achieve an erection and ejaculate through self-masturbation, and possibly oral sex, his sexual confidence will usually return and with it the ability to enjoy successful sexual intercourse with his partner.

Premature ejaculation

Premature ejaculation is a relative concept, and "coming too soon" can be a problem in one relationship but not in another, even for the same man. It is a problem that may exist from the start of a man's sexual life, or it can develop after many years of perfectly satisfactory lovemaking.

In the former, the man's sex drive is unusually high and he comes too soon because he is "trigger happy". This can make some men go off sex because they fear letting their partner down.

The latter is often seen as the man ages, and frequently goes hand in hand with a loss of sex-drive. There is occasionally an obvious factor that starts the problem off, but more often the starting point is less clear.

Premature ejaculation can take several forms. Sometimes, ejaculation occurs even before the penis erects, but this is very rare. More commonly the man ejaculates as soon as his penis is inside the vagina. Finally, there is the man who thrusts once or twice and comes.

Whatever the causes, men who suffer from premature ejaculation often cannot recognize the sensations that other men know mean they are about to ejaculate. They reach the point of no return and do not realize until it is too late.

An alternative explanation is that these men do recognize the sensations but, for any one of many subconscious reasons, do not act on them.

Perhaps one of the most common causes of premature ejaculation is bad sexual training. Many young men become used to having sex very hastily, perhaps in their girlfriend's parents' home, or in the back of a car. They simply mis-learn and end up seeing intercourse, and indeed ejaculation generally, as a very

WHEN TO SEEK HELP

Although in many cases premature ejaculation is a problem that can be solved with the care and sensitivity of a loving partner, for some people its roots are more complex, and they may need professional help. If you think you or your partner have a problem because of any of the reasons listed below, it makes a lot of sense to seek professional help. Delaying matters while you try do-it-yourself methods is pointless and frustrating, while qualified people outside the relationship can identify the problems and offer solutions more easily. Start off with your general practitioner and take it from there.

The following are all possible reasons for premature ejaculation:

♥ *Infections of genital organs.*

♥ *Diseases of the nerves, such as multiple sclerosis.*

♥ *Any painful conditions of the penis.*

♥ *Psychological causes such as a fear of women and their genitals, and seeing intercourse as an assault.*

♥ *Anger or anxiety about sex generally.*

♥ *Serious relationship problems.*

brief affair. It then becomes difficult to unlearn their training. The guilt that often accompanies such early, furtive intercourse can also make a man want to come quickly.

Just as with any other sexual problem, power and control lurk very close to the surface. Many couples run their relationship (often quite unconsciously) on the basis of one controlling the other.

A very effective way of exerting control is to take the lead in bed – and many people know this, however unconsciously. Some premature ejaculators, annoyed and resentful of their partner in some other area of life, realize that they can exert the ultimate control by coming too soon and thwarting all her sexual hopes and plans.

A man might be in control here, but he often knows deep down that his partner is controlling him much of the time when they are out of bed. A couple who interact in this way need professional help to sort out their relationship.

In general, however, premature ejaculation is one of the easiest problems to treat yourself. A loving couple who really want to make things work can usually sort things out using the following self-help programme.

Step 1:
Have orgasms more frequently. This is especially useful in young men who are "trigger happy". They are greatly helped by masturbating a few hours before they are about to have sex. If you are going to be apart from one another for any length of time, it makes sense for the man to masturbate at some stage close to his return so that your first bout of lovemaking does not end prematurely.

If the woman straddles her partner she can stop any thrusting movement if the man feels he is about to ejaculate.

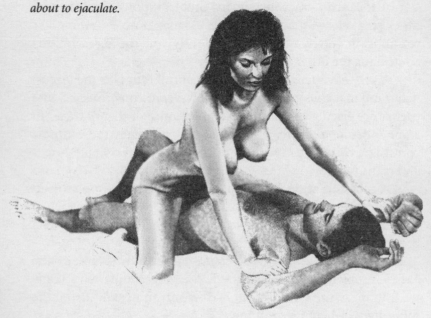

Step 2:

Talk it over between yourselves. Perhaps there are simple answers that could easily be arrived at. For example, some women become so excited after a lot of foreplay that they overstimulate their man with kisses and caresses. He, understandably, cannot take too much of this and climaxes very quickly. She may simply have to indulge in less foreplay, or not stimulate him quite so powerfully if she wants him to last longer.

Step 3:

Masturbation training. The next stage is for the man to teach himself to masturbate in such a way as to be able to learn to recognize the sensations associated with impending ejaculation. He should start off by reading erotic material, watching sexy films or videos, or whatever turns him on in reality or fantasy. In this way, he obtains a really good erection. He then concentrates on all the sensations in his genitals and continues to masturbate, being very aware of the physical changes and different sensations in his testes, penis, scrotum, breathing, heartbeat and internal sex organs. The key sensations that have to be noted are those that occur in the immediate run-up to ejaculation. As the man feels he might be nearing these mini-orgasms deep inside his pelvis, he should stop stimulating his penis and let his erection go down.

He can repeat this stop-start exercise until he learns what it feels like to be getting very close to an orgasm. He should then be confident that, after recognizing these changes, he can do something to prevent them from going on to produce an orgasm.

Wearing a sheath during intercourse can work wonders for some men. The latex reduces penile sensations just enough to make them last longer. Together with his masturbation training, this can do the trick for many men. It breaks the cycle and after a few weeks he can dispense with the sheath.

Some men have success with weak anaesthetic creams. These also reduce the sensitivity of the penis.

Contracting the anus tightly at the end of each thrust can also help. Some men find that really deep penetration with very small penile movement is an answer. In a highly aroused woman, the top end of the vagina balloons out and, ironically, actually

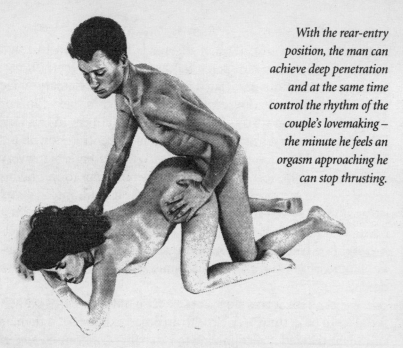

With the rear-entry position, the man can achieve deep penetration and at the same time control the rhythm of the couple's lovemaking — the minute he feels an orgasm approaching he can stop thrusting.

stimulates the penis tip less rather than more. This is why really deep penetration can be good for premature ejaculators. The most stimulating sex (from the man's point of view) occurs when the penis tip is in the lower part of the woman's vagina. As blood collects in the blood vessels in her pelvis, a "barrel" of vaginal tissue forms and grips the penis.

Stop-start intercourse is another useful tool that can work very well. The man inserts the penis tip and then keeps still. Slowly, over several stages, he inserts it deeper and then cautiously thrusts and stops when he feels he is near climaxing. Such a "teasing" approach can greatly excite the woman, but it is best in the early days if she tries not to show it. This could so arouse her partner that he will yet again come too soon.

Some men find that once they are advanced in their premature ejaculation training they can concentrate more on pleasing and pleasuring their partner. Concentrating on her takes his mind off himself and can work wonders.

"Non-come" intercourse

As well as premature ejaculators, and those men who cannot come there are also some who simply choose not to. The technique of "non-come" intercourse has long been practised in the Orient, where one man might have had to keep many wives satisfied. It enabled the man to have sex several times a day, perhaps with all his partners enjoying several orgasms while he would come only at the end of the day with his last act of intercourse.

Non-come intercourse is, to some extent, a case of mind over matter, and involves the ability to control the degree of arousal felt during intercourse to such an extent that ejaculation can be delayed indefinitely.

A simple first step is for the man to try and concentrate on something other than what he is doing – analysis of the pattern of the bedroom wallpaper or counting the curtain rings. By doing this, he can delay ejaculation a little more each time until, eventually, he will be able to concentrate on what he is doing yet still be able to control his state of arousal and delay his ejaculation until his partner is about to have her orgasm.

Once learned, this technique can be quite excellent if his partner takes a long time to come. It is useful also for men who fear a loss of vitality or get tired if they have sex in the morning. Indeed, men who use this technique say it greatly adds to their sense of well-being and vitality during the day.

THE DESTRUCTIVE INDIVIDUAL

There are some people who never seem to make a success of any relationship. These are destructive types who compulsively destroy whatever is good in a partnership. They meet a new partner who seems absolutely right for them, then they make sure something goes wrong.

There are others who do manage to sustain a permanent relationship, but at great cost. It is clear to outsiders that the relationship is some sort of living hell and that the destructive partner is eroding the happiness of both of them.

The main types of destructive partners tend to fall into definable and easily recognizable categories:

The nagger: He or she destroys the peace of mind of his or her partner and their children, creating an unpleasant atmosphere in the home. Classically, the nagger takes an issue large or small and goes on and on about it. The constant reiteration shreds everyone's nerves and makes a happy relationship almost completely impossible. The subconscious reaction of the nagged partner is often not to do whatever it is they are being nagged about.

The selfish partner: The selfish partner comes in many forms. What they all have in common, however, along with supreme selfishness, is the inability to see their selfishness for what it is. Often a long-suffering partner positively revels in the selfishness of the other. But that is pure luck and quite incidental.

The insecure partner: Sometimes very insecure people are attracted to others who are very confident. As partners, the meeker ones often pick at a relationship when it seems to be going well, simply because they cannot believe that anyone can really love them, and that the relationship will stand the test of time. Other insecure people destroy relationships by coming on too strong too soon. They dare not be anything but pleasant and anxious to please their partner because they fear that if they relax and let themselves behave normally, they will be found out, and their partner will not want to stay with them.

The unforgiving partner: He or she suffers throughout life because of an inability to forgive and forget anything that their partner may have done. They make particularly destructive partners, because no relationship develops without problems, bad behaviour and hurtful episodes, yet each one lodges in the mind and heart of the unforgiving partner. If they are not going to forget it, their partner is certainly never going to be allowed to.

The silent partner: Some people find communicating their feelings and thoughts to someone else extremely difficult. Men, who are not encouraged to be verbal or to show emotions, often have this problem more than women do. This lack of communication can be destructive because what it often reveals is a lack of trust in a partner.

The emotional sadist: This is the easiest type of destructive partner to spot. The sadist rarely uses physical violence (which implies lack of control) but indulges in mental torture, which is ultimately more hurtful. Unlike many other destructive partners, the sadist is usually quite aware of what he or she is doing.

The addict: This kind of destructive partner usually has an obsession or addiction that pushes their relationship into secondary place. Often, alcohol is the problem, especially when the drinker refuses to recognize his or her addiction. Usually, the

When a woman can't come

Problems with orgasm are more common than is generally realized. According to a large recent survey, one in three married women experienced orgasm difficulties at least half the time they made love, and only one in five never had any difficulty.

While the male orgasm is fairly durable, the female's is not. Women have more emotional concerns that seem to interfere, and a greater degree of cultural inhibition to contend with.

In some cultures or families, young girls are brought up to think of sex as something that is dirty and unmentionable. These notions may lurk in their subconscious mind, and control what they do and what they enjoy.

Some women say they never feel sexy or even have any sexy thoughts or dreams, either because of physical factors or because of inhibitions stopping them from doing so. Perhaps the most common form of orgasm failure is seen in the woman who feels sexy and becomes aroused but does not actually experience orgasms.

Some women can have an orgasm in a particular position, but not in others. Other women have difficulties experiencing orgasms early on in a relationship, but find that things improve as they become more relaxed and their lover becomes more expert at stimulating them.

Some women have orgasms early on in a relationship when sex is "naughty" or "forbidden", but lose them after marriage when sex is "allowed".

But what are the causes of orgasm failure? As with erection problems, causes can be physical or psychological, and again, as with erection problems, once the cause has been identified, a loving couple should be able to solve the problem.

The following is a list of physical factors that can lead to orgasm failure in a woman:

● *Almost any illness, especially an acute one.*

● *Gynaecological surgery – many women can feel mutilated after this and it is not uncommon for a woman to go off sex entirely after a hysterectomy or mastectomy.*

● *Certain drugs including anti-depressants and blood pressure drugs.*

● *Hormone deficiencies.*

Emotional and psychological causes may include one or more of the following:

● *Shyness, especially in new relationships.*

● *Fear of letting go.*

● *Depression.*

● *Inability to relax – this applies particularly to young, busy mothers.*

● *Bereavement, including miscarriage.*

● *Being safe through contraception– some women do not reach orgasm because they feel they should not enjoy the pleasures of orgasm without the possibility of having a baby.*

● *Being contraceptively unsafe – women often feel tense about the possibility of an unwanted pregnancy.*

● *Adverse sexual experiences during childhood, including incest and rape.*

● *Identifying with their mother who many women see as sexless. Consequently, a woman who has had a baby may stop having orgasms because she is now a mother, not a lover.*

Probably the most valuable time a woman can spend learning – or relearning – to have an orgasm is spent on her own, relaxing and exploring her own body.

The first step towards solving the problem of orgasm failure is for the woman to become more confident about her own sexuality. There are several ways in which this may be achieved:

● *If you do not usually stimulate your vulva by hand, you should start to do so and try – by clitoral stimulation – to bring yourself to orgasm in this way.*

● *Join a therapeutic group where you can discuss your problem with other women having the same difficulties.*

Once a woman is relaxed, her partner can slowly tease her clitoris while she caresses her breasts herself.

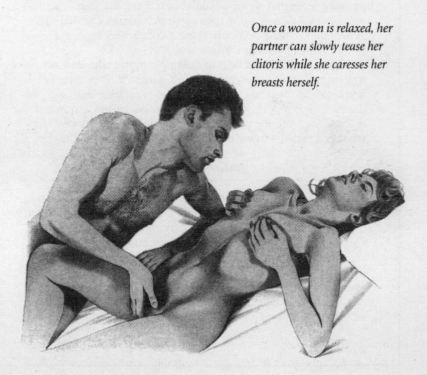

JEALOUSY

Love leads to pairing, caring and, in many cases, having children. Fear readies us to resist attack. But what of jealousy? At first sight it appears to be totally negative, causing misery both to the jealous one and their partner. It is a suspicious and questioning emotion. It can break up marriages and relationships and, in extreme cases, can even lead to violence. But is there more to it than this?

Positive effects of jealousy

Jealousy may have a positive side as well. It can be argued that jealousy strengthens the sexual bond between partners, and prevents individuals going their separate ways on a sexual whim. Where the bringing up of offspring is concerned, this has to be a benefit to the species as a whole.

Jealousy can also help to split up couples who may not be well suited to each other anyway. If a marriage or an affair is breaking up, jealousy often provides the language and the dramatic framework. Sometimes it produces the grounds for divorce, too. And the pain of the emotion can spur the two now separated partners to set about making new lives for themselves.

Jealous minds

Researchers have found that the feeling of jealousy does seem to be different for men and for women. For men, jealousy is often based on sexual issues, while women may say that they are more concerned about the loss of time and attention from their men.

One study by psychologists shows that men tend to be more jealous if they have a low opinion of themselves, while women's jealousy depends more on how dependent they are on the relationship. Equally, men are more concerned about the loss of self-esteem involved in finding that a partner has been unfaithful, while women are more concerned about completely losing a sexual partner. Women also say that the intensity of their jealous reaction depends on the attractiveness of their rival. A man might actually take it as a back-handed compliment – and thus a boost to his ego – if a particularly handsome man is attracted to his wife. But out of concern for his ego he is more likely to ask himself: "Is the other man a better lover?"

The major difficulty in coping with a jealous partner is that jealousy has an enormous appetite. It can feed on anything. A man's glance at a pretty girl in the street is fuel for his partner's jealousy. But his studied effort not to glance at a pretty girl in the street can be taken in the same way. She may say: "I saw her looking at you as if she knew you. Funny, the way you avoided her and kept your eyes on the ground. Are you quite sure you don't know her? Are you hiding something?" And if there are no real events on which it can feed, jealousy will always find fuel in the imagination.

Where does jealousy lead?

The jealous person has an uncontrollable fear of being replaced by somebody else in the affections of their partner. Jealousy involves massive doubt and uncertainty about being loved and wanted – feelings that lead to anxiety. Mild forms of jealousy are common, and do not initially threaten a relationship. But they can cause discomfort and unhappiness, which is a good reason to try to do something about them. Frankness and discussion between partners can often help put jealousy into perspective.

Sometimes, though, attempts to cope in a positive way, by dealing with the feelings behind jealousy, may be thwarted by the fact that the couple simply do not recognize or know what these feelings are. If loving understanding cannot uncover them, then it is time to seek out professional assistance such as counseling.

*Eventually, the man can use his mouth to bring
his partner increased pleasure.*

● *Buy a vibrator. Provided they really want to, most women can
have orgasms with a vibrator. Women who take a long time to
have an orgasm may also come much sooner in this way.*

● *Learn to fantasize more. Many women who do not have
orgasms find fantasizing difficult. Some have fantasies but
always as onlookers, never as participants. Erotic books and
videos help many such women, as does reading about other
women's fantasies. Reading this kind of material in a warm
bath, perhaps after a small alcoholic drink, may also help.*

Once a woman feels more confident she can start to involve her partner. A caring man should be only too delighted to help. Gradually, the woman can teach her man to masturbate her, perhaps using a vibrator on her while making love or using some other variation that pleases her.

Oral sex can be introduced as well. For many women, this is one of the most relaxing parts of making love as they do not need to make any effort. The partner should do this in exactly the way that the woman likes. She should feel that no pressure of any kind is being forced upon her. The only goal must be to give the woman every encouragement to gain orgasmic control.

During intercourse, the woman can now add to her own sensations and help her progress to orgasm. She can experiment with various ways of broadening her experience of lovemaking – perhaps by sweeping the penis around the inside of the vagina, rotating her pelvis, extending her fantasy life and learning pelvic muscle control.

If, despite this kind of training programme, a woman is still unable to experience orgasm, she would do well to seek professional help from someone trained in psychosexual therapy.

The therapist will attempt to find the reasons why a woman is unable to enjoy an orgasm and will try to find ways to resolve the problems. Then the woman will commence a course of training which will start with teaching her how to masturbate herself to orgasm. In virtually all cases, once a patient is able to overcome any guilt she may feel about enjoying sex, the problem can be solved.

Imbalanced sex drives

Just as our feelings about other activities vary, our sex lives vary too – a great deal. Not only from person to person either, but within any one individual at different times. Because of the variety of different libido levels we all experience, some people think that they are much more or less sexual than others, but this is not necessarily true.

Clinical evidence suggests that we all have much the same sort of interest in sex, but that some of us can express that interest more easily than others. Many individuals, especially women, who undergo sexual or marital therapy complaining of poor sex drive, are transformed into very sexy people within a few weeks, simply by altering their views of themselves.

But a lack of interest in sex is not the end of the world. One study found that 35 per cent of men questioned said they were totally uninterested in sex, yet at the same time they thought their marriages were fine. And the fact is that there are far more marriages that persist with little or no sexual activity than is generally recognized.

There are many factors that affect a person's sex drive, and any – or all – of them may be present at any one time.

Drugs, particularly sleeping tablets, medication for reducing blood pressure, some water tablets and some angina drugs can cause problems. Depression is also a very common cause, as is falling out of love.

If a couple already have a sexual relationship before they settle down together, sexual mismatching should not occur. Some couples, however, decide not to have sex at all before marriage and therefore lose the opportunity to find out whether they are sexually well matched or not before they make a commitment.

If either partner is not interested in penetrative sex, the 69 position, where both can indulge in oral sex, is a good substitute.

This decision to enter marriage without the benefit of knowing each other's sexual needs can lead to problems of mutual unfulfilment, and fluctuations of libido levels in either or both partners.

Sexually mismatched partners

If you suspect you have become mismatched sexually ask yourselves whether you were well matched in the first place. If you think you never were, there are a variety of things that can be done. The first option is for the one who is getting less sex than he or she needs to seek sexual outlets elsewhere; secondly, the couple can seek professional help to sort out the problems, usually by removing inhibitions; thirdly, they can agree to part, leaving themselves free to look for more suitable partners.

CHILD SEXUAL ABUSE

Sexual abuse suffered as a child can have lasting effects, and is increasingly being recognized as a catalyst for disturbed behaviour in teenagers and adults. Recent studies have shown that one third of abuse is carried out by people who are under the age of eighteen, and it is now known that many abusers themselves were abused as children

There are no definite figures telling us how many children are abused, but it is an alarmingly high proportion. The majority of offenders are male and, very frequently, they are members of the child's family, or someone the child knows well.

The effects of abuse

When sexual abuse happens within the confines of the family, a term that is often used is "dysfunctional", which literally means that the family is not functioning properly. The child is not being nurtured correctly and is not receiving accurate and positive reinforcement of the person he or she is. Abused people suffer a lowering of self-esteem. The ability of abused children to be themselves, to develop normally, ask questions, receive honest answers and simply feel safe and secure is badly affected.

Abuse creates a distorted image of what relationships are about, especially if the abuse is perpetrated by a family member or a figure of authority. Abuse establishes patterns of behaviour to which every thought, feeling and action become connected. More often than not it is the abuser who sets up these patterns and it is only by breaking these established patterns and habits that the abused person can break the abuser's power over them.

Recovery from sexual abuse takes determination and support. Abuse doesn't take place in a void and it often happens with the consent or collusion of parents or carers. It is easier to recover if a person can allow themselves to trust friends and partners. Support can allow an individual to feel liberated from their past.

Social workers and psychologists dealing with children are still unravelling the complex behavioural knot that abuse creates. As the behaviour of children directly reflects whatever is affecting them, similarly, behaviour will change if an unusual experience or something traumatic has occurred. Not all the signs of abuse are obvious, and any unusual fluctuations in behaviour should be investigated. Things to look out for include:

❤ *An uncharacteristic onset of bedwetting*

❤ *A return to "babyish" behaviour*

❤ *An unusual tendency to be flirtatious, or to manifest forms of sexual behaviour*

❤ *Furtiveness, solitariness, preoccupation*

❤ *Fear or mistrust of familiar adults*

❤ *Medical signs, including irritation or pain in the genital and anal area, urinary infections, chronic stomach or head pains*

❤ *In older children, depression, suicide attempts, self mutilation, anorexia or bulimia*

Many people choose the first course but then regret it, usually because sex is only one of many ties between a couple.

Some couples are advised – wrongly – by friends or even professional therapists that all is lost in their relationship if they are sexually mismatched. This is not always true by any stretch of the imagination, and a change of attitude towards sex can put matters right: if one or other partner's libido appears to be flagging, they might, for example, rethink their work schedules in an effort to spend more time at home. Something as simple as going to bed just half an hour earlier would allow more time for making love in the evening without being exhausted in the morning.

If the woman's sex drive appears to be greater than her partner's he might try practising "non-come" intercourse which will allow him to satisfy his partner without exhausting himself.

She might compromise too by getting herself a dildo and sexy publications and pleasuring herself whenever necessary. By giving herself permission, so to speak, to masturbate, she would experience no guilt because it would be seen as just another addition to a rich and varied sex life.

Everyone's libido fluctuates from time to time, and it can be frustrating for the partner whose libido has not hit a slump to cope with the diminishing desires of his or her partner. The problem isn't always insurmountable, however, especially if there are no other problems in a relationship.

Couples should not be afraid to see a psychosexual therapist or a counsellor and reveal their innermost feelings as a way of finding a solution to the problem.

Common fears

Sex is closely linked to the emotions and, in a culture where we tend to have only one partner at any given time, it is not very difficult to appreciate why many people encounter sexual fears.

Whatever sort of relationship you are in, there is always an implicit pressure to please your partner and, however much you may care for or love them, there is always the fear that the sexual failure of one will hurt the other. Indeed, the more a couple are in love, the more likely they are to feel anxious about sex.

One of the most common male fears is that of failure to feel emotionally "strong". This can be a hazard in any man's sexual life because, instead of opening up to his partner and so gaining the solace, practical help and understanding that a healthy relationship can provide, he labours on, bottling up any problems he may have. The situation may become so bad that he may seek solace in alcohol or even a less committed relationship with another woman. He will then shut himself off from his partner and she will end up feeling hurt, taken for granted or ignored.

As a consequence of this, their sex life and ultimately the relationship as a whole will inevitably suffer. A fear of letting go and allowing a partner to get to know them intimately is sometimes linked to men's fear of displaying emotional vulnerability. This is usually because they are worried about appearing soft or silly, which would run contrary to the macho expectations placed on them by stereotyped notions about men. Many men who are afraid of displaying any sort of emotional vulnerability find that they cannot really relax and enjoy themselves in sexual situations.

We all have at least a few hang-ups about our appearance. A scar, a spot in a prominent place, hair loss, blemishes and physical imperfections can all create anxiety in the man or woman who has them. In our culture, we are brought up to believe that we should look perfect – or as near to perfect as possible – if we are to be sexually and socially acceptable. In Western society, where physically perfect models both male and female are used to sell everything from aftershave to cars, there is now as much pressure on men, as there has always been on women, to be

Inspecting her vagina using a mirror allows a woman to view her genitals intimately.

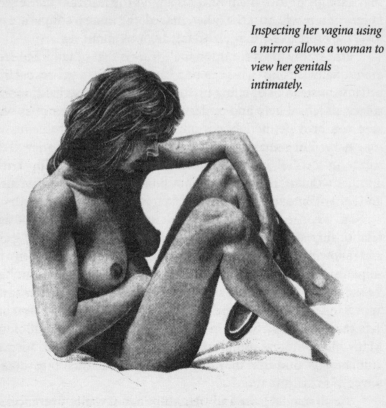

beautiful. Women fear not matching up to the images of beautiful models that fill the pages of magazines and peer down at us from advertising hoardings, and go to great lengths to avoid being or appearing overweight. Men, too, often fall prey to the fear that their bodies are not up to scratch, or that they do not have sufficient body hair or other male characteristics to appear "manly" and therefore attractive to women.

Allied to fears about physical appearance is, of course, for men the age-old and extremely common concern over penis size. Despite the fact that the subject of penis size has become a joke, and that an overwhelming majority of women insist that when it comes to the quality of lovemaking it's not what you've got it's what you do with it, many men, no matter how well or poorly endowed they are, fear that their penis is too small and they will not be able to please their partner.

Many women also harbor genital fears. Most women will not have seen another woman's genitals, or have any idea of the enormous differences there can be between women's bodies. Indeed, many women have never even looked closely at their own vagina. The vagina by its very nature is almost hidden away, unlike the penis, and the only way a woman can get a good look at herself is to use a mirror. If the woman is shy this is unlikely to happen and consequently, she is more likely to believe the myths about female genitalia and what they should look, smell or taste like. Some women are appalled at the size of their vaginal lips, or feel that their vagina has become much wider after childbirth, and will therefore feel unsatisfying to their partner. Factual information and reassurance from a partner can help dispel some of the myths.

Fear of letting go and behaving in a sexually uninhibited way is particularly common among women. They often find it very difficult to let go sexually in case they will be thought "loose" or "tarty". Perhaps they fear that their excited responses won't be appropriate. Many women who have been conditioned into thinking this way experience trouble reaching their sexual potential, or even enjoying themselves sexually. Every part of their sexuality can be affected by this lack of confidence, from finding it difficult to reach orgasm, to feeling uncomfortable about wearing sexy clothes. The success rate among women seeking sexual or marital therapy to help with such problems is, however, very good and their futures are normally bright.

*Learning how best to
please your partner
and concentrating
on her pleasure goes
a long way to
allaying fears.*

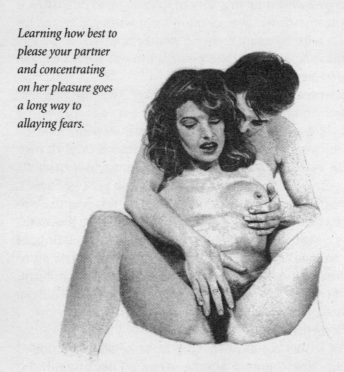

A fear of disappointing our partner is often the result of sexual fears, and can occur at any stage in a relationship. Early on, we all want to impress our partner and get a new relationship off to the best possible start, which can be nerve-racking. Later on, the fear is often that if we do not come up to scratch, particularly in sexual situations, our partner might begin to look outside the relationship for sexual satisfaction. This should be one of the easiest fears to combat. Talk things through with your partner and let them know about your fears. You can then discuss how you both feel and talk about your likes and dislikes. But always remember that not every sexual encounter is a success and that unrealistic expectations will inevitably increase any fears you may have about letting your partner down in bed.

Fears about performance are very common, particularly in some men who feel that they should be the sexual "doers", and who, as a rule, usually make things happen. *Will I be able to keep going for long enough before I come? Will I give her an orgasm? Will I be as good as her previous lovers? Will I know what to do to turn her on?* These are just some of the common performance fears that men have. Most can be overcome with enough loving behaviour, encouragement and discussion from a partner who is sensitive and understanding. Many people fear that if they masturbate rather than have sexual intercourse, they might get hooked on it and then not want sexual intercourse with their partner, but this is not really something to worry about. Most men and women masturbate occasionally and most say that they view solo sex as something completely separate from sex with their partner.

For many people problems arise because they do not know what to say to their lover as they make love, or perhaps more importantly, how to say it. Some fear that they might say something silly or inappropriate. Although some couples talk a lot while making love, sometimes to profess their love or their lust for each other, it is not necessary to say anything at all, especially if talking during sex is something you find difficult or which makes you feel uncomfortable.

Fear of pregnancy, a common female fear, can affect women whether they are teenagers or mature women. Avoiding pregnancy, on the face of it, may appear fairly easy, taking into consideration the array of contraception devices and methods available. Any woman who has ever had a pregnancy scare, however, knows that it is not as easy as it seems, and any woman who has had to make the choice to have an abortion is aware of the risks that pregnancy itself can carry. For some women, the fear of becoming pregnant affects them, and their relationship, in a very sexual manner. They need to gradually develop confidence in their chosen contraceptive built on an understanding of how it works, and, of course, confidence in their partner, through discussion.

Many people, of either sex, worry that if they indulge in unusual sex, such as bondage, they might become so hooked that they will not be able to enjoy what they regard as "normal" sex ever again. This fear is usually quite groundless. People who like to experiment with sexual practices which are a bit different generally do it for a change or a treat, and don't suddenly stop having so-called "normal" sex because they happen to like occasionally doing something out of the ordinary.

We are not born with our various fears and anxieties, we learn them, and just as we have assumed negative attitudes associated with our bodies and sexual behaviour, we can also reverse those negative assumptions, turning them on their heads. This, however, takes considerable commitment. The best way to unlearn fears and anxieties is to desensitize yourself gradually, over a long period of time. Remember that it is natural to have fears and doubts when it comes to sex – everyone does, but with patience and understanding even the worst problems can be overcome.

Men and women who avoid sex

Most couples go through a stage where one or the other partner avoids sex for at least some of the time. In some relationships, however, one partner avoids sex for much of the time. When this happens, the other partner feels a strong sense of rejection and frustration.

When thinking about sex avoidance, a few points are worth considering:

First, while the term gives the impression that the person who is doing the avoiding is behaving in this way consciously, this is often not the case. The majority of sex avoidance occurs for reasons of which the person concerned is not consciously aware. The problems lie deep in the unconscious mind and usually have their origins in the person's early life.

Second, many sex avoiders can perform sexually in other ways but go to pieces when intercourse is involved, and women can allow intercourse to take place while avoiding actively participating in it.

Third, we all avoid sex from time to time, but for some people sex avoidance has become a way of life or at least a common occurence. The man who sits in front of the late night movie while his wife goes to bed alone is a sex avoider. He may have a problem, or the relationship may be in trouble. Such avoidance is hard to sort out, even for a professional counsellor.

Lastly, it is important to bear in mind that a person who avoids sex often does not want to behave in that way. They realize by avoiding sex they are hurting themselves and their relationship.

Why do people avoid sex?

There are some men who avoid almost any contact with women, while there are some who avoid sex only in certain situations or with certain women.

Some male sex avoiders fear ridicule for what they think is poor stature, or even poor personality.

Childhood conditioning leaves some men with both conscious and unconscious notions that women, especially those they love, are somewhat sexless, only having sex because they love them and do not want to let them down.

Other common unconscious notions are that women are very powerful and can punish men for their sexual interests in them, or that women reject men who show an interest in sex with them.

Many men who have these unconscious notions and who see women as boring, or unapproachable, can still function quite well much of the time, but are easily tipped into sex avoidance.

Often the man involved cannot achieve an erection when he wants to and this failure can last for months or even years. If he, even unconsciously, sees his partner as the cause of his distress, he may equally unconsciously avoid sex in order to punish her.

This in turn may confirm many of his fears about women, especially if the woman scorns or rejects him for his failure. Even an apparently straightforward and sympathetic remark such as "don't worry, lots of men have problems like this" can lead to rows, because the man may all too easily become preoccupied with thoughts about her previous lovers and how they made love to her.

It is easy to see how, once on the slippery slope, the man becomes afraid of making sexual advances because, having failed once, he expects more failures to follow. He focuses all his attention on his genitals, and this makes him actually more likely to fail again. It is a vicious circle.

Some men start to avoid sex after years of happy love-making. It can occur as part of the gradual loss of excitement that can so easily come about as the years pass. Sometimes, the birth of a baby may reawaken male anxieties about sexual wishes he had for his mother. A man who feels this avoids his wife now that she has stopped being a lover and become a mother in his eyes.

As with men, there are women at one end of the scale who go out of their way to avoid any contact with the opposite sex, and, at the other end, there are those who conduct a normal relationship with a man for most of the time, only to be tipped into sex avoidance when a specific set of circumstances arises. The big difference between sex avoidance in men and women is that the man has to get an erection before intercourse. Any avoidance mechanisms are obvious, because they will often prevent him from being able to have an erection.

A woman, on the other hand, can have intercourse whether or not she is aroused, so it is a lot more difficult to perceive when a woman is avoiding sex.

There is a subtle side to sex avoidance that occurs when someone sublimates his or her sexual drive and directs their energies into some non-sexual activity. Some people, women

THE VIOLENT PARTNER

For some people violence is a natural form of expression. It may be that they are inherently aggressive, inarticulate or even driven to the edge of reason. Luckily, the seriously violent partner is relatively rare, but a significant minority of people feel obliged to express themselves in a violent fashion, and an even smaller number find themselves gravitating towards violent partners, hating, but needing, such a relationship.

The violent partner can be male or female. The battered wife syndrome is well recognized, but there is also a growing number of battered husbands. There are many types of violence and violent people:

Verbal violence: This can be just as menacing as physical violence. People use it to tyrannize with threats and gestures although they may never follow through with violent actions. Others use threats against themselves, promising suicide if a relationship fails.

The bully: This is more often a man, because usually they have superior strength, although this is not always so. The bully is probably the most common type of violent partner. They maintain control by using superior force, but there are elements of cowardice in their actions. They pick on the weakest people who are in the poorest position to retaliate – such as a wife and children.

The maimer: They use objects to wreak violence, and the intent is usually to hurt seriously. This type is as likely to be a woman, because superior strength is not needed. Knives, vases, or any other weapon may be used to beat, stab or disable. The maimer is much more likely to be lashing out in anger than the bully.

The destroyer: Some people stop their violence just short of attacking their partners physically, but will deflect it on to anything else within close range. They often seem almost to pride themselves on their history of home wreckages, perhaps because they have never hit or hurt the real target of their anger – their partner.

The inherently violent person: This person has usually grown up in an atmosphere of violence. He or she was usually beaten at home, and witnessed violent confrontations between their parents. To people like this violence is a way of life, and is a natural form of expression.

Driven to violence: People who do not see themselves as essentially violent partners, but who are driven to violence in a particular relationship, are not uncommon. This can happen because they are living with someone who is so emotionally cool and withdrawn that violence seems the only way to get through to them.

Frustration: Violence is used by some people simply because they have difficulty expressing themselves, and the frustration of this causes them to lash out. People who suffer in this way are often the most deeply contrite afterwards.

Drunken violence: Some people reserve their violent moments for times when they are "not themselves" – when they have been drinking or taking drugs, for instance. These people are usually much more violent than they are prepared to acknowledge, but are constantly holding themselves in check. Drinking, taking drugs, or whatever else, gives them licence to behave violently.

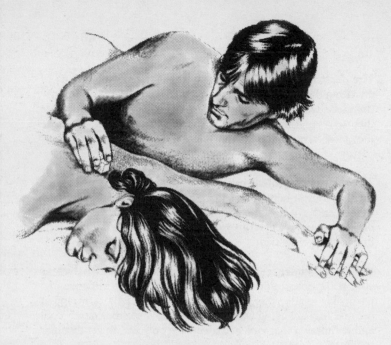

Try turning a relaxing massage into an all-over touch sensation by investigating all your partner's hidden nooks and crannies.

especially, can become almost totally immersed in other pastimes and exclude sex from their lives.

    Babies are a common focus of women's subliminated sexual feelings. Some women go off sex for a long time after giving birth – they focus all their needs for loving and caring onto the baby and seem to switch off totally from sexual involvement with their partner.

    A complicating factor in both sexes, but perhaps more so in women, is the fact that almost any woman can avoid sex with one man, yet be able to enjoy it with another.

Women also tend to follow the sexual style of their partner. If he is inhibited, shy, avoids sex, or is even deviant, she will tend to behave similarly, whereas if he is free and open, she will usually follow suit. This means that if a woman is off sex, her partner could look at himself to see if he is the cause.

Overcoming sex avoidance

Solving the problem of sex avoidance is not always simple. Most people find it very difficult, without professional help, to accept that they are in fact avoiding sex. Often it is the rejected partner who goes for help because they cannot stand the strain. Or a man may go for help with his impotence, the real cause of which is his wife's sex avoidance. Cure the latter and the husband's impotence probably disappears.

Many people who avoid sex and who recognize they are doing so, have, to them, perfectly rational and convincing reasons for their behaviour. The truth that emerges in therapy, however, is often quite different. All this can be very difficult to disentangle and, in very complicated cases, can stretch the professional skill of even the best counsellors.

Once you can come to terms with the possibility that you might be avoiding sex, start to look at your background to see what factors could have played a part. You may be able to pinpoint several things in your childhood and adolescence, or even in your current relationship, that would have contributed to your avoidance of sex.

When you think you may have identified the problem areas in your life that have contributed to your avoidance, talk things over with your partner. This can be very difficult at first, especially if you are not used to discussing intimate details of your lives which, in itself may be a cause of sex avoidance, particularly if one of the partners is much less outgoing than the other.

This is where a professional counsellor can be helpful – if only because he or she will be at ease with such discussions and will know how to bring things out into the open.

It can be very helpful to take the pressure off intercourse and go back to courtship games and rituals.

Or, take a sensual break. An evening, a weekend or a week spent together devoting yourselves single-mindedly to one another again can work wonders. The idea is to get out of your normal love-life and to experiment and be inventive both in and out of bed. Share fantasies and act them out if possible. By re-educating each other sexually, you can slowly put back the eroticism into your life.

Perversion

Although the words "pervert" and "deviant" are often bandied around as general forms of abuse, they have very specific meanings within the context of sex. Strictly speaking, a pervert consistently bypasses so-called "normal" heterosexual activity in favour of other sexual pursuits. Likewise, someone who is deviant literally deviates from the norm when it comes to sex.

Most of us enjoy unusual practices or pastimes that enhance our sex life; they vary, they're not compulsive and can be given up in favour of other sexual enhancers. These activities may include dressing up, making love in unusual places, the use of sex toys and so forth.

An individual with a perversion, however, cannot be easily persuaded to give it up. Indeed, it may be the only way in which he, or less commonly she, can have or enjoy sex at all. Perversions are occasionally caused by personality disorders, mental illness or brain disease. More often, they arise because the person, after a normal upbringing, finds straightforward sexual intercourse intimidating for one reason or another.

The vast majority of perversions are found amongst men. Freud's theory was that when a boy first sees his mother's naked body, he is so shocked that she doesn't have a penis that he averts his eyes. Whatever object his gaze falls on next becomes the object on which he will fixate and "fetishize". In severe cases, such men find that, as adults, they cannot function sexually unless their fetishized object is present.

The vast majority of perversions among women occur as a result of psychosexual development problems. They are generally locked into a problematic way of life that makes normal sex difficult or impossible.

Coping with perversion can be very difficult. Most of us carry with us some sort of low-level perversion but it usually does not interfere with our sex lives. The true pervert, however, cannot overcome his or her problem, even through fear, shame, the threat of punishment or exposure.

Some people – for example, paedophiles – are driven by their perversions to commit crimes. Even if they are imprisoned for their crimes, many come straight back out and indulge again, unless they have had appropriate therapy. Unfortunately, however, much of the therapy aimed at perversions is of little help, perhaps because the compulsive nature of the activity is so deeply embedded in the individual's personality.

Low-level perversion is not, however, something we need fear, and it can often be accommodated within a loving relationship if it is understood and enjoyed by both partners.

Pleasure or perversion?

Sado-masochism involves the link between pain and sexual pleasure. Sadists get pleasure from inflicting pain, and masochists from having pain inflicted upon them. In general, it is believed that men tend to be more sadistic and women more masochistic, but both men and women can be either, and – within the sex industry at least – dominant, sadistic women are much in demand by masochistic, submissive men.

Sadists are, in actual fact, usually so afraid of retaliation by the opposite sex that they have to control their sexual partners. Masochists, on the other hand, are afraid of their own sexuality and have to hand over control to their partners. Usually, for a sadist to enjoy himself the masochist must also enjoy it.

Although the majority of couples are not sado-masochistic in the way that many pornographic books would suggest, many like to inflict at least a small amount of pain on each other, or receive it, during sex. Men often like their testes to be squeezed as they approach and have an orgasm, for example, and some women say that they like their whole breasts or nipples squeezed very hard as they climax.

Many women like to have something inside their vagina as they climax. If it is not their partner's penis, then it tends to be his or her own fingers. They enjoy the feeling of penetration and feel that their orgasm is heightened by being able to grip with their vaginal muscles, or they may enjoy pushing or thrusting against something hard and firm.

Some women go further than this and put some sort of object in the vagina. Perhaps they use a vibrator, a penis-shaped fruit or vegetable, or even a household object such as a candle. None of these is especially harmful provided that it cannot break and tear or otherwise damage the vagina. Ideally, it is safest of all for a woman to use something that is specifically designed for the purpose, such as a dildo or a vibrator.

Sex aids have been popular for many thousands of years. Some women become hooked on their vibrator as a source of orgasms but even this "unnatural" practice gives little cause for concern in the average bedroom. In fact, some men actually encourage their partner to use a vibrator if it gives them a better quality orgasm. This in turn will also often make him more excited and, therefore, both partners benefit. Who is to say they are wrong or perverted for doing so? More often than not, sex aids are used as part of foreplay and intercourse proceeds as normal later.

Anal sex is another very ancient practice and one probably enjoyed by about one in every ten women at some time or another, although it is still illegal in many countries. It has always been held as a perversion by the Christian churches because it is not procreative: that is, it does not result in the conception of a child.

There are many taboos around anal sex, often considered "dirty, because of the connection with faeces. There is no need for this version of penetration to be any dirtier than any other form if a condom is used and the woman doesn't need to empty her bowels. Anal sex holds a far higher risk of transmitting the HIV virus than any other form of sex, so taking precautions is not only hygenic, but wise. If a woman wants to have anal sex and her partner does not, it is possible to use a vibrator or dildo in her anus instead of his penis. If he wants anal sex and she does not, then by favouring rear-entry positions he can fantasize that he is actually having anal sex and overcome the problem that way.

Any form of "domestic" voyeurism or exhibitionism – in broad terms, men getting pleasure from looking at women's bodies and woman showing off their bodies – is usually acceptable between a loving couple. In fact, it is often a part of the stock-in-trade of their love life. However, someone who looks outside the relationship, or who perhaps indulges in such practices because they have no relationship, such as spying on neighbors or strangers, may need help.

But perversions within reason can be enjoyed and used to enlarge a couple's sexual repertoire. Sharing fantasies, whether they are intended as scenarios to be acted upon or not, encourages open sexual communication between partners and that is surely a good thing.

CHAPTER 9

Relationships

The dynamics of relationships of all kinds are complex, requiring a huge investment of time, energy and emotion. Every individual has their own needs and expectations and there are inevitably very many different situations to be experienced and coped with – meeting, moving in together and possibly affairs, breaking up, bereavement and so on. Making a relationship work is not always easy, and, often, it is not even possible, but it is nearly always something worth having at the time, and something to learn from for the future.

Healthy relationships

We usually feel vibrantly alive when we are in love, but recent research indicates that there is considerably more to it than that. Good relationships actually improve your health, while bad ones can damage it. Showing love and affection for your lover can help keep him or her healthy and happy. The equation is simple – good relationships make you feel valued, whereas bad relationships make you feel the opposite.

It follows that the most important element in keeping your relationships healthy and, by extension, keeping yourself and your partner healthy too, is making your partner feel appreciated and hoping that these expressions of love and caring will be returned:

● *Express love for your partner openly. This can be done by verbal or non-verbal messages – non-verbal ones are probably the more powerful. The arm around the shoulder, the gentle hug, the squeezed hand, the loving kiss and, of course, good sex are all*

*important ways to indicate the value and appreciation that you
have invested in your partner.*

● *React when your partner says or does something that pleases
you. The verbal record of appreciation for a job well done or a
simple reminder that your love is as strong as it always was can
help to sustain your partner's feelings of worth. If you ever feel a
sudden surge of passion, do not keep it to yourself – let your
partner know about it.*

● *Comment on the little things that you appreciate as well as on
the big ones – this shows that you are paying attention to your
partner and noticing and valuing what he or she does. People
like to have the changes in their behaviour recognized and noted
rather than just taken for granted. Attention to these changes
can show that you appreciate that he or she is developing as a
person, that you like and value the personal growth that is
taking place and that you would like to be an active part of it.*

● *Make an effort to share time and activities together. This is a
good way of indicating attachment to another person, and of
binding your lives together. By making time to be with someone
you express the value that you place in that person and in the
relationship.*

Lovers with an excellent relationship, marital partners with a
strong sense of mutual involvement, and families who are very
close to each other all have much lower rates of psychiatric and
neurotic problems than those in troubled relationships or
dysfunctional families. They are also much less likely to suffer
from severe depression.

LOVING AND HEALTH

One of the most striking studies on the effects of love on health was conducted in California. Of those studied, researchers found that healthy subjects were generally happier with their life, with their marriage and with many other aspects of their personal relationships.

The studies also showed that the healthy subjects had more friends than other unhealthy neighbours did. Their views on life were more positive and they felt more successful and able to cope generally.

In addition, they suffered less from depression, and dealt with stress more effectively than those people who had fewer friends, were unmarried or had no long-term sexual relationships. These findings indicate that friendships and good relationships with sexual partners can help to improve our outlook on the world.

People who are lonely or socially isolated, however, stand a higher risk of coming down with a variety of illnesses and disorders ranging from the common cold to heart attacks. The lonely are especially prone to psychological disorders, attacks of depression in particular.

Generally, it is clear that both men and women who have close relationships with their partner are better able to stand up to times of extreme stress. In a way these relationships act as a buffer.

The feeling of being needed and wanted, of being important to somebody else, and the knowledge that someone else will care and be upset if you suffer because of a problem, is what gives a person strength. Being loved seems to be central to overriding crises and dealing effectively with stress.

Additionally, it has been found that recovery from illness is quicker and the general ability to cope with life's problems is stronger when the person has a strong "support network" – that is to say, good friends to whom he or she can rely with confidence, and by whom she feels valued.

If good, close relationships help to keep us healthy, what do bad ones do to us? Research indicates that they have the negative effects that you would expect – bad relationships are bad for your health, particularly, although not exclusively, if you are male.

It is a general feeling for both sexes that the widowed have a much higher rate of health complaints during the year following bereavement than do other people of the same age. The problems reported by widowed and separated men, however, are generally more serious than those reported by women.

Recent surveys have shown that one of the most dangerous things to be, in terms of health, is a man who is in the process of separating from his wife. After separation, it is in the six months before final divorce that men are much more likely than normal to suffer from stress-related illnesses, whether they are as serious as heart attacks or as minor as headaches. A surprising proportion of these illnesses affect the respiratory tract, often impeding the person's breathing.

Such dramatic consequences seem to be specific to divorce, but any form of disturbance in a close relationship can have a detrimental effect on a person's health. And it is worth remembering that, when you next tell your partner you love him or her, or you offer a hand of friendship to someone, you may even be offering them a life-line.

ATTITUDES TO MARRIAGE

In Western societies, such as the USA, Canada and Australia, where parental influence has gradually grown less significant during the twentieth century, marriage is seen as involving a romantic type of love. It fulfils the desire of each partner to find an intense, emotionallysatisfying and long-lasting relationship – ideally "till death do us part".

One of the most important aspects of marriage in many societies is that it legitimizes the birth of any children and creates a stable family framework for their upbringing. Children are generally seen as desirable, and high infant mortality in developing countries encourages large families despite the influence of education for birth control. Children form an important part of the workforce in many developing countries, and are also expected to care for their parents in their old age.

Religion and marriage

In the traditional culture of countries like India and most Muslim nations, parental emphasis remains paramount and couples often have no say in the matter of marriage partners.

Other countries fall somewhere between these two extremes. In Catholic Spain, Italy or Ireland, young people are rapidly becoming more independent, although there is still considerable influence from the family and the community, often leading to a situation of conflict. Although young people are allowed to mix freely, they may face severe disapproval if they indulge in pre-marital sex.

In countries like India where arranged marriages are the norm, it is recognized that there exists – and there always will – a natural attraction between young men and women. Society, however, draws a sharp distinction between such attraction – seen as primarily sexual – and the true happiness of married love, to the extent that teenage girls and boys are often kept strictly segregated. Most Indians would say that love comes after marriage, not before it, and would argue that their system of arranged marriages ensures the best possible chance of success. They regard pre-marital sexual experimentation as irresponsible and immoral.

In Muslim countries, marriage has traditionally involved a contract between the groom and the bride's father Even today, the bride only signs the contract as a witness, sitting in a separate room at the marriage ceremony. Younger Muslims and Asians who have grown up in Western countries, particularly women, often face great conflict between traditional family values and those of their Western environment.

Sexual fidelity within marriage is an area where double standards still exist, especially in particularly male-dominated cultures such as in Islamic or some Far Eastern countries.

This sexual discrimination may even be enshrined in law, as in Egypt, where an adulterous husband can be punished by up to three years' imprisonment, but only if his infidelity occurred in the matrimonial home. His wife, on the other hand, is always considered guilty, no matter where the adultery takes place.

Does marriage have a future?

In the West, certainly, the aim of marriage seems to be becoming less defined by these factors, and some people even recognize "marriages" between homosexuals, although society has not given its official blessing.

Despite all these changes, marriage in its traditional form is holding its own and, whatever other form it may take in the future, the monogamous one man/one woman marriage looks likely to be with us for a long time to come.

How relationships progress

"Why aren't things like they used to be?' is a common question asked by couples after a few years, or maybe even a few months, of being together. Where once they leapt into bed at every opportunity, or went everywhere hand in hand, they find that

Physical affection is very important in reassuring your partner, not just in the early stages of relationship.

almost imperceptibly they start to take things more casually. Desire – at least partially – has been replaced by something else.

Before anything that can be called "love" has appeared in a relationship, there is an initial stage – a kind of grey area between ordinary friendship and something special when two people tacitly agree to explore each other as potential partners. The key features of this early phase tend to be a mixture of curiosity, sexual attraction, elation and a tinge of anxiety.

During these preliminaries of a partnership it is possible to enjoy the nother person's company in a fairly intimate way, but still be able to stop the whole thing progressing without causing any serious emotional pain.

For some, the initial stage might include sleeping together; others may keep the relationship open-ended for months, with only a few shared dates and most of the contact by telephone or letter. After the early barriers have been broken down, a relationship may very well start taking over a couple's lives. The feeling is not that you would merely enjoy seeing the other person, but that you actually need to see them. Somehow, those involved begin to lose control over their rational feelings.

Suddenly, the whole world is different: there is hope, happiness and heady excitement. Falling in love changes your whole being – your whole way of looking at the world. Everything your lover says or does is viewed in a special light.

The blindness of love at this stage in a relationship, however, can sow the seeds for disaster later. For some, the urge to share experiences with their lover and to please them, becomes an urge to agree with everything their lover thinks.

From here it is easy to make compromises which can eventually mask your true self. The experience of being in love can be so strong that it hides the real facts.

Naturally, falling in love has different effects on different temperaments, but probably the one common factor is that it feels like it is the first time even if it is tenth time. What is more, it feels as if something as wonderful as this has never happened to anyone else before. And in a sense, it has not, since all relationships are unique.

How long can the excitement and intensity of love last? Although some might claim that it can last a lifetime, this seems unlikely, since being in love is so closely connected with a sense of newness and feeling of discovery. This second stage of a

Once the intensity of the early passion has passed, a more mellow, comfortable sex life can replace it.

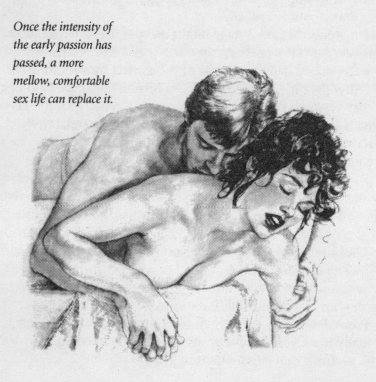

relationship is often marked by a lack of interest in the practical matters of the world. Yet sooner or later, most people tire of spending yet another night squashed in a single bed, and make the decision either to break up or move in together.

At this point, if it is to survive, a relationship needs change – to exist in the context of other people and not simply turn inwards on themselves. After the initial introspection, a couple is likely to open out more to the world, re-establishing old friendships, entertaining and perhaps even finding new interests to stop them spending all of their free time together.

It is important to remember that a relationship is not finished because it changes into something different. The bonds between a couple are still there and can become deeper, if the partnership is given a chance to develop further.

Most couples find that the sense of progress their relationship has initially can fade away as they become immersed in the business of everyday living. In particular, the years between twenty-five and thirty-five are usually full of distractions – houses to decorate, children to rear or career ladders to scale – all of which can force the central relationship to take a back seat.

Sometimes a staleness creeps into a relationship which is not noticed by either partner, or is noticed but never mentioned, because of these and other pressing demands. But for many couples, the importance of having someone with whom to share the joys and crises of life far outweighs the long-term problems that must be faced.

The greatest test for the majority of relationships comes in the lull that follows the children starting school. The man's career may be established by then and the woman is able and eager to assert her own needs. Life can be suddenly much emptier for both partners with fewer common goals to aim for.

SAVING YOURSELF FOR MARRIAGE

Sexual freedom has given us the opportunity to explore whatever sexual avenues we choose to go along, and a growing number of people are choosing no sex at all, at least until they are married.

Back in the radical sixties, losing your virginity was considered a political act, but these days saving yourself for marriage is thought by some to be just as potent a symbol.

The True Love Waits campaign in America has more than 100,000 followers, proudly announcing that it's hip to be a virgin. The campaign's founder, Southern Baptist minister Richard Ross, claims that it represents the biggest shift of social behaviour since the free-love movement of the sixties and he may well be right.

Why wait?

Many people abstain from sex before marriage for religious reasons. Orthodox Jews and practising Catholics are brought up to believe what their respective religions teach them – that the only purpose for sex is procreation, that it should happen only within the traditional marital structure and that any sexual act indulged in outside of this structure is a sin. To be a virgin is to be blessed because surrendering virginity before marriage falls foul of traditional religious systems of punishments and rewards.

Other reasons given by the True Love Waits supporters are moral, perhaps even moralistic: the breakdown of the family unit with sexual freedom is cited as a contributing factor. Some schoolgirls involved in the campaign view sex as a power tool employed by their male peers to control and bully them. It's the old story of being labeled as a prude if you don't have sex or a slut if you do, which has been practised on young girls for aeons, but these girls are getting back at the stereotypes by reasonably withholding their virginity.

For many, resisting sex is a question of strong physical and mental control, an act which differentiates them from "wild", uncivilized creatures. Many also advocate the virtue in waiting, viewing virginity as a gift which can only be given once and is therefore worthy of deliberation. And anyway, as far as the True Love Waits contingency is concerned, sex is somewhat overrated.

These days, health reasons are probably the main motivation for people abstaining from sex until they are married – the fear of unwanted pregnancy and of sexually transmitted diseases, especially AIDS. For some the fear of AIDS has made them abstain completely, believing sex will only be safe when they are married and then only if they have married another virgin.

Young people who abstain from pre-marital sex may give any or all of the above reasons for making this choice but the ultimate reason for waiting is the best one: love.

Both may start to wonder why they got together in the first place. When the couple stop to think about their relationship after maybe years of just observing the outward form, they can be shocked by the distance between them.

For some, damage is too difficult to repair and the relationship may break down. But for others, the sudden realization that they no longer know their partners is a signal that it is time to make positive changes

Pay attention to each other's moods and needs for understanding, affection and support.

Living together

For people who need a close sexual relationship, but want to delay marriage, one alternative is a live-in loving relationship. Consequently, many couples today are choosing to cohabit – to live together without getting married. In almost all aspects, this results in a relationship that is very similar to marriage – except that it is not a formally recognized arrangement, with the weight of a legally binding document behind it.

For some people, living together is a viable alternative to marriage – they co-habit for many years without formally "tying the knot". But these people represent only a fraction of the population. A much greater percentage uses cohabitation as a prelude to marriage. Indeed, one study showed that as many as 70 per cent of couples who married in the last ten years had lived together before they acquired a marriage license.

For those couples who are thinking of moving in together there are a number of things to bear in mind:

Considerable research leaves little doubt that cohabiting couples show less commitment to one another than do engaged or married couples. Generally, married and the "traditional" courting couples report a greater dedication to continuing their relationship and also feel that there are more external restraints against them breaking up. They are more likely to be influenced by family and friends to stay together, and they feel that their commitment to the relationship is public as well as private.

If things do go wrong, they also feel that they will receive more support from outsiders and more help at patching up the relationship if they want to.

But the relationships of couples living together can survive for years and the level of satisfaction with the relationship reported by cohabiting couples is actually the same as that of married couples.

One possible reason for this is that cohabiting couples seem to manage to successfully work out ways in which to handle traditional male and female roles within their relationship. They are unhappy with the traditional perception of husband as bread-winner and wife as glorified domestic, and noticeably in favour of equality in relationships.

Several studies now confirm, however, that such attitudes are not, in fact, borne out in their behaviour. After several months there is little to distinguish the majority of relationships in terms of the distribution of domestic duties.

Sexual behaviour, however, does distinguish cohabitors from married couples. Some 30 per cent of cohabiting partners have active sexual partnerships outside the cohabitation. Studies of married couples report, by comparison, that roughly 25 per cent have had a sexual relationship outside of marriage.

Cohabitors tend to be rather more sexually experienced than are members of the typical marriage. Studies show that they have had more partners, that they engage in more sexual variations and that they have oral sex more often than married couples do.

Another notable feature of cohabitation is that the female partner tends to take the initiative in sexual behaviour much more often than do married women. Also, cohabiting partners are more active in, and more satisfied with, their sex life, whatever form it takes.

But what is the likelihood of a cohabitation being successful in the long run?

One long-term study showed that about 65 per cent of all cohabiting couples were still cohabiting (but had not got married) some eighteen months after they were first investigated, 21 per cent of cohabiting couples had married between the first and the second investigation whereas only 14 per cent had broken up entirely.

When cohabitors do eventually marry, the quality of the relationship does not alter significantly but the picture is less rosy in terms of its potential success. In a study conducted in 1985 it was found that 22 per cent of partners who had cohabited before marriage had divorced within nine years.

Cohabiting couples who decide to marry often find that their relationship deteriorates, but if they are able to communicate well they should be able to sort out the problems.

MONOGAMY

There are two schools of thought regarding the exact meaning of monogamy. One group believes that it means being sexually and emotionally faithful to one person for the rest of your life, whereas the other maintains that it means being sexually and emotionally faithful for as long as the relationship lasts. The former is known as monogamy, and the latter is now recognized as serial monogamy.

Attitudes to monogamy

Recent research reveals that a large proportion of women believe monogamy to be unnatural and old-fashioned. But if monogamy is so unnatural and difficult, why is it deemed so important throughout Western society?

Perhaps because it is the ideal romantic scenario. We all dream of meeting Mr or Ms Right, falling in love, marrying and living happily ever after. The most likely explanation for the importance of monogamy, however, is that, providing the people involved are happy together, it creates a stable environment for the rearing of children. Two parents consistently caring for children as they develop through all the stages from babies to adults is, like the idea of being with one person for eternity, the stuff of everyone's dreams.

This is not always possible, however, and it could be that dreams of the ideal set-up actually prevent us from having a chance to find happiness in a relationship. Perhaps the pressures we put on ourselves and our partners are unrealistic. Can we really expect one person to fulfil all of our needs for all time?

Still, society, and often governments, advocate monogamy as the "norm", an attitude which has been strengthened in the age of AIDS. We can't dismiss the impact that AIDS has had on people's feelings towards monogamy – nearly two-thirds of women say it has made them more likely to stay with their partner, regardless of how dissatisfied they may or may not be.

Is monogamy all-important?

Is the importance placed on monogamy dangerous or negative? Certainly, on a personal level, it can be. For fear of not being monogamous, you might stay in an dissatisfying and unhealthy relationship, or, if one partner is not monogamous when the other expects complete fidelity, an otherwise successful relationship might be destroyed. No matter how attractive you find your partner and whether you could never dream of being with someone else, over time attraction and sexual feelings can fade while the love, respect and personal compatibility remain. If non-monogamy was more acceptable, if fidelity was not the lynch-pin for successful relationships, perhaps there would be fewer divorces and break-ups.

Not being monogamous does not necessarily mean the end of the relationship. It could be the importance attached to monogamy which destroys relationships that may have survived if the possibility and the meanings of affairs had been recognized.

For some couples, monogamy is the perfect set-up – being sexually and emotionally committed to one person for ever, secure and stable, works for them – but for others it isn't. It may always be perceived as the ideal – perhaps it is – but it is also possible that there are better, broader and more natural options for those of us who find monogamy unworkable options which hold promise for more individual fulfilment and a richer, more satisfying society as a result.

In contrast, only 10 per cent of the couples who had not cohabited before marriage had divorced within the same period. Some cohabiting couples begin to feel trapped once the arrangement is officially sanctioned. They are also more likely than other couples to feel that their personal freedom has been infringed by marriage.

A number of other experiences are reported by cohabitors which suggest that the move to marriage is more stressful for them than it is for other, more traditional, couples. For example, many cohabitors report that they experienced loss of love for their partner once they married, and others describe a strong increase in conflict about the household tasks and traditional roles to be played.

Most people believe that premarital cohabitation helps in learning to live with one another and in sorting out problems ahead of time, but this assumption does not seem to stand up to scrutiny.

Open relationships

It is not unusual to question how you feel about your partner. Will you always love them? Will you meet someone else and leave them? Will you stay with them but have an affair?

There are some who know the answers to these questions from the outset – that the partner they are with is not enough, and that sooner rather than later they will want and need a relationship with someone else, whether it be brief and sexual or longer and more important.

Most people keep these doubts and conclusions to themselves, but a very few have a far more radical way of dealing with their feelings. They make a pact with their partner that other relationships are permissible and are to be conducted openly, without deceit or secrecy. This small minority then enter into an "open" relationship.

In the classic open relationship, once or twice a year, one or other of a couple has a relatively brief affair with someone else. It may happen that they have their affairs at exactly the same time.

Where this differs from an ordinary couple couple in a similar situation is that they tell each other most – if not everything – of what is going on. They consult each other about the new relationships, especially if there are problems and difficulties, and comfort each other when things break up.

Despite their affairs, a couple with a classic open relationship see themselves as a permanent pair in the long-term. A couple in this situation can be living together or married but they make a firm commitment to each other that they should be allowed to have other relationships, usually sexual, whenever and however they want.

Open relationships do not follow a set pattern. They vary in their degrees of openness from couple to couple, each having to arrive at a formula that works for them. For some couples this kind of pact simply means the occasional sanctioned fling or one-night stand, while for others it means playing the field.

Whereas one couple may be quite open about their philanderings, another may be relatively discreet about them. They may decide right at the beginning that both are free to pursue other relationships if they really want to, but they will not talk to each other about them.

One couple whose relationship was like this never asked questions when no information was volunteered. Every so often, one or other would say, "I'm going away this weekend", and if

Sometimes the discovery of an affair can revitalize the original relationship – but it's a big gamble to take.

they didn't add anything to that, then the other would know it was with someone else but would not know the details.

A variation on the "open" theme is "swinging". "Swingers" set out to swap partners on a regular basis and often join circles where "wife swapping" is the norm. For them, fidelity is boring: they get their sexual kicks form constantly changing partners. Sex is a matter of fun and new experience.

But occasionally for some people, an open relationship means more than just sexual games, it provides the freedom to build up a proper relationship with someone else if the opportunity presents itself.

Some couples decide to act as if they are single, pursuing all sorts of relationships in exactly the same way as would someone who is unattached. They want to stay together with their "partner" but feel hemmed in by the confines of a traditional monogamous relationship.

Do open relationships work?

The theory of open relationships is all very well, but in reality the balance is very fine, and often one partner wants it, and the other goes along with it simply to keep the peace. It may well go against everything they believe about love and marriage but they endure it in order to hold on to the one they love.

Some reluctant partners agree to an open relationship as a way of forestalling jealousy. Knowing about a new liaison from the beginning often helps them to cope with negative feelings. Without the element of deceit, they are more likely to feel in control of the situation, rather than feeling outwitted or fooled.

The kinds of people who find an open relationship ideal are the types who keep an emotional distance, whose deepest feelings are never engaged by another person, and who do not experience jealousy. For them, sex is essentially a physical release. Love does not have to enter into it.

But such people are extremely rare, and research indicates that, in fact, open marriages are not very popular. In one study only 4 per cent of the people interviewed thought the concept either possible or practical – so the number of people who are actually trying it out must be even lower.

Couples sometimes start out believing in the virtues of non-exclusive relationships and then find jealousies and insecurities get in the way, forcing a sudden re-evaluation of the contract.

Open relationships rarely last because of the pain they cause. Jealousy is a normal and natural emotion. Trying to control it means cutting off emotionally from the other person if they become involved with someone else, and that is almost impossible.

Also, there is the ever-present threat of one of the new and casual encounters turning into something serious which would cause more permanent damage to the relationship. Inevitably, the end result is that the open relationship cannot survive and is brought to a close.

Having an affair

Open relationships aside, most people enter an important relationship at least planning to be faithful to each other. But as the years go by and the relationship settles down into something different from the early romantic days, some people stray.

An affair is very different from a casual fling or one-night stand. An affair, however long it lasts, implies a commitment to the new person as well as to the existing partner.

Usually it is exciting to begin with. But once the affair goes on for any length of time, all but the most insensitive people begin to suffer in one way or another.

The new partner is miserable about the restrictions of the relationship, such as being unable to phone at certain times, or see their lover whenever they both would like. The original partner, whether aware or not of the affair, notices a change in the relationship, usually for the worse, and may feel unhappy or guilty about it. Even the central figure, who is apparently having the best of both worlds, carries the burden of responsibility for two lovers and has to lie and use up a lot of time and emotional energy in just trying to keep things going relatively smoothly.

In fact, few people would choose to be part of a love triangle. But it happens over and over again, for many reasons.

Some people are simply more likely than others to have affairs. This may be due to a number of factors. Some people find the secrecy involved a turn-on. It makes them feel clever and in control. Others have an affair as a convenient way of making sure that they are never on their own. They build up a new relationship before relinquishing the old.

Other people are drawn into affairs because they have a misunderstanding about the nature of relationships. They do not realize that the feeling of being totally wrapped up sexually and emotionally in another person is transitory, is part and parcel of the early days of a relationship, and is bound to evolve into something else. When the euphoria disappears they think that something has gone wrong, and start to look for it elsewhere.

For others, the feelings that go with the start of a relationship produce such a high that they become hooked. They know these feelings will not last, which is why they do not leave their steady partner. They opt instead for a series of affairs, which means that they constantly have the buzz of a new relationship.

But even those who are not inherently affair-prone may have one given a certain set of circumstances. For example, there are difficult times in any relationship, when the idea of an affair becomes very attractive and the problems that it is likely to cause seem less important. Then, if the opportunity comes along, it may be taken.

There are times when one or other partner may feel entitled to have an affair. If the relationship is going through a bad patch, and you are rowing a great deal so that your home life becomes fraught, being with someone else somewhere else might seem to be your right.

Sometimes if a partner feels rejected for some reason – as men often do when they lose the main focus of their partner's attention during pregnancy, or while the woman is caring for young children – they seek the attention they need elsewhere.

Similarly, if one of you has lost interest in sex, or neither of you can be bothered to make love except in the most perfunctory manner, an affair can seem necessary.

However, if any of these situations arises in what is essentially a good healthy relationship, an affair need not be the only answer. Rational discussion with your partner and maybe even a marriage guidance counsellor can help you discover just why your relationship has changed, and how you might restore it to its former state.

The effects of an affair

It is impossible for an affair to have no impact at all on the people involved, especially on the relationship of the original couple.

Even if the affair is never discovered, the lying that is involved takes its toll on the relationship. Lying puts a distance between a couple. It destroys true intimacy, because you must watch yourself in case you contradict something that you have said, and therefore give yourself away. It can also make you doubt the truthfulness of your partner.

Guilt also harms the relationship. It can take the form of making you extra loving, as in the classic situation of buying flowers to make amends. But it can also make you aggressive so that you goad your partner into a row or into behaving badly to make you feel more justified in the way you have behaved.

Sometimes the straying partner conducts the affair so carefully that it is never discovered. Other times, it is apparently not discovered because the innocent partner turns a blind eye – pretending not to notice any tell-tale signs, rather than risk further, more serious disruption of the relationship.

But often the affair is discovered and the consequences must be faced. The discovery though not always leading to break-up can alter for ever the nature of the original partnership. With trust gone and suspicion ever-present,it can be hard to recreate a harmonious atmosphere at home.

Often, the discovery of an affair means the end of a marriage or live-in relationship. This is usually the case when it was shaky to begin with, and the affair filled more than a casual need.

Relationships can also break up because the discovered affair was of real importance. Sometimes the erring partner wants to be found out so that without the trauma of telling the other partner the issue is brought to a head, and he or she can leave.

Sometimes the truth can have a positive effect. If the affair has been embarked on because a couple have stopped communicating on any serious level, it can be the catalyst needed to make them talk out their problems.

Quite often an affair ends without discovery at all, either because the lover has had enough, or because the straying partner wants it to end.

Whether this has a knock-on effect on the original partnership depends on the feelings of the straying partner. If he or she needed the affair because of gaps in the existing relationship,

COPING WITH DIVORCE

It is all too easy to think of divorce as a single event that happens to people – or as something that they cause to happen by their own actions. However, we tend to overlook the fact that most divorces are long drawn-out processes and do not just happen overnight.

In reality, divorce is a whole chain of events which affects every single aspect of a couple's life. It is a process which begins with the first differences within a marriage and which may peak at separation or legal divorce proceedings. Its effects may well continue for a long time after the actual divorce, until each individual learns to stand on their own two feet confidently.

Divorce patterns

Two researchers in Pennsylvania, Hagestad and Smyer, have mapped out various types of divorce. They have detected several distinct general patterns.

The first type they identified is the "orderly divorce", where both partners accept that they have fallen out of love, that they are not unhappy about losing the status of "being married", and that they are positive about readjusting the routines of their daily life. In such cases, there does not seem to be much of a problem for either partner. Generally, they accept the divorce and are glad that it has released them from an unsatisfactory situation.

Many more couples have "disorderly divorces", where one or other partner – or, in some cases, both – find it difficult to let go in one way or another. Some stay in love with their partner, while others cannot adjust to the status of being unmarried again. For example, many women prefer to keep their married name and call themselves "Mrs . . ." after the divorce rather than going back to their maiden name.

Others find that they cannot not adjust to the changes in routine, handling their own finances or housework, making decisions on their own or simply being on their own in the evenings or holidays.

During their study of disorderly divorces, Hagestad and Smyer discovered some intriguing ways in which people handle their divorces. In one group, which they called "Business as usual", the couple had been legally divorced and did not love one another, but continued to live in the same house and go out together – and some even went on holidays together.

In another group, at least one of the couple – and in many cases both of them – still loved their partner and wished the divorce had not happened. Such partners kept in touch with one another and often saw each other. In many cases they left clothes, tools or possessions in the other person's home and sometimes tried to patch up their relationship quite a long time after the divorce. Some even remarried their former partner.

Facing the future

Divorce is by no means straightforward. There are many difficult social, psychological, economic, legal and sexual changes that follow the decision to take formal steps for a divorce. After the partners have gone through the business of legalizing the divorce, they have to face up to the new social status of being unmarried, with all its attendant problems and advantages. They may, for the first time in their lives, find themselves faced with the scary, depressing but also exciting prospect of living on their own.

Dealing with the practicalities of dividing up possessions is not the only problem that must be overcome. Nor are the divorcing partners the only people involved. Parents, children and friends may have a lot to say about the whole affair and will exert different pressures on the couple. Some couples manage to loosen the ties of marriage relatively easily and painlessly, while others find it traumatic.

then a search may be on for a replacement. In other cases, the straying partner may become unhappy and depressed after the affair has ended, which could affect the original relationship in a way it never did when the affair was in full swing.

Occasionally the straying partner will breathe a sigh of relief that things are back to normal again, and that they no longer have to endure the strains of leading a double life. and weaving an elaborate web of deceit. They may have started out thinking

Falling in love has many physiological symptoms – your heart beats faster, you exude particular scents, your pupils dilate – and it may feel as though there is nothing you can do to prevent it.

that an affair would be exciting, but end up valuing those aspects of a settled relationship they had previously scorned.

Loving two people

No one really questions anybody's capacity to love more than one person. You love your partner – but you also love your parents, your children, possibly your best friend. It can be hard to say for sure who you love "best". So different are the people that you may, at various times, feel that you love each one with "all your heart".

Loving like this is totally acceptable. But loving more than one person romantically and sexually has very different implications.

Theoretically, we can love any number of people. We are not issued with a certain quota of love which gradually becomes used up as the years go by. If anything it is the other way round – the more love you receive, the more you have to give. Just as the physical heart increases its capacity with exercise, so does the loving heart when given the chance. So falling in love with two or even more people can certainly happen. In practice, however, it happens rarely. We guard against it. It is not acceptable to maintain two equal love partners at the same time. Most people, while recognizing the potential attractions of another person, inhibit their own responses so that nothing ever happens, but if they do accidentally fall in love they have to quickly decide what to do about it – whether to try to balance the two loves or to let one of them go.

In simple terms, falling in love involves being attracted to certain qualities, perhaps physical, mental or spiritual, that

If a couple cannot discuss problems between themselves, then the relationship is obviously in trouble.

someone else possesses. It would be quite easy to fall in love with two people because what attracts you is different in each case – and the ways in which you love them also vary.

One person may make you feel protective and tender, another may arouse your respect and admiration, or perhaps your sensuality and lust. Falling in love is the easy part. It is maintaining the love subsequently that is difficult.

Falling in love when you are already involved with someone else can happen at any time. At work, for example, if you are open and friendly, friendship can easily slip into something more serious with someone you instinctively like and admire. And the transition to loving can occur almost without your noticing it. You see each other every day, laugh, joke, spend time together, and suddenly you find the friendship has gone beyond the usual professional relationship. Your pulse quickens when they come into the room, you find yourself worrying and missing them when they are ill, you contrive to spend more and more lunches together, sharing your worlds over sandwiches and coffee.

People caught in this situation find themselves unable to see one relationship as subsidiary or less important than the other. Their quality of life would be diminished if either was lost. They are in love with two people, and sometimes they are at a loss as to what to do about it.

Although loving two people can happen to anyone, many people would not be able to tolerate such a situation. If they found themselves falling for another person they would feel compelled to make a choice – loving them both would be unthinkable. For them the new love either marks the fact that the old relationship is over, or reinforces the strength and importance of the existing relationship. It cannot be just a matter of having room in their hearts for two.

If one of the relationships is emotional rather than physical it is often easier. Many people are able to accept their partner's need for a platonic friendship outside of their relationship, and do not see it as a threat. Others, however, feel excluded and cannot cope with this second "love" in their partner's life.

Breaking up

The end of a relationship is rarely quick and clean. The longer you have been living together the more likely it is that the decision to part becomes increasingly difficult.

Part of this is to do with the fact that most people feel that saying goodbye to someone they have loved very much is an admission of failure. *If it was so right once, then something must have happened to spoil things. Was it something I did? Or didn't do? Or something we both neglected to do?*

Another important factor in slowing down the process of parting is the realization that all relationships go through bad patches. Couples who are considering parting should ask themselves if what they are going through is just a bad patch. Is what they've got essentially sound and worth fighting for? Would they always regret it if they broke up?

Breaking up is often delayed because a couple fear what will happen next. The sheer practical problems that arise when they have been living together, especially if they have bought their flat, or house, can be daunting.

Both parties may know that their relationship is dead and should be buried, but what will they do on their own? Will they be able to find someone else? Isn't being together, however miserable, really preferable to being alone which will be just as

TO PART OR NOT TO PART

The right reasons

There are good reasons for deciding to part and it is important to consider them. These are just some of the right reasons:

✔ *Basic incompatibility.*

✔ *The things that are wrong with your relationship badly affect the rest of your life.*

✔ *You no longer like each other.*

✔ *One of you is making the other very unhappy and is not prepared to do anything about it.*

✔ *You want very different things from life – one wants children, for example, the other adventure.*

✔ *You prefer to live on your own as a single person.*

✔ *You have genuinely fallen in love with someone else.*

The wrong reasons

The wrong reasons for breaking up might seem very right at the time – but they may be transitory. Here are some of them:

✘ *A passionate affair – often a symptom rather than a reason.*

✘ *You are very angry about something that has happened recently – let the anger cool before you make a decision.*

✘ *You are bored – do not immediately blame the relationship, rather investigate further.*

✘ *You cannot talk anymore – how hard have you tried?*

✘ *Your job is making demands on you that is affecting your relationship – do you want professional success above all else?*

miserable, at least for a while? These and many other questions, doubts and fears go through the mind of everyone who believes a relationship is heading for the end.

But there comes a time when you have to admit that your relationship has reached make-or-break point. It's more than likely that you have been having a lot of rows, which have not been resolved as easily and fully as they once were. Some people come to realize that apart from rows and day-to-day practicalities they have almost entirely ceased to talk about anything important. Conversation which was affectionate and friendly is now more wary and barbed.

Your sex life is also an excellent guide to the true state of your relationship. Usually, when it deteriorates, your sex life suffers too. Some people find it ceases altogether, others find that it changes in nature, becoming more aggressive and less tender.

Sometimes things get so bad before the crunch that couples on the brink of parting find themselves hating the atmosphere at home to the extent that they will do anything rather than face it.

But often it is when one or other of a couple find themselves seriously assessing other people as possible partners that they realize how distant they have become from their existing partner.

There is no single reason why some relationships fall apart after a certain time and others go on indefinitely. Sometimes there is just a fundamental incompatibility. A couple may like each other, even love one another, but if they are incompatible it will be unlikely that they can live together for ever.

It is rarely as clear-cut as that, however. Relationships can go wrong for any number of reasons, even when the two people concerned seem to have a real chance of making a go of it.

One problem is that people continue to change and develop throughout their lives. With luck, a couple will grow together in a

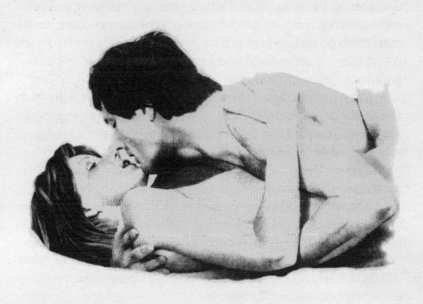

Sexually the death of someone we love can have a profound effect. We may alternate between feeling afraid of physical intimacy and craving sexual comfort.

complementary fashion, but it is no one's fault if, instead, they grow apart.

If you are coming to believe that your relationship is in danger, you have to make the difficult decision of choosing between trying to make up or agreeing to break up.

The first thing you have to do, which might mean breaking the habits of years, is to discuss it together. Nothing is going to resolve itself satisfactorily until you sit down and talk. If you find that talking to your partner always ends in a row or one of you dominating the discussion, consider using a marriage guidance counsellor or another intermediary. You do not have to be married to do this, and the advantage of consulting professionals is that they are uninvolved and know what you ought to be talking about – even if you do not.

Carrying through a decision to break up, even when it is obviously the right thing to do, is very difficult. The emotional impact of a separation is as traumatic as the feelings of grief experienced on being bereaved.

And as if grappling with this trauma was not enough, there are almost always complex practical problems to be overcome.

If you do decide to split up – which in some cases may be the best decision from everyone's point of view – the next stage is to "go public". Friends should recognize the need for the couple involved to create face-saving stories about the break-up. They should not be encouraged to lie, but some biased interpretations of ambiguous events are allowable.

Remember that once the pain of a break-up has gone there is the rest of your life to look forward to, and it is up to you to make it as happy as you can. Relationships break up all the time. If yours does so, use the experience to learn a little bit more about what a relationship needs to make it work, and you can apply it the next time you fall in love.

Bereavement

None of us can really know or understand what grief is like until we lose someone we love, and no two people experience loss in exactly the same way, even if they are lovers. Grief is what we feel when we suffer a major loss, and when we grieve it can be for a lover, a friend, a pet or even a limb – anybody or anything that has meant a lot to us in our lives.

How we grieve and how long each of us takes to heal depends on how close we were to the person who has died, the time in his or her life – and in ours – at which the death actually occurred and the unique, individual circumstances of that death.

The one thing that all people who are grieving have in common, however, is the pain they experience. When we lose someone we love, we feel unbearable emotional pain, and in order to heal and begin to live fully again, we must move through it.

The way we define ourselves as sexual beings depends on the people around us, and with each new person we love we have a different relationship. Sexuality is not just about making love, and the death of someone we love can, therefore, affect us sexually just as much as the death of a lover.

Coping with grief

From the beginning of our lives we are taught to bury feelings of pain, and, at a time of bereavement, this training works against us, leaving us with little space to let our grief out, and less knowledge of grieving. This is unfortunate, given the wealth of evidence now on record which indicates that people who express their feelings recover much more quickly than those who don't. Grief is an isolating and lonely experience, but we don't have to be isolated in our grief or pretend we are not sad.

Research carried out among Maoris, who spend three days with the dead person, crying and yearning, concluded that such a complete expression of grief helps the bereaved person enormously. Other studies have shown that people who allow themselves to mourn – for instance, weeping openly – recover more quickly from the loss than those who repress their grief.

Grief is felt on many levels at the same time and can manifest itself physically, psychologically and sexually. When couples grieve together it is unlikely that they will feel the same emotions at the same time, and there is a danger that one person will take his or her frustration out on the very person they expect the most support from – their partner.

When we lose someone we love we also experience social isolation and alienation because we now see ourselves as different from other people and different from the person we were before the death occurred. The insecurity we feel awakens all our childhood fears of abandonment and leaves us feeling scared, alone and unsafe. It is unsurprising that many couples find that their relationship suffers during the grieving process and often cannot withstand the strain at all.

It is impossible to generalize about how grief affects people, but there are five discernible stages of grief upon which most experts agree. It should be remembered, however, that grief is not a linear progression, and that the stages of grief are not platforms which, once reached, herald a decrease in the level of pain we will feel from that point onward.

● **Shock:** *this is a general term used to describe our reaction to the trauma we sustain at a time of loss, and the circumstances in which the death occurs affects the severity and length of this initial phase. Numb and confused, we will be heavily affected by fear – the fear of dying and of being alone. Many people report feeling as if they are turning inward, losing interest in the outside world. It is also common at this stage to be preoccupied with thoughts of the deceased person. We may feel an incredible yearning for physical comfort – to be held – and we may seek out sex for comfort, or find ourselves wanting a lot more sex* *than usual from our partner. Depending on age and on how he or she is feeling about the bereavement, this may or may not be possible.*

● **Chaotic emotions:** *once the initial shock has passed, the second stage will be a period of chaotic emotions. Searing separation anxiety and conflicting emotions will be intensely felt. Guilt, shame and anger are all emotions with which people who are grieving will be familiar. We may find ourselves about to phone our lost loved one, make their bed or otherwise do things which, while perfectly natural things to do when the person was alive, are inappropriate now that they are dead. This is the period during which most people feel they are going insane – after losing someone special the world is a dismal and bleak place. Physically our bodies are being pumped with adrenalin, so we have excess energy and sleep is difficult. Sexually, we equate sex with life, and experience a surge in libido, but if we feel angry we may equate guilt with sex and want to abuse our bodies. If we are angry at our partner and blame them in some way for hastening the death, we may withdraw sex to signal this anger.*

● **Conservation:** *this feels familiar to depression. Previously volatile emotions will have taken their toll and we now find that we need to rest and recuperate, to try to regather our dwindling resources. It is during this time that others will begin to withdraw their social support, thinking the worst is over. But the grieving individual may still feel helpless and out of control. There is evidence that prolonged grief physically affects us, by suppressing our immune system, so we may also find ourselves developing coughs, colds and other maladies. Psychologically we find ourselves in hibernation – stagnating as the world moves on*

SHYNESS

Learning to trust other people is essential if we are to form successful relationships. But first we need to like ourselves and trust our own feelings. Many shy people so lack self-confidence that they are unable to relate or respond to others. Attempts at communicating with them make them blush bright red, stutter, stammer or gaze fixedly at the floor. Their shyness makes them so ill at ease that they are incapable of even carrying on a conversation.

Although such shyness is off-putting, it is, in fact, part of the person's emotional defence system – a sort of first-strike weapon to deter potential enemies from getting too close and inflicting hurt.

What makes people shy?

Our self-esteem and ability to get on with others are chiefly determined by our upbringing – especially important is the first year of life. The close, loving relationship formed between a mother and her new-born baby establishes a pattern for future relationships.

A mother who not only feeds and protects her child, but cares for and cuddles it, helps to ensure the baby's later emotional security. Research has shown that babies who are fed, but not "mothered", are less able to relate to others in later life.

Infants and young children instinctively imitate their parents' mannerisms, gestures and social behaviour. Prejudices and preferences are similarly learned through the parents' friendly response to other people, or the lack of it.

Attitudes to the opposite sex are also formed while we are young. Family rows may implant the idea that men are only after one thing, or that women are devious and not to be trusted. Almost certainly, such ideas will affect the degree of commitment an individual brings to relationships and ultimately their ability to love and be loved.

Shyness is not necessarily an automatic barrier to a loving relationship. Some men and women prefer a partner they can dominate – or be dominated by. At best, a stable and happy partnership can be the turning point in building up the shy person's self-esteem.

But when shyness is linked to basic insecurity, a fear of losing their partner's affections can fuel the flames of jealousy or initiate a claustrophobic togetherness which may eventually undermine the relationship.

Sadly, true intimacy is rarely achieved. Persistent fears of rejection mean that the shy partner holds back physically and emotionally. Without mutual trust, the free exchange of pleasure will be missing from the couple's lovemaking, thus further chipping away at the relationship. This is the destructive side of shyness – inhibiting responses, narrowing choices and casting a shadow of fear over all relationships.

Overcoming shyness

It is advisable for shy people to ask themselves some simple but searching questions: when did the shyness begin? Was it linked to a change in lifestyle, such as starting at a new school or job, or moving to a new area? Did it follow in the wake of a disastrous love affair?

Writing down both questions and answers will help to provide an explanation for the shyness, which is the first step towards overcoming it. It also has the psychological advantage of allowing the shy person to get to grips with the problem. Making a list of specific, achievable goals is the next step, which once down on paper, is contained and made more manageable.

*without us. We feel left alone with our grief. Although this
period seems empty and meaningless, we are moving towards a
resolution, a letting-go of the loved one and an acknowledge-
ment that our lives will never be the same again. It is during this
phase that we reach a turning point. If we make a decision to
move forward with our lives, knowing that things have
irrevocably changed, we will start to feel the first glimmer of
hope for the future. Sexually, at this time, it is difficult to be
intimate, and any sexual advances made towards us can feel
intrusive and aggressive.*

● **The turning point:** *this is the fourth stage in the grieving
process and is a healing phase during which we begin to
establish our new identity and relinquish roles which tie us to
the past. As we begin to accept that the past is over, our life force
and natural optimism will begin to resurface. On a personal
level, we will now forgive ourselves and the loved one for dying,
and begin to let go of them. We may find ourselves seeking out
new friends and a more realistic picture of the deceased person
will replace the often idealistic portrait we have, which has
enabled us us to cope with the loss so far. Sexually, we can now
seek new partners, practices and adventures without feeling
shackled to the past and without feeling guilty about enjoying
our life.*

● **Renewal:** *at this stage we recognize that slowly we have come to
grips with a world which no longer includes the person for
whom we are grieving. We experience a surge of self-awareness
and confront our loneliness and isolation, realizing that we don't
have to be beaten by them. We begin to live again, and to feel an
emotional independence from the loved one we have lost. Now*

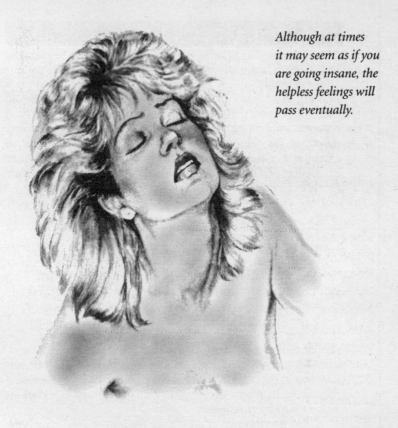

*Although at times
it may seem as if you
are going insane, the
helpless feelings will
pass eventually.*

*we can reach out and accept new people and relationships. We
also begins to experience a greater perception of the long process
of grieving.*

Many relationships break up after the death of a child. The role of
the father and mother are often very separate, and while this can
and does work effectively when things are going well, when
things go wrong it can cause communication to break down.

LONELINESS

Loneliness is being alone and not liking it, or being with others and still feeling alone. Researchers have drawn a distinction between two types of loneliness know as "trait loneliness" and "state loneliness". Trait loneliness is the most serious and involves permanent feelings of loneliness. State loneliness describes the temporary feelings of loneliness that we all experience now and then, for example when we are somewhere unfamiliar or far away from friends. Everyone becomes state lonely from time to time. Only a few are trait lonely.

What causes loneliness?

Loneliness results from a discrepancy between the number of relationships or social contacts that you have and the number that you want, irrespective of the absolute number itself. So if you feel you need two friends and you have two, then you will not feel lonely.

The feeling of loneliness can be brought about by anything that lowers our self-esteem and increases our need for other people. One piece of research, for example, found that teenagers often felt lonely at weekends – not because they saw their friends less than at other times, but because they expected to be seeing them more than on a week night. It is a question of expectations rather than objective reality.

Another factor that affects our feelings of loneliness is the way that we feel about ourselves. Anything that makes you feel good about yourself can have the effect of making you feel less lonely in the short term. It does not have to be the company of other people that brings it about – it can just as easily be a piece of good news or a job well done that helps to reduce loneliness.

But loneliness is not just a question of our state of mind. If we move to another town, we will probably feel lonely fairly soon because we have fewer social contacts, but this will not necessarily make us feel bad about ourselves as a result, because we blame the loneliness on the situation rather than on ourselves. We can see that it is quite natural to be lonely in this situation and that it has nothing to do with our personal qualities.

Some lonely people, however, lack the skills and interact easily with others. To outsiders, they seem to be uninterested in other people, when really thay are just awkward or shy. If this is the case, the problem may require more drastic solutions and there are therapists who are trained to improve social skills. Coping successfully with loneliness is made possible and more effective by a person's belief that he or she has control over the factors which have caused it.

Long-term loneliness

Sadly, some people become so used to being rejected that they become chronically lonely – they turn into lonely personalities. They develop a style of behaviour and thinking that cuts them off from other people. Their self-esteem is so low that they always blame their loneliness on themselves, seeing it as a permanent feature of their make-up and one that they can do little to change.

Researchers have identified a set of behaviours called "sad passivity" that some lonely people show. What this means, essentially, is a type of helpless, hopeless inactivity. Sad passivity is characterized by overeating, oversleeping, watching television non-stop, crying, drinking alcohol and taking tranquilizers.

Lonely people of this type have often decided that their loneliness is a permanent state, which is due to their own style of behavior and is uncontrollable. They feel that they may as well involve themselves with things that will help them to forget it.

Men, often trained to carefully hide their emotions, can appear stoic and wooden, and appear to have no grief at all, and women, more conditioned to a nurturing role, now need to be nurtured themselves. If the woman turns to her husband or partner for support and finds that he is withdrawn and unable to communicate, this is often misinterpreted as lack of love for the child – or worse, for her. There seems to be no way to bridge the communication gap and the couple's sex life may begin to suffer because the ability to trust or feel close has now been lost.

There is no time limit on grief, and no correct length of time to remain in any one stage. Some people find that they have become stuck in grief, and feel overwhelmed. There are professional grief counsellors who can help people who feel this way. Most bereavement counselors have been bereaved themselves and can offer a listening service which perhaps nobody else can. Ultimately, however, it is time which is the great healer.

Staying single

One result of the sexual revolution is that more people are choosing to stay single. Now that marriage is no longer a requirement for a full sexual relationship, and illegitimacy no longer carries any great social stigma in most Western societies, people are thinking long and hard about the question of marriage.

It is no longer automatic to consider marrying even if you are deeply in love. In fact, many financially independent people are not even sure that they want to live with anyone. Be sexually involved, in love, be committed to – yes. But share living space? That requires more thought.

Sex by yourself can feel very lonely sometimes, but very comforting at others.

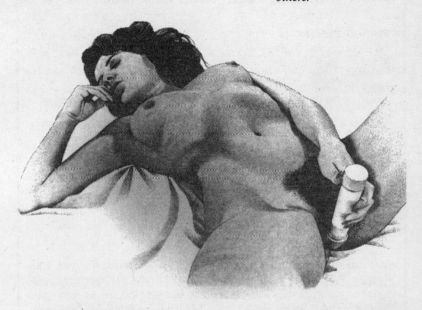

The image of people who choose to be single is slowly changing. But it is still seen differently for men and women. While men may be considered to be carefree bachelors "on the loose" and keeping their options open, single women are still thought by some to be "on the shelf" – single because no one will have them.

The ironic thing about society's attitude to the male and female singles is that in reality the roles are reversed. Far from enjoying their single status, research has shown that single men

STAYING SINGLE

Both men and women today are finding that far from being a daunting prospect, staying single may actually be desirable. Here are just some of the advantages and drawbacks of the single life:

	PROS:	**CONS:**
Men:	More disposable income	Childlessness
	More career mobility	Possible loneliness
	No commitments	Social stigma: "homosexual"
	More sexual freedom	
Women:	Option of further education	Possible childlessness or
	Greater career choice	single motherhood
	No domestic obligations	Less financial security
	Freedom to travel	Possible loneliness
		Social stigma: "old maid"

Many of the advantages of staying single are the same for men and women. Both have the freedom in terms of work, leisure time and travel to do what they like, when they like and exactly as they like. Similarly, the main disadvantages – not having a family of their own and potential loneliness – are also true for both sexes.

Financially, the issue does have slightly different implications in that single women are more likely to be discriminated against. However, they may have advantages in this area if they marry and subsequently divorce.

Interestingly, research has shown that men who marry do come out of it better in some areas than women. They tend to be more healthy and more successful in their careers than their single male counterparts. However, it seems that for women – especially those in their mid-thirties – the reverse is true. They are likely to be more successful and wealthy if they remain single.

in their late twenties and early thirties are a conspicuously unhappy group – far less content than married men of the same age. Further research has shown that single women of the same age are much happier than their married counterparts.

Quite why this should be has never been made clear, but it must be partly to do with the fact that couples, married or simply living together, still tend to fall into their traditional roles. So a married man is "looked after", free to concern himself with his job and his own needs, with all domestic arrangements taken care of. A married woman – even if she has a full-time job – has the additional responsibility of the home and possibly children to fit in where she can.

There are people who make a statement quite early on that they are going to remain single, and then stick to it. But the rest, even those for whom staying single is definitely a matter of choice, are rarely so categorical. What they have in common though is a reluctance to compromise by becoming involved in a relationship they know not to be right, just for the sake of not being on their own.

Most people who choose to remain by themselves, rather than marrying or living with someone, do so because they are prepared to wait for the right person to come along. Consequently, determined "singles" are usually far more confident and secure in themselves than people who feel incomplete when they are not half of a couple.

Well-adjusted single people have a lot going for them. They are not bored or frightened by their own company. They can control their social life, seeing people when and where they choose, which is not always the case with couples.

They do not have to do anything they do not want to, and can indulge themselves regardless of what anyone else thinks.

Some single people – used to making their own decisions – find the idea of consulting and debating with a partner irritating. It can be one of the hardest adjustments to make if they finally do decide to marry or live with someone, and it can be a source of friction.

Fear of commitment

Not all people make the decision to remain single for "healthy" reasons. Some are terrified of the idea of commitment – either because of events in their childhood, or because of past relationships which have gone wrong. But even when singleness results from fear of commitment, it is not necessarily a bad thing. Some people are genuinely happier alone than they would be if they were living with a partner.

Others, though, long for the mythical perfect lover who will never let them down, yet are scared to give any one a chance. For them being single is a matter of choice but not a happy one.

Most people who are single by choice live a normal social life, the only difference being that they do not have a partner in tow. Long-term singles will probably find they actually prefer to see their single friends, but may find it hard when they drop away, as they turn into couples.

Many of the people who start out wanting to remain single may change their minds over the years, perhaps when the right person comes along, or they change their idea about what the right person should be like or they realize that they want a child.

Some people, however, are happy to remain single throughout their lives and, by relying on themselves and no one else, are able to build a life that is rich and rewarding and exactly tailored to their desires.

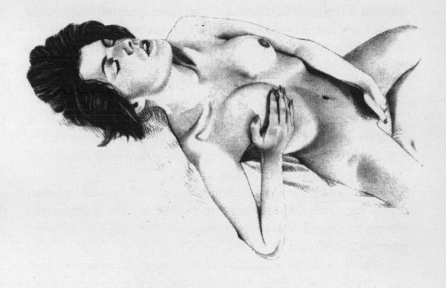

Being single means having the freedom to choose when you want to have an orgasm rather than waiting for somone else to provide it.

Bisexuality

Bisexuals are people who are equally attracted sexually to both men and women. This completely balanced sexual preference actually applies to relatively few people. But there are still many others who, although they are predominantly attracted to one sex, do recognize the attraction of the other.

Most people's idea of a practising bisexual is of someone who sets up with a homosexual and heterosexual at the same time. This is called troilism, and in fact it is very rare.

A bisexual who is genuinely equally attracted to both sexes is still most likely to be in a single close relationship with one partner – homosexual or heterosexual. He or she may, however, seek sexual gratification with a member of the opposite sex.

Practising bisexuals often have a number of explanations for why they need partners of both sexes, but their reasons can be broadly divided into two main areas – sexual and emotional. These are of course, interrelated.

Many men, for example, find that with a male partner there is less emotional baggage, and they are able to achieve an equality as "good friends". Women, on the other hand often report that while sex with their male partner may have become mechanical, with no sensuality or spontaneity, with a woman the entire process is about "making love", and giving each other pleasure.

Recognizing your bisexual nature is one thing, acting upon it is quite another. Even nowadays openly living as a bisexual is fraught with obstacles and difficulties. If a relationship does not "just happen", to set out to form a new attachment to someone of your own sex usually means venturing into the gay world, and if you are a bisexual who is socially heterosexual that can be an unnerving, alarming or even distasteful experience that could make it difficult to search for a partner.

Where bisexuals are involved with either entirely heterosexual or homosexual partners there is also the problem that the people they are closely involved with may be out of sympathy with their sexual orientation.

Bisexuals who choose to continue relationships with both sexes often compartmentalize their natures, getting different things from their homosexual and heterosexual partners. They need to do this rather than look for one person who offers it all. For some people this proves to be an entirely satisfactory and successful way to operate and conduct their lives.

❖

A to Z
of
Love
Play

■ *Introduction*

For sex to stay exciting in a long-term relationship, both partners should use their imaginations and be prepared to experiment. Fantasy role-playing can be highly erotic – although there will be times when you will both collapse on the carpet in fits of giggles!

Try to think yourself into each role, as any good actor would do. Be a little mysterious. Surprise your partner. Keep him or her guessing.

Some of the love play suggestions in our A to Z may strike you as far-fetched, but your partner might find the same ones intensely arousing. Take your pick. Close your eyes and open the pages at random then try whichever one is shown. Or make up your own love-play situations, based on fantasies your partner and you particularly enjoy.

■ *After-sun Sex*

How can you plan for a really sensual holiday? Flirting on the beach is a popular pastime. Try wearing clothes that particularly appeal to each other. Men could try buying their partner a nice swimsuit or bikini. Women could dare their partner to wear a sexy thong on the beach. Try flaunting your sexy beachwear in front of each other by lying in provocative positions and walking around in a sensual manner. You can do this quite discreetly – no one else need realize.

Try to extend the excitement. Rub in suntan oil as erotically as you dare all over each other, inflaming your longing.

After hours of luxuriating in the warm sun and being rubbed down you'll both feel an urgent need to make love. Hot and distinctly flustered, you rush back to your hotel knowing full well

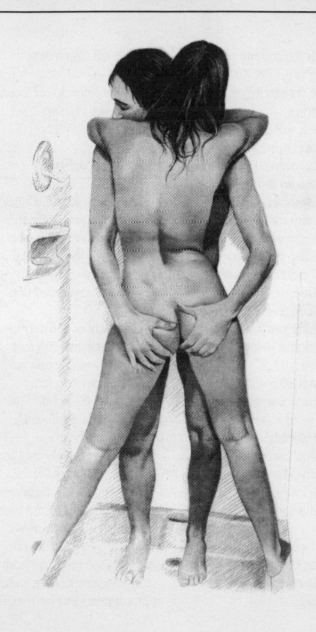

that the first thing you want to do is fling yourselves at each other. But try extending the agony further, because the lovemaking will be so much stronger and impassioned.

Slowly undress each other and take a cool shower together. You can take it in turns to soap each other down, paying special attention to the genitals. Linger over them a little bit longer than usual. This is a huge tease for many people. Then let the jets of water prickle your naked flesh as you embrace behind the curtain.

If you have a shower en-suite then the intimacy will be wonderful – if it is a shared one the sense of naughtiness will add an edge. Many people find the slippery warmth of a wet body deliciously erotic.

Leaving your skin slightly damp, then dabbing on lotion, is a highly charged way of prolonging the interlude before you get down to serious lovemaking.

You fall onto the bed entwined in each other's arms, lips passionately glued together and tongues probing.

■ Al Fresco Fun

A picnic on a summer's day is the perfect aphrodisiac for lovers whose sexual palates have become jaded with the constant round of work, household chores and family duties.

A delicious leisurely lunch of gourmet food with fine wine will put you in the mood for love, and now you have nothing left to do but devote the rest of the day to each other.

Lay close to one another and shut your eyes, let the warmth of the sun caress your skin, and breathe in the heady fragrance of the cool sweet grass mingled with the familiar smell of your partner's body.

If you have chosen a shady spot, remove your partner's

shirt or T-shirt and watch the dappled light play on his warm smooth skin.

Write secret messages on each other's bodies using twigs, blades of grass or pine cones, or revert to simple childhood pleasures like making daisy chains.

Undress as much as you dare, but remember that ramblers and curious children can seek out lovers in the most secret of places.

If she has come prepared, wearing a loose, voluminous skirt, he can slide his hand up into the soft regions of her thighs, lingering on the aspect of pleasure and caressing her sensitive skin with a plucked flower head.

Tickle her until she cries out for mercy, or until she slides her own hand into the fly of your jeans, making you groan with desire.

Thus hidden by long grass, thick bushes or a clump of trees, you can make love to the sound of the wind rustling in the leaves. Let your inhibitions drift away with the summer breeze and enjoy the warm sensation of the sun on your skin, the hard earth beneath you and the deep blue eternity of the sky above.

■ Arabian Loving 1

The sixteenth-century Eastern sex annal *The Perfumed Garden* cites eleven classic Arab positions for intercourse. Here are some of them:

● *"Make the woman lie upon her back, her thighs raised, then getting between her legs, introduce your member to her. Pressing your toes to the ground, you can move in her in a convenient, measured way."*

● *"If your member is short, let the woman lie on her back, lift her legs into the air so that they are as near her ears as possible, and in this position,* with her buttocks lifted up, her vulva will project forward."

● "Let the woman stretch herself upon the ground, and place yourself between her thighs. Then, putting one of her legs upon your shoulder and the other under your arm near the armpit, get into her."

● "Make her get down on her knees and elbows, as if kneeling in prayer. In this position the vulva is projected backwards. You then attack her from that side and put your member into her."

● "Place the woman on her side and squat between her thighs, with one of her legs on your shoulder and the other between your thighs, while she remains lying on her side. Then you enter her vagina and make her move by drawing her towards your chest."

● "Let her stretch herself on the ground, on her back with her legs crossed. Then mount her like a cavalier on horseback, being on your knees, while her legs are placed under her thighs."

● "Place the woman so that she leans with her front, or if you prefer it her back upon a low divan, with her feet set upon the ground. She thus offers her vulva to the introduction of your member"

● "Let her lie upon her back on the ground with a cushion under her posterior. Then, getting between her legs and letting her place the sole of her right foot against the sole of her left foot, introduce your member."

■ Arabian Loving 2

Sheik Nefzawi, author of *The Perfumed Garden*, believed that every "act of combat" should end in orgasm for both partners. Here are some of the more popular positions he recommended, derived from his readings of Indian scripts.

● *Pounding on the spot. The man sits down with his legs stretched out. The woman then sits astride his thighs, supporting herself on her hands, crossing her legs behind the man's back.*

She positions the entrance to her vagina opposite his penis and guides it into her entrance. She now places her arms around his neck and he holds her sides and waist, helping her to rise and fall upon his penis.

● *The screw of Archimedes. The man lies stretched out on his back. The woman sits on his penis, facing him, and holds herself upon her hands to make sure that her stomach does not touch his.*

The movement of the woman is up and down, and, if the man is fit, he can assist her from below.

● *The stopperage. As this position can be painful for the woman, Nefzawi only recommends it if the man's member is short or "soft". Place the woman on her back with a cushion under her buttocks. The man kneels between her legs and bends her thighs against her chest as far as possible. The man can now place his penis in her vagina. At the moment of ejaculation the man should draw the woman towards himself.*

● *The tail of the ostrich. The woman lies on her back and the man kneels in front of her. He lifts up her legs until only her head and shoulders remain in contact with the bed. He enters her vagina and holds onto her buttocks.*

Movement is created by his pushing and pulling on her buttocks.

■ Art Lovers

Visit an art exhibition with your partner. Arrive separately, and don't acknowledge each other. By pre-arrangement, though, neither of you should be wearing any underwear. If you are sufficiently daring, the woman could also wear a very short skirt.

Wander around looking at sensual works of art such as luscious eighteenth-century

nude paintings of voluptuous women reclining on sofas; brush past each other as if by accident. Drop your catalogue at an appropriate moment and bend down to pick it up, when only your partner is looking, giving him a tantalizing glimpse up your skirt.

When you've both done enough looking and want to progress to some touching, grab your lover by the hand and rush home to create your own works of art.

■ *Artist and Model*

Painting your lover naked is an interesting experience. Whether you have artistic talent or not, it is an extremely sensual exercise and can be highly erotic and very satisfying.

It is an erotic experience for the "model" too, to have such care and attention lavished upon their form as they lie comfortably and quietly in a warm room.

Choose any medium you like – charcoal, poster paints, pastels. With brightly coloured kids' paints, you can go for an abstract, pop-art style figure, with pencil or pen a simple sketch, with oils a more traditional style of painting.

Set up your equipment, then, making sure the room is warm enough for your partner to sit nude, decide upon a pose. It must be comfortable if it is to be held for more than five minutes, so reclining on a bed or sofa is perhaps the one to go for, with lots of cushions for support. Cover the surface he or she is to lie on with a plain sheet or blanket so the background is not a distraction.

You will be looking at your partner in a new way, and may well discover aspects of them which seem unfamiliar – a mole here, a patch of darker skin there – it's not a question of having been inattentive before, just that now you are forced to look at every inch and reproduce it on paper.

As soon as you arrive at a sketch you are happy with, you can start to paint. As your colours start to bring the picture to life, your passion will begin to rise. The delicate bloom of the skin, the smooth tautness of the muscles or the dark shock of pubic hair, might just be enough to distract you from your work of art.

Give in to the urge, as artists are entitled to be wild and impetuous, and make dirty, painty love to your muse on the studio floor.

■ *Barnyard Fun*

Never forget that making love can be wholesome as well as naughty, so don't be ashamed to face the open sky and declare your sultry passion.

You may want to become the lord and lady of the manor, dressing in smart day clothes and surveying your fields when suddenly the urge to make love strikes and you take each other up against a tree. Or you could be a farming couple, going about your chores in rustic overalls, hats and boots when you are overcome by incontrollable desire.

The best thing is being there – you can actually go on holiday and revel in the perfect pastoral setting – but you can pretend just as well in your own home or back yard.

For play at home, why not buy a bale of hay and scatter it around the yard over a plastic sheet so that it is easy to clear up afterwards. Or, if you intend to play in the daytime and your yard is too exposed, clear a space and lay the sheet and hay on your kitchen or living-room floor.

Of course, you'll want to look as though you've just got back from an exhilarating horse ride across open country. Dress perhaps in riding clothes – for her, jodhpurs, barbour coat, tall shiny boots and perhaps a lacy camisole underneath; for him, tight jeans, casual shirt carelessly unbuttoned to the waist, a big leather belt and boots.

When the erotic urge strikes, let it consume you entirely as you tear off each others' clothes in a frenzy. One partner can take a strong lead and pull the other down onto the hay.

The man may want to tear open the woman's blouse and hungrily suck her breasts. The woman might then push him down on the hay as she greedily makes a grab for him. Now the scene is set, just let nature take its course and enjoy your farmyard frolic!

■ Bikes and Sex

Speed is an aphrodisiac, and a fast ride in an open road, coupled with the proximity of the leather-clad pillion passenger is a certain recipe for arousal ...

Start by sliding provocatively back and forth on the leather saddle of your partner's motorbike to adjust your position. Then begin a slow langorous striptease, easing yourself as sexily as you can out of your clothes until you are on the bike saddle in nothing but your underwear.

Let him come to you and, as he does so, spin round to sit side-saddle, wrapping your legs around his waist, and running your fingers up and down his spine. Kiss his lips, nibble his earlobes and breathe hot passionate words into his ears.

His hands may be dirty, but don't back off – let him cover you with his greasy fingers, touching your face, your breasts, your thighs. Hold him tightly, writhing under his oily touch, until he succumbs, and starts to remove his own clothing.

While he undresses, lay back on the tank and slide your fingers into your panties and down towards your clitoris. Masturbate in front of him until he is hard and erect, then let him straddle the bike as though he were about to ride it.

With his body leaning forward over yours, his hands clutching the rubber handle grips, guide his penis into you. Then, with your legs twined around his back, and your hands on his shoulders, you can start to move slowly in time with one another.

As he is in the riding position, he will have the pleasure of watching you both reflected in the chrome of the handlebars and in the wing mirrors of the bike.

Of course, you can change position if you choose – you could try sitting face to face or with woman on top, but any change should be effected carefully so as not to rock the bike.

■ Blindfold Games

If sight is taken away, even for a short period of time, we can "see" with our other senses more fully and intensely. First explore your sense of touch. Try different textures to tantalize your partner.

Feathers, and bits of velvet, silk and linen are good to start with. Have your partner lie on his or her back and then slowly begin to tickle the back of their neck. Work your way down the length of their spine with feather-like strokes, then heavier brush strokes.

Tickle the back of their calves with a bit of velvet, alternating with the other materials. Try brushing his or her buttocks with a soft baby brush.

Now turn them over to stimulate their sensitive front. For her: lightly dust her nipples and the areas around her breasts with a piece of linen. Its slightly rough texture will make her tingle. For him: wind a piece of silk loosely around his penis and slowly unwind it.

Brush the insides of their legs with wide, gentle strokes. Come seductively close to their genitals and then change tactics when they least expect it.

A deep and lingering massage using deliciously scented oil can be all the more sensual when the recipient is wearing a blindfold.

Alternatively, have your partner wait in a darkened room blindfolded as you raid the kitchen. Place little morsels of food in their mouth, or perhaps just smear them across their lips for a brief moment. If they like the food, you can feed them more of it in tiny bits. Tease them with kisses in between these bites.

Try making love to your partner while he or she is blindfolded. The new sensations which this can bring can be quite amazing. Keep feathers, scarves and scented oils handy so that you can carry on the love play, if you wish, or pop on a blindfold yourself and join in the fun.

■ *Body Painting*

Before you start, make sure you have bought special washable non-toxic body paint. Also, don't paint each other's most sensitive areas, as very tender skin can react to the paint. Areas to avoid are the tip of the penis and the woman's genitals, as well as the eyes and mouth.

Try following the contours of the body to make great swirls of colour. Or incorporate features of the body as part of your design. You can make a face using the nipples as eyes and the belly button as a mouth. Or you can use the nipples as the centre of a flower, painting petals radiating from it.

Concentrate on one small area – maybe one that you know to be especially erotic – or cover your lover's entire body with colour. For those

with a taste for something bolder, try making the navel into another vagina.

The fun of body painting is seeing the results as well as in the feeling the sensations involved, so it appeals to both tactile and visual senses

You could do your body painting in your bathroom. When the sensation starts to drive you crazy, you can make love right there, while the water washes you clean.

Of course, you may not want to see your artwork washed off right away, and you may want to take care what positions you use for lovemaking. If you've both painted each other's fronts then try making love in a seated position, both leaning slightly away from each other. Keep the lights on to enjoy the sight of your lover's body highlighted in bright colors.

But once you start making love, you may get too turned on to be so careful. It can be just as much fun to rub against each other, smearing your paints as you make love. This can be especially exciting if you've both painted naked figures or genitals on each other. The paintings then make love as you do.

■ Bondage

One of the great sexual fantasies of all time, bondage can be wildly erotic and deeply passionate, adding a hint of danger, spice and abandon to your lovemaking.

The idea is not to hurt, or even create discomfort, but simply to immobilize your partner, making them completely helpless and at your mercy.

Choose soft materials as bindings – silken dressing-gown cords, featherlight chiffon scarves, stockings or strips of lace and don't tie them too tight. You can theme it – the adventurous can use climbing ropes, naughty schoolgirls or boys can use ties; many sex shops sell handcuffs that are fabric or fur-lined so the metal does not cut into your wrists. But make sure you don't lose the key.

For him: his whole body is yours to explore and discover as he lies there bound and helpless. You can tempt and tease to your heart's desire. There is no need even to touch him.

You have the power to inflame him simply by being there. Undress in front of him, or dress up in something he really likes. Then run your fingers up and down the length of his body.

The fact that he cannot reciprocate will drive him wild. When you know he can hold out no longer, give in to him, and guide him inside you.

For her: her body is open to you, and you have the power to please or deny. Cover her with kisses; let her feel the weight of your body on hers. Tease her with your tongue and give her the pleasure of long and sensual oral sex. Then enter her, and watch her pleasure as it mingles with the sweet frustration of being unable to touch your body.

Whichever kind of bondage you choose, the most important thing is to remember that it should be a pleasure for you both. Should either of you wish to stop – have a prearranged code word which means "stop, untie me immediately", and have a knife or sharp pair of scissors to hand, in case of a real emergency.

■ Boss and Secretary

Is your fantasy a smouldering vamp of a secretary, oozing sexuality? Or a powerful, sexy boss who transforms her- or himself at a moment's notice into an electrifying lover? Then, why not act out the scene with your partner at home.

Scenario 1: it is very warm in the office, and you find your secretary's proximity disconcerting. Her heady perfume fills the air and, as she leans forward, you find that your eyes are level with her breasts. You try to move away, but suddenly she is behind you massaging your shoulders.

She loosens your tie, and slides her fingers down between your shirt and your skin. You are being seduced, and there is nothing to do but surrender.

She removes your clothes, and covers your body with kisses, teasing your nipples with her teeth and running her tongue down towards your genitals. She takes your penis in her mouth, tracing patterns along it with her tongue.

When you are about to orgasm, you find yourself beneath her. She takes your penis inside her, and begins to gyrate, while your body explodes in an orgasm.

Scenario 2: your boss calls you into her office to ask your opinion on some photos for a lingerie advertising campaign.

As you look through, the pictures become more wanton and, embarrassed, you feel yourself becoming aroused by them.

Your boss leans closer. You are almost finished when suddenly she takes you by the arms and pushes you down onto a chair, kissing you hard on the lips.

Before you have recovered your senses, her hand slides up your thighs and rubs against your erect penis, before moving up to unfasten your trousers and slowly slide the zipper down.

Your boss pulls your trousers down then lifts her skirt to reveal her stockings and crotchless panties. Then she climbs onto your knee, kneeling either side of your hips on the chair, and lowers herself onto you to make love wildly and passionately.

426 BREAKFAST IN BED

■ Breakfast in Bed

There are few simple
pleasures greater than a lazy
Sunday spent in bed with your
partner. But busy lives make
such lounging a luxury.
Whether your peace is
shattered by children, or
unsocial working hours, the
mornings you can call your
own are rare.

To make the most of your
time together, tease your
partner from the depths of
slumber with a breakfast
banquet in bed.

Whatever your preference
for a morning meal, make it
bite-sized and instantly edible.
And choose food which will
give you energy, rather than
send you back to sleep again.

As it's more likely to be
brunch than breakfast, finely
cut cold meats, like honey roast
ham, Parma ham and turkey,
make great appetizers. Served
with chilled melon, olives or
rye bread, they make a
wonderful start to the day.

Select your food for the
look as much as the taste.
Asparagus is a traditional
aphrodisiac, but gained its
reputation possibly more for
the phallic shape than any
magical properties.

Cooked in advance and
arranged individually on
plates, together with two cherry
tomatoes and a large sprig of
parsley, they may just amuse
and excite enough to effect
your partner's libido.

Hot coffee, tea, freshly
squeezed orange juice, lox and
scrambled eggs, and Bucks
Fizz, can turn breakfast into a
leisurely feast.

And bear in mind that the
food you prepare may not
necessarily be just for eating.
Not only can you titillate by
suggestive presentation, but
you can use each dish as a
prelude to yet more
lovemaking.

If yogurt is on the menu,
don't restrict it to the pots. It is
the perfect natural
accompaniment to oral sex.

Grab a towel from the bathroom to save the sheets, then pour, spoon or finger the yogurt over your partner's genitals. Hold them while they squeal in response to the cool and creamy liquid, then slowly and meticulously lick the yogurt off their body.

■ Butler

Arrange an evening – or a weekend – when he has to do everything you say and fulfill your every whim. When you come in from work, there must be a delicious candlelit meal on the table and mellow music on the stereo. Ask him to pour you a glass of wine and give you a footrub before you sit down to eat. He is your servant for the evening, and bound to do as you say.

After dinner, you could demand that he runs you a fragrant bath and washes you from head to toe. And what better, after your bath, than a sensual massage on the rug in front of the fire?

After that, just instruct him to do whatever you feel like – maybe you are in the mood to have him kiss all the way up your legs, tease your nipples and stroke your bottom, before moving on to direct genital stimulation. And when you are making love, tell him exactly what positions, speed and mood you want – and you choose how long it has to continue!

■ Cabaret!

Recapture the essence of sexual freedom in pre-war Berlin with its nightclubs and smoky caverns where life was one long cabaret. Watch the movie *Cabaret* starring Liza Minnelli to put you in the mood.

You enter the stage and are blinded by the spotlight, which follows your every move as you sing to the assembled crowd.

They appreciate the spectacle, with its raunchy songs and suggestive gyrations, and applaud you loudly, while the top-hatted MC in the corner of the stage adds his own lewd comments to the proceedings.

Around midnight the place is packed, and you play to the throng. Your verbal sex play with the MC increases, and the more daring it becomes, the more the crowd cheer.

By 4am the tables have emptied and the last of the stragglers are sitting up at the bar. The MC joins you in a final duet, his lithe body perched on the edge of a chair. You approach him, and swinging your stockinged leg over onto his lap, entwine your body around his in the most explicit manner, continuing your song.

The MC reaches around your basque, and slowly pulls it undone to expose your breasts, which he then starts to kiss, while the music plays on.

You reach down and slide your hand between his legs, where you can feel his penis harden between your fingers, and with dexterity you work your way into his stage costume.

You take his penis into your mouth, teasing it gently with your tongue until he is on the brink of orgasm. Then, before he comes, you pull off the red panties that form part of your costume and, still astride his lap, take his penis inside you.

Moving in rhythm to the music and still bathed in the spotlight, your hands feel their way over every inch of his body, while he kisses you with passion. You can feel the eyes of the remaining clients watching you appreciatively, enjoying the impromptu spectacle.

■ *Camera Shy?*

Before you start you need to know where you are going to

get your photographs developed – if you have access to a darkroom, or a Polaroid camera, you are free to take as daring photographs as you like, but if you are taking your film to a standard laboratory you will have to be more restrained. As a rule, if it is permitted on television, it is permitted in your prints.

With a Polaroid camera, the results are instant. You have no control over the lighting – a flash will fire if the camera senses there is not enough light. But the slightly fuzzy quality of your final print can work to your advantage. Curves and lines are softened and flattered, and the flash tends to even out the tones of the skin.

Compact cameras with built-in flashes are the easiest to use as the settings are automatic and they regulate everything for you, but this often means you have no control over the results. Why not stretch a black stocking

over the lens? This gives a soft focus effect to the prints.

Single lens reflex 35mm cameras are the most flexible and can be used for artistic shots, but again, the lighting is of prime importance. Use natural daylight if you can, experimenting with shadows to create areas of light and dark across the body.

Often, simplicity is the best policy, and spontaneous snaps work well. Pick a moment when your partner is particularly happy and relaxed, then just snap away. Encourage them to pose in clothes they feel comfortable in – a silk dressing gown that slips casually off her shoulder or a small towel wound round his waist.

Then once you have warmed them up, you can start to direct a little more carefully. If they are dressed, for example, ask them to remove an article of clothing very slowly, and take a series of photographs to give you a frame-by-frame striptease show you can enjoy at any time.

■ Card Games

The most famous of all erotic card games is the traditional strip poker. This can be played using any form of poker game, in which you bluff your opponent into thinking that the five-card hand you hold is the highest around the table.

However the object is always the same – the loser on each round has to remove an item of clothing, while the winner is the one who manages to retain their modesty the longest.

The thrill of the game is the ultimate aphrodisiac, as each hand played brings you closer to what is to come.

The best clothes to wear are, for him, boxer shorts, button-fly jeans and a front fastening shirt. For her, layer the clothes on top of the right underwear. Choose a basque or bra and panties rather than a teddy.

Stockings with a suspender belt are a better choice than tights, and they count as three items, not one! Finish with an easily removable blouse together with a skirt or button-fly jeans.

Once you have succeeded in gambling all the clothes from your partner's body (or lost all of your own), why not prolong the anticipation and play on for forfeits and favours. This time the loser, has to perform an act dictated by the winner, the cards enabling you to enjoy a new kind of foreplay.

You can be as chaste as you like – a kiss on the cheek, a stroke of the thigh – and you work up to the more exciting favors until the game becomes a secondary consideration.

Alternatively you could play for just one big favour – the loser becomes the winner's slave for the night. The winner can then decide when and where to make love, which position, or combination of positions to use, and how long you have to make love for.

■ *Chinese Sex 1*

When the Yellow Emperor inquired of his goddess-instructress, the Wise Maiden,

as to how the right mood for love could be induced, she advised him to follow the "Five Natural Humours of the Male".

The first "natural humour" was to be relaxed and unassuming, the second to be generous of spirit, the third to be controlled in breathing and the fourth to be serene in body. The fifth humour – a desire for solitude brought on by feelings of loyalty – was the only legitimate excuse a man could give for the failure of his Jade Stem (penis) to stiffen.

The Wise Maiden proceeded to advise the Yellow Emperor to be guided by the Five Responses of the Female. First, when she became flushed, the man should approach her. Then, as her nipples rose and beads of perspiration appeared on her nose, he would know his advances were welcome.

The next stage in the Chinese sexual act was foreplay. This held great importance for the Taoist Masters, who believed that only if the Yin and Yang forces were stirred slowly into action could they reach full potency.

After the initial embraces came more intimate touching, with the woman fondling the man's Jade Stem and causing her own Yin essence to flow.

The man should allow his Jade Stem to hover over the Cinnabar Gate (vagina) while kissing the woman lovingly and gazing down at her Golden Gully. He should stroke her breasts and stomach while allowing his Male Peak to flick the sides of the Examination Hall (labia) and caress the Jewel Terrace (clitoral area). And if necessary, he should kiss and lick the Pearl on the Jade Step (clitoris) to ensure that the Yin essences were thoroughly stirred before the Clouds and the Rain (intercourse).

As the Jade Pavilion reached full lubrication, so the man should plunge ever deeper, slanting to the left and right, sweeping in circular motion, and alternating deep thrusts with shallow strokes.

■ *Chinese Sex 2*

Retiring to the bedchamber in the wrong mood is the most common cause of impotence. This advice, given by the Wise Maiden to the Emperor Won Hung Lo more than 5000 years ago, is as worthy of note today as it was then.

Pillow books suggest setting the scene with care. In ancient China erotic wallhangings, subdued lights and scented sheets were employed to create a romantic atmosphere.

In a modern context, this means thinking about simple touches such as subtle lighting, plenty of pillows or perhaps glossy satin sheets – all of which can transform a bedroom into a warm inviting love nest.

Soothing background music helps too, and with a modern hi-fi you can go one better than the wealthy lovers of the Orient, who frequently had a maidservant stand nearby reciting poetry while they made love.

In their teachings Taoist philosophers accept that one or even both partners might feel hesitant or inhibited. To overcome this they suggest that couples, before even touching each other, place a pillow book on the bed and look through it together.

This way, the more hesitant partner – in ancient China, it would probably be a shy young bride – can become aroused without too much performance pressure.

The pillow books recommend that a couple move on from this stage of subtle excitement of the senses to more direct stimulation only when they have let each other know they are fully aroused.

Starting with general caresses and the whispering of sweet words, a man is then advised to move on to kissing the breasts and the Jade Step (clitoris) until the time is right to begin his assault on the Jade Pavilion (vagina).

Taoist sexual teaching can have many benefits. When a couple set out together to explore each other's bodies in a playful and relaxed way, the pressure to "perform" is removed and both partners can let their senses take over.

■ Correspondents

This works particularly well for partners who are temporarily separated – perhaps one has business in another city. But you could also write to a partner that you live with or see regularly, and leave the letter in a place where only they will find it.

There are several forms your letter can take. It could be a sensuous description of a love-making session you both enjoyed very much. It could be a fantasy that you would like to try one day, or a far-fetched fantasy that you would never dare to attempt in reality. One particularly erotic type of letter would be a detailed list of everything you are going to do to your partner the very next time you see them. You might start:
"When we meet tomorrow night, the first thing I am going to do is give you a long, luscious kiss . . ." and then go on to describe the parts of their body you want to lick, stroke nibble and caress. You'll find that by the time you meet, your partner will be more than ready to let you have your way.

■ Cops and Robbers

Knock loudly on your partner's door and when he or she answers, say "Freeze! You're under arrest. Move inside and face the wall with your hands where I can see them." You may wish to use props like a toy gun or even a policeman's uniform from a costume-rental store.

With your leg, move your partner's legs apart as they face the wall, and get them to put their hands high up against the wall. Do a thorough body search, on top of their clothing, patting and rubbing up the inside leg, round the crotch and bottom and up to their arms, looking for concealed weapons. Once you're finished though, announce that it is not enough – they could be hiding contraband in a more intimate place and you'll have to strip search them.

You should then order them to strip while you watch to see they don't make any sudden movements or try to escape, and insist they take off every last item of clothing. Then your search proper can begin. Feel carefully in every crevice of your partner's body,

making sure your search is very thorough.

When you have finished, produce a set of handcuffs and cuff their hands behind their back. Sex shops often have fur- or fabric-lined cuffs that don't hurt the wrists. Once they are cuffed, march them off to "jail" for further searches of an even more intimate nature.

■ *Courtesans and Geishas*

Offer your partner a taste of the exotic East and make love to him using the special skills of the revered Japanese courtesans and geishas.

For centuries, their training and expertise in the ways of love and pleasing men superseded that of their Western sisters, and their charm inspired legends as great as that of the tragic Madame Butterfly.

Begin with a long, solitary, scented bath. Choose flowery

essential oils – vanilla, ylang ylang or tea rose, and bask in the perfumed water, thinking of the divine form of your partner's body.

Pat yourself dry, apply some perfume and slip on a kimono (or a slinky dressing gown). Prepare a pot of jasmine tea, put on some soothing music and present him with the mild scented tea on a tray.

The aim is to please, so you have to use all your powers of seduction to drive your lover wild, while taking your lead from him.

Start by giving him a gentle massage – go for whichever part he likes best and caress him with supple fingers until he becomes aroused.

Let your kimono slip slowly apart, and when he has given you an indication of what he wants you to do, carry out his bidding with passion and fervor, bringing him to new heights of sexual pleasure.

Imagine you are a high-class courtesan and he your powerful client, and your aim is to give as much pleasure as is humanly possible within the walls of your perfumed boudoir.

You might even have a novice, who you are tutoring in the ways of love, watching you from a crack in the door, and it is your duty to reveal to her all the tricks and skills you have learned in the course of your sexual training.

When your repertoire has been exhausted, and your partner too, you may want to persuade him that playing the courtesan is fun, and that there is no reason why he shouldn't take on the role and please you next time you make love.

■ Cowboys and Indians

Pick up a hat, put on some warpaint and prepare for an afternoon of cowboys and Indians – grown-up style ...

Stealth and silence are all-important in the cowboy and Indian game, for it is up to you to take the enemy unawares if they are to become your captive. This may mean much creeping around and hiding in wardrobes and under beds, but if you can touch them with your hand or your "weapon" before they have seen you or sensed your presence, then you have all but won the game.

Once you have found and grabbed your prisoner, bind them with a rope or perhaps silk cord, tight enough so that they cannot escape, yet loose enough to enable them to move around.

Using her feather the "Indian" should subject her cowboy prisoner to tickle torture. She can remove his trousers and run the feather up and down the inside of his thighs, and even around his genitals.

When she feels he has suffered enough physical torture, she can loosen her clothes and, keeping her captive at a distance, tempt him with the delights of her body, knowing that he can look, but not touch.

She can slowly reveal her breasts, moving close enough for him to feel the heat of her body, then back away.

If he becomes aroused, she can treat him to more visual thrills. Standing above her captive, legs either side of his helpless form, she can raise her skirt, and seductively lower her panties, swaying her hips hypnotically while tempting him with the potential delights of her femininity.

Only at the end may it be necessary to free him, as the passion of each lover reaches fever pitch.

If the cowboy is the victor, he can treat his Indian captive in much the same way, using the cold metal of his toy gun to elicit frissons of desire from her warm skin.

■ Cross-dressing

This comes under the category of love play that could have you both rolling around the floor laughing rather than making love – but one can always lead to the other! Some men may be turned off by the thought of trying on women's underwear and clothing, while others get a secret thrill from it. A lot of men get excited, though, by seeing their girlfriend parading around in their underpants, plus a cut-away vest.

Choose your sexiest undergarments for him to try – peep-hole bra and crotchless panties, if you have them, and possibly even stockings and suspenders. Don't worry if they are a tight squeeze – you're going to be stripping them off again very soon!

■ Cupboard Love

In a past survey of sex in strange places, cupboards figured surprisingly high.

Whether it's because you are overcome with desire and have nowhere else to go, or if it's just the thrill of the unusual, provided the cupboard is big enough for two and there is no danger of being locked in, feel free to experiment.

In an old-fashioned larder you can make love with the sweet-spicy smell of food around you.

In a linen cupboard, let the crisp smell of freshly laundered sheets and lavender potpourri accompany your antics, while in a washroom you can use a washbasin as a support for any quickie position you care to choose.

But the wardrobe is possibly the most erotic of all cupboard spaces. The faint odours of perfume and aftershave on the clothes, freshly washed cotton, shoe leather, and the unmistakable smell of your partner makes it a highly charged experience.

Hide out in your partner's wardrobe and when he opens the door pull him towards you, drawing him into the folds of fabric and rows of coat hangers.

He may be shocked, horrified, or simply delighted to find a woman among his shirts and ties, but whatever his reaction, he will soon find the situation to his advantage.

If he is dressed or partially dressed, loosen his clothing and slide your hands over his body. In such a confined space and in the absence of any comfort, don't linger over foreplay.

Take his penis in your hands and guide it into your vagina, positioned either face to face or with him approaching from behind. If he is making love to you from behind, bend from the waist until you are touching your toes (if there is the space) to vary the angle of penetration and therefore the sensation.

■ Desert Fling

On a warm, sultry evening, create a passionate oasis of pleasure in the guise of prince and princess of the exotic East. He could wear a turban made from a fine cotton sarong, or a traditional Arab cloth headdress, and she a pair of flimsy harem pants, tiny bra top or waistcoat, and perhaps several floaty, filmy chiffon scarves.

Pile the bed with cushions, and if it is at all practical, hang rugs and throws around the room to make the scene look exotic and inviting.

As slave to his every whim, she should run a damp sponge over the contours of his body, then cover him with oil, massaging every inch of his skin with the unctuous liquid. When he is in a state of high arousal, she should withdraw, rinse her hands, and, in a spacious part of the "tent", start to gyrate slowly – out of his reach – removing her "veils" one by one in the manner of the skilled temptress.

Reveal ankles, wrists and thighs, dancing and twirling with each veil then letting it fall to the ground, wrapping the filmy fabric around your partner's body, between his legs and over his genitals.

Imagine yourself as a luscious exotic fruit, peeling off each layer to reveal a ripe and succulent centre.

When she is all but naked, she can approach him, and together they can continue the foreplay until they are both on the brink of orgasm.

Next she should mount him, then to increase his pleasure, lean back and cup his testicles in one hand, caressing them while moving her hips slowly up and down.

They should rise and fall as one, locked together in the ritual of love which is as old as humanity itself, and only when he can feel her giving in to her approaching orgasm should he allow his semen to flow into the innermost reaches of her body.

■ *Dinner for Two*

Everyone enjoys the luxury of having a special meal cooked for them and there are few things more romantic than a meal together in the privacy of your own home.

A casserole, curry or a similar "one-pot" meal may not appear to be the sexiest food around, but such dishes are easy to prepare and will keep for hours in the oven if you happen to get distracted before the main course is served.

Lay the table in true restaurant style to make the occasion special, and fill small dishes with peanuts and potato chips for your partner to munch with an aperitif.

At the table unfurl his napkin and place it on his lap, smoothing it out around his thighs and over his trouser fly. Or tie her napkin around her neck, adjusting it over her breasts while softly kissing her hairline.

Now you can serve up the other specialities of the evening. On the dining chair, on the floor, or even on the table, she can take his member into her mouth, closing her lips around it to make pink lipstick marks on the shaft.

She can toy with his foreskin with her teeth, first sucking to raise it over the tip, then running her teeth gently down the shaft to send electric shivers up his spine.

He can caress her all over, performing cunnilingus while stroking her thighs close to her stocking tops and her breasts through her special outfit. He can take his time. Everything is planned so that the dinner won't spoil.

When each partner has climaxed, there's no need for the fun to stop. Consider the first orgasm as the "starter". Then move on to the "main course".

Before he achieves erection again, she can swing round on the dining chair to sit astride him, moving her body rhythmically against his until he becomes hard once more with desire.

■ Dirty Dancing

It has been said that the tango is the vertical expression of a horizontal desire. Performed well, it is certainly the sexiest, most evocative dance imaginable.

Unlike all the other sexy, suggestive dances that have thrilled and horrified audiences, the tango retains a dignity which allies it more to the sexual act than any other dance.

To get some of the spirit of the tango in your blood, put on some tango music. Then draw the curtains, lower the lights, turn up the volume, and let the wild melody course through your veins.

In the land of your imagination there are two people – your alter egos. It is a sticky, humid night in a poor South American town and they are sitting in the corner of a crowded, noisy bar, drinking ice-cold margueritas to quench their thirst in the heat of the tropical night.

As the band strikes up the familiar chords of the tango, he leaps to his feet, catching her round the waist and spinning her onto the tiny dance floor. Their dance becomes ever more sexual in its movements. In the gloom of the bar they could almost be making love in time to the cheers of the crowd on the dance floor.

Once aroused by the image of your tango fantasy, coax your partner out of his or her seat – change the music if necessary, to something more familiar, and modern. Hold him tight against you, and start to move, thinking of the dance more as choreographed sex in an upright position.

When you can wait no more, make passionate love. The athletic can try it in the dance position, standing up, or the man can sweep her up into his arms and take her to the bed or sofa. Keep up the rhythm of the dance, and have sex in time to the music.

■ Dressing for Your Partner

To dress successfully for your partner you must turn detective. Look for those clues by which everyone betrays their sexual desires. When your partner tells you that you look "nice" they probably mean "sexy". Make a note of what you are wearing, and try to find out more about what prompted that response.

Once you have completed your basic training, become more adventurous by turning conversations round to the subject of sexy dress.

Magazines and videos can be particularly helpful here, by providing a starting point.

Having assembled enough information put your plans into practice. You know your partner better than anyone else, so you will probably be able to come up with your own fantasy outfits, tailormade to drive him or her wild, but here are some tried and tested favorites:

FOR HER

● *The age-old "frilly underwear" combination of stockings, suspenders, lacy brassieres and exotic panties is still a classic turn-on for men.*

● *Skin-tight leather and latex with zip fastenings point to female domination.*

● *The "Sexy Schoolgirl" is popular, particularly when combined with adult underwear.*

● *The fresh-faced "Tomboy" look: keep things as natural as possible – freshly washed, casually worn hair and little or no make-up.*

● *The "Professional Woman" look – strict school ma'am, tough businesswoman or even "Miss Prim".*

FOR HIM

● *The classic "Wild Boy", such as Marlon Brando in the movie* The Wild One. *Choose leather jackets, denim jeans and white T-shirts.*

● *The "Sportsman" look – sports gear which somehow manages to show off all the right bumps and bulges.*

● *The "Latin Lover" look – your clothes should spell M.O.N.E.Y. White tuxedos or expensive casual clothes would both be equally appropriate.*

● *The "Little Boy Lost" look –*
big woolly sweaters, shirts
hanging out and tattered
jeans give some women the
irresistible urge to scoop the
wearer into their arms.

■ Earthling and Alien

You have just landed on this
planet from outer space on a
mission to find out about the
strange creatures that inhabit
Earth. Your first explorations
have brought you to the house
of an attractive Earth creature,
and you are questioning her
about their species. In
particular, your fellow aliens
back on the home planet are
keen to know how Earth
creatures reproduce.

The Earth creature tries to
describe what they call
"making love" but you are
incredulous. It sounds very
strange and you can't believe
that they actually enjoy it as
well as producing young in
this way.

The Earth creature offers to
demonstrate. You both take
your clothes off and she
explains what all the different
parts of the body are. It seems
you have the same parts as the
male of her species and as she
strokes your part, a strange
thing happens and it begins to
grow hard and erect. She kneels
down in front of you and puts
it in her mouth which, you
think, is very odd because
surely you can't make babies
that way. But it feels extremely
good, you have to admit.

The Earth creature takes
her mission very seriously and
goes to a lot of trouble over the
next few hours to show you
many of the different ways in
which Earth creatures can
reproduce – and you find
yourself agreeing that it is very
pleasurable indeed.

■ Explore Yourself

Exploring your own body is an
exciting way of discovering
what turns you on. To do this,

you need a warm, comfortable room and guaranteed peace and quiet. You'll need to be naked, so after a bath would be ideal.

Once you are comfortable and relaxed, explore all over your body, not just those parts usually associated with sexual pleasure. Take time to really feel the textures of skin and hair on different parts of your body.

Then move on to your breasts, running your hands over them. What feels better – a firm or gentle touch? Use your fingers to circle your nipples – what sort of touch makes them erect?

When you are ready you can start to explore your genitals. If you want to see what you are doing, sit up against some cushions and use a small hand-held mirror.

You will see the hair-covered outer lips or labia majora. These meet at the top of the vulva to form the clitoral hood which covers the exquisitely sensitive clitoris, below which lies the entrance to the vagina.

Once you have familiarized yourself with what it all looks like, concentrate on where and how you most like to be touched. It's important that your fingers are well lubricated.

It's well worth spending time on your clitoris. Try rubbing and stroking, hard and fast or soft and gentle. Sometimes the best sensations are produced if the clitoris is stimulated indirectly through the clitoral hood or by squeezing your legs together to exert pressure on it.

Next try inserting a finger into your vagina. You may enjoy the sensation of thrusting your fingers in and out or prefer a more gentle touch. If your finger is long enough you may be able to stimulate your own G spot.

By this stage of your exploration you will probably feel really turned on and be wanting to orgasm – go ahead!

■ *Feather Fantasia*

First make your partner warm, relaxed and comfortable with a bit of pampering. Gently remove their clothes and lay them naked on the bed or on a soft rug on the floor.

Kneel or sit beside your partner's head, and begin. Start at the top, running the feather slowly and lightly across the forehead, down to the tip of the nose, then over the top lip – linger on this particular spot for a while as it is extremely sensitive to the feather's delicate fronds.

Tickle the ears, one at a time, then move down across the jawline to the chin. From there spiral the feather down the neck and onto the body. Lightly dust the chest or breasts, caress the nipples with the very tip, then whip it away quickly just to tease.

Stroke the rest of the body, swirling the feather over the thighs, the arms, the wrists, the knees. Use just the tip for a delicate, teasing stroke and the full plume for a rich, soft caress.

To induce a state of shivering excitement, lift the feather away and touch it again to another area, so that your partner never knows what to expect. If you want to soothe your partner into a deep melting sensuality, use a long slow stroke that never loses contact with the skin.

Once you have completed one side of the body, turn your partner over and start on the next. Then go for the grand finale – the feet!

Push the tip of the quill between the toes and pull the rest of the feather through after it. Use the quill again to press gently on the sole, running the point up and down the arch of the foot and around the base of the toes.

Women can use a feather boa effectively as a wonderful prelude to lovemaking. Just wrap the mass of feathers seductively around your naked body and proceed to dance, never quite revealing what your partner longs to see.

■ Fireside Frolics

After a long country walk, a romp in the snow or a special evening together, making love beside a warm fire can complete a perfect day.

Lay pillows or cushions on the floor, or better still, spread a thick sheepskin rug or feather comforter in front of the fire. Pour yourself a special drink to get you in the mood – make it something you rarely have, like a rich liqueur or Schnapps, to warm you on the inside while the fire heats you without.

Draw all the curtains or blinds and stop any draughts at floor level that may take the heat out of the moment. Turn off all the lights – if you find the light of the flames too dim you can light candles all around the room. Then fetch plenty of wood and stoke up the fire so that it will burn for as long as possible.

When you are ready, lie down in front of the fire and undress your partner. Remove each article of clothing carefully, kissing and caressing arms, shoulders, neck, breasts, chest and thighs as each new erogenous zone is revealed. Lay your partner back on the comforter or pillows and caress them gently. Then let your naked partner undress you.

Let your bodies bathe in the heat, and watch the firelight flicker and play on each other's skin.

Caressing the mounds and hollows with the tips of your fingers, slide down to kiss your partner's genitals. Take them in your mouth and suck, lick and tease to the point of orgasm. Then it's your turn to enjoy the same warming treat.

When the pleasure of oral sex has been given and received, you can lie satisfied in each other's arms, with no sound but one another's heartbeats and the crackle of the flames.

Try not to drift off to sleep. Instead, coax your lover back to arousal and make passionate love again.

■ *First Meeting*

Remember the thrill of the time you first met and the conversations you had as you began to get to know each other? Remember also the excitement of the very first time you made love? Well, it's possible to have the whole experience all over again – with a little help from an understanding friend.

Next time you are invited to a party or dinner, explain your plan to a friend and, when you arrive (separately), ask her to introduce you to your partner as if you were meeting for the first time. Look at each other and smile and shake hands. Ask him how he knows the party's hostess. Tell him you met her through work and

explain what your job is.

Show that you are interested in each other with subtle eye contact and casual touches on the arm or knee. Gradually work your way round to seduction techniques, complimenting each other on clothes, eyes, hair, sense of humour – whatever is appropriate.

At the end of the evening, one of you can tentatively ask the other if they would like to come back to your place for coffee. And you can see how the evening develops from there!

■ *Food Fun*

Taste is an essential sense in the sexual act. Along with touch, sight, hearing and smell, it completes our sensual map of our partner and makes the experience of lovemaking complete.

Whipped cream is one of the most sensual of all sweet

toppings. Its rich, cool, mousse-like texture feels gloriously smooth and silky on warm skin.

For him, start at the chest with swirls and patterns, then apply a thick, soft, piled line down to the navel. For her, cover the breasts in peaks and mounds – you could even finish with a cherry on each nipple or in the navel.

Work fast, as the cream has a tendency to melt as soon as it comes into contact with body heat. Decorate still further, with silver balls, "hundreds and thousands", fruit such as peaches, strawberries and cherries, or chocolate flakes to create the ultimate in dream desserts.

Once the topping is complete, you can begin the delightful task of eating your creation. Begin with a silver spoon, gently running the cool of the metal down the centre of the body, circling the navel, then down between the thighs, offering your partner small mouthfuls as you go.

When the temperature really heats up, you can meet fire with ice and share a tub of ice-cream or frozen yogurt. Allow a spoonful to soften slightly, then let it slide slowly down her cleavage – it should send shivers of delight. Try the effect on different parts of each other's body to test the response.

Honey, maple syrup and chocolate are the ultimate sweeteners, and can add extra flavour to your lovemaking. Like the whipped cream, the application is as much fun as the removal. For those who prefer their sex a little more savoury, try mayonnaise, peanut butter or salad dressings – you can raid the refrigerator for imaginative ideas. Daub each flavour in a new place, then explore them with your tongue, kissing them and licking off the remains of the food.

■ *Games of Pleasure*

For those well versed in the ways of love, the sex manual of the Chinese writer Noble Tung has much to offer.

Art of the Bedchamber includes thirty different "advanced" position, and many suggestions for lighthearted play. Here are a few:

● *Awakening the Sleeping Beauty.* Here, Lady Yin lies quite still, pretending to be asleep while Lord Yang undresses her slowly. His gentle kisses and caresses fail to have any effect so he begins to fondle her breasts and the Pearl on the Jade Step (clitoris).

Lady Yin becomes more and more aroused until she can stand no more and springs up to meet Lord Yang's Iron Implement (penis) as it strikes passionately at the Jade Gate (vagina).

● *Blind Man's Buff.* This is another playful romp in which both partners are blindfolded and search for each other around the bedchamber. When Lady Yin is caught, intercourse takes place while her blindfold remains in position.

● *The Lady Submitting to the Leaping White Tiger.* This offers plenty of scope to lovers of outdoor sex. Here, Lady Yin is bent low over the extended, almost ground-level, branch of a tree with her head resting on her folded arms. Lord Yang then approaches her Vermilion Gate (vagina) from the rear.

And for really deep penetration:

● *The Kicking Mule.* Lady Yin positions herself in the center of the bed, with Lord Yang above her. He places his left hand under her head, and his right hand under her right leg.

Lord Yang then inserts the Jade Stem (penis) while raising her head and leg together, and continues raising and lowering to the rhythm of his thrusts.

● *The Tandem Ducks in Flight.* Lord Yang lies back facing upwards for this position. Lady Yin sits on his stomach, *facing his feet and begins to caress the Jade Stem. When it is fully erect, she uses both hands to guide it into the Golden Gulley.*

■ *Gangster and Moll*

The gangsters of Prohibition America had it all – sharp suits, plenty of money and sex appeal. Why not spend a night as Mob King and Moll and enjoy a gangster-style romp?

Dress up in something provocative – stockings, a basque, or bra and panties, a long robe and a feather boa. Your partner can wear a hat and suit, white shirt and shiny shoes.

Ask him if he's had a hard day, and if he would like to relax somewhere soft and warm. Move closer and tell him you know a way to increase his assets, if he dares to take a gamble on some hot property!

If you don't think he will give in to the soft approach, pull out your weapon – a toy machine gun, or a pistol – and order him to remove his clothes or you shoot. Under supposed threat of fire he should be like putty in your hands.

Once you have him down to just his underwear, slowly run your hands over the muscular contours of his body. Then, with the very tips of your fingers, lightly move your hand downwards towards his genitals.

Now, peel off his underwear and take his penis firmly in your mouth, tugging at it gently with your lips. Cup his testicles with one hand, and hold his penis with the other, while your mouth and tongue move rhythmically back and forth along the stem of his member.

Let your imagination run wild and picture yourself in the bridal suite of a Chicago hotel. Together you have just pulled off the biggest bank robbery of the decade.

In a few hours he has to get away to safety, leaving you behind. Who knows when you are going to see him again, so in the few hours left together, you must give him something to remember you by . . .

■ *Gymnasium Gyrations*

Whatever happens on the gym mat, working out together can be tremendous fun, and extremely stimulating – you can help each other with the trickier exercises, all the while appreciating the unique beauty of your partner's body.

Put on some music with a good beat if it helps, and start with some simple warming-up exercises. Straightforward stretching or jogging on the spot will do.

Then follow your usual routine, adding some simple movements where you have contact with your partner.

Let your imagination take you to a faraway gymnasium, deserted but for yourselves. The faint odour of rubber exercise mats, the old wood and suede of the gymnasium horse and the polished, sprung wooden floor will take you back to your school days. But now you are an adult with adult desires to match!

As you watch him vault the horse several times with ease, you marvel at his strength and lust after the fine form of his muscular body.

Your desire inflames: as he performs press-ups on the gymnasium mat, you imagine you are lying naked beneath him and he is teasing your taut, waiting body with his penis, the form of which is just visible through his exercise shorts.

Now it is your turn to vault the horse. You leap and clear the horse with ease, but he is waiting to catch you. With a swift movement, he removes your singlet and shorts and lifts you back onto the horse, caressing every inch of your body with firm hands.

His fingers find your clitoris with ease and he brings you to a sensational climax.

Before you have recovered your senses, he spins you round to face the soft suede body of the horse and enters you, firmly but gently, holding your hips and teasing the soft skin of your back with his tongue. You reach orgasm simultaneously, and your fantasy dissolves in a rainbow of light and pleasure.

■ Hairdressing

Everyone loves the feeling of lying back at the hairdressers and being pampered, their hair coaxed and styled into attractive shapes. You and your partner can play hairdressers in the bedroom, with one major difference – it is not the hair on your heads you're going to be styling but your pubic hair!

Start off in the bathroom by washing the hair with shampoo and conditioner then rinsing it off with the shower spray. Comb it through with a small, fine-toothed comb, and then decide what style you are going to create. You may wish to trim the hair carefully with a small pair of nail scissors. Some couples even like to shave each other's hair, but remember that it will feel very itchy for a while as it's growing back in again.

You can finish off your hairstyling with little coloured ribbons, if you like; and then sit back and admire your own handiwork!

■ Happy Hooker

Playing a happy hooker to a lad with lusty loins allows you both to turn a run-of-the-mill romp into a steamy sex scenario.

No matter where he is importuned by his partner the first thing he notices is that she is wearing very little under her coat: a glimpse of bare breast and a flash of aroused nipple sees to that.

She may tantalize him by kissing him full on the mouth and, when he responds, draw away mockingly.

Lowering her voice to a seductive husk she tells him what's on offer, letting her tongue flick around his ear as she whispers the various ways she can pleasure him and for how much.

Keeping her coat on, she unknots his tie and lazily pulls it from under his collar, making it plain that there's something else she'd rather be pulling!

Still in her coat, she unbuttons his shirt, one button at a time, licking his chest as she bares it.

Kneeling down, she takes his shoes and socks off, massages his feet and then gradually lets her hands run up and down his calves and thighs.

She helps him out of his trousers, then lazily shrugs her shoulders and lets her coat slowly fall to the ground revealing the special outfit that will bring him to a peak of passion – maybe a black bra, black stockings or fishnets and a suspender belt made of soft, yielding leather, or a white, lacy bra, and snowy-white suspender belt with a gleaming pair of split-crotch panties.

Let his fantasies take flight! The more aroused he becomes, the sexier you will feel, too, until the voluptuous volcano erupts into your every nerve ending for just a few fantasy-filled moments and you climax together in a simultaneous explosion of ecstasy.

And then? It's his turn to do the work, and her turn to let him do it.

■ *Honeymoon Suite*

If you are spending your first night as husband and wife in a hotel, the luxury and novelty of your surroundings should inspire you to partake in some extraordinarily pleasurable lovemaking.

Making love in wedding clothes is an erotic fantasy in itself – sinking into the honeymoon bed in a cloud of satin and lace.

Unless your clothes are really restrictive, there is no need to undress. Take off only what is necessary and make love in your wedding attire. The sensation of skin moving rhythmically against fabric, the rustle of silk, the stiffness of net, together with the familiar, delicious sensations of penetration, will bring you both to new heights of ecstasy – don't be tempted to follow your normal routine. Tonight is the night you discover your partner anew.

If you arrive at the hotel in a special "going away" outfit, make sure your underwear is of the most exciting and erotic kind. You won't have the pleasure of making love in your wedding clothes, but you can still enjoy the sensuous thrill of watching your partner's desire rise to a crescendo when you peel off your outer garments.

Go for lace and satin basques and stockings in virginal white or devilish red for her, and designer briefs or boxer shorts for him.

If you are both tired and weary after the day's drama, it may take something radical to rejuvenate body and soul. If you have time before the wedding, you can prepare a special surprise for your partner. Daring girls can trim their pubic hair into the shape of a heart (there are some beauty parlours in big cities who will trim it for you and even dye it!).

Presents are always appreciated, even more so those of an erotic nature. Give something you would not usually think of to make an exciting and interesting end to what should be a perfect day.

■ Ice Screams

Start by exchanging a piece of ice between your lover's mouth and your own, until it melts, then let your tongue travel across their forehead, chin and eyelids.

Holding the ice between your teeth, move it down your partner's body, right down to their feet. Now move on:

HIM FOR HER:

Start by rubbing your cooled lips around the insides of her thighs, close to the genital area. You may want to surprise her with a few tiny love bites. Next, run your cold tongue between the folds of her labia. Take a piece of ice in your mouth and gently insert it into her vagina, pushing it in with your tongue – be careful not to push too far inside or you will not be able to continue to suck it.

She may feel an electric sensation at first, but the sharp contrast in temperature will make this a highly erotic and sensual experience. Now suck on the ice cube, at times holding the ice between your teeth, and move it in and out, simulating intercourse. Of course, if you desire, you can complete your loveplay with full penetration.

HER FOR HIM:

Prop your man up on pillows so that he is comfortable, and has a full view of what you are doing to him. Begin by holding a piece of ice in your mouth and then running your tongue down along his chest.

Let your tongue linger at the point just above his genital area and play along the folds where his legs begin, then tease your tongue along the inside of his thighs. Do this for a while before taking the ice back in your mouth.

Now put your cold tongue on the tip of his penis and swirl it around. He may jump at first but will be ultimately thrilled. Work your tongue around his testicles before giving him full oral satisfaction. Or you may want to finish by getting on top of him, using one of the "woman on top" positions.

■ *Indian Loving 1*

Of all the ancient treatises on the art of love, the Indian *Kama Sutra* has had the greatest impact on Western society. It is attributed to the sage Vatsyayana, and represents the cumulative experiences of a thousand years of sexuality, as practiced by one of the world's greatest civilizations.

According to the *Kama Sutra*, when lovers meet, their

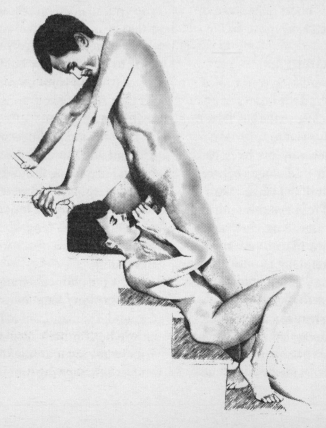

bodies may touch slightly, rub against one another, "pierce" each other or be pressed against a nearby object such as a wall.

From here, they progress to one of the four classic embraces:

Standing, the couple may be entwined – The Twining of the Creeper – alternatively the woman may grip the man with one foot off the ground and the other on his foot – The Climbing of a Tree.

Lying down on a bed, the lovers can entwine their limbs passionately in The Mixture of Sesamum Seed with Rice. Or, the woman can sit on the man's lap in the embrace of Mixing Milk with Water.

The *Kama Sutra* states plainly that it is a man's duty to please a woman, and that this cannot be achieved successfully unless he correctly gauges her disposition and acts on this accordingly.

When she is ready, he has the following options:

● *Moving forward – straightforward penetration of the yoni (vagina).*

● *Churning – holding and moving the lingam (penis) in the yoni.*

● *Pressing – pushing the lingam hard against the yoni.*

● *Giving a Blow – removing the lingam from the yoni and striking the yoni with it.*

● *Piercing – penetrating from above and pushing against the clitoris.*

● *Blows of the Boar and Bull – rubbing the lingam against the sides of the yoni.*

● *Sporting of the Sparrow – moving the lingam rapidly in and out of the yoni.*

When the woman takes the initiative she may also try different movements:

● *The Top – turning round on top of the lingam.*

● *The Pair of Tongs – grasping the lingam, drawing it into the yoni and squeezing it.*

● *The Swing – swaying from side to side.*

■ *Indian Loving 2*

The great Indian love manuals all laid emphasis on the various components of foreplay:

In the *Ghatika*, or "neck-nape" kiss, the woman covers her lover's eyes with her hands and then, closing her own eyes, thrusts her tongue into his mouth in a series of deep, slow, rhythmic movements which are a parody of the act of intercourse itself.

In the *Uttaroshtha*, or "upper-lip" kiss, she takes his lower lip between her teeth then chews and bites it very gently. Her partner, meanwhile, does the same with her upper lip.

In the *Pratibodha*, or "awakening" kiss, one partner, on finding the other fast asleep presses their lips to them and gradually increases the pressure until they wake.

The ancient sex counsellors of India were firm believers in the power of the fingernails to titillate and arouse during foreplay. Pages of the manuals are devoted to describing how – and even when – lovers' nails may be used to best effect.

Light, dabbing movements on the breasts, back, buttocks and thighs are designed to produce a delicious shuddering sensation in the recipient.

Another favoured foreplay technique was biting. The bite said to require "great practice" to perfect is the *Pravalamani-dashana*, or "coral bite" – a protracted and passionate union of a man's teeth and a woman's lips, in which sucking, nibbling and nipping all play their part.

Alone among the ancient civilizations, the Indians exhibit a great fascination for hair and the *Ananga Ranga* lists four ways in which the erotic potential of this much neglected part of the body might be explored.

First, the man may clasp his lover's hair. From here, he can draw her towards him, sliding his hands around her head. As passion mounts the man should grasp a knot of her hair tightly while embracing her. Then as the couple come together, they can run their fingers through each other's hair, ruffling and pulling it as they do so before moving onto lovemaking.

■ Indian Spice

According to one Indian sex manual, the *Ananga Ranga*, "the chief reason and the cause which drives married men to the embraces of other women, and their wives to the arms of other men is the want of varied pleasures and the monotony which followed possession." So don't delay, light some incense sticks, dim the lights and experiment with some Eastern passion:

● *Most seated positions involve the man sitting cross-legged with his lover perched on his lap facing him. From here she can draw her legs up under her arms and manoeuver herself over his erect penis, from side to side or back to front.*

● *One of the* Aranga Ranga*'s suggested standing positions is for the man to raise his partner to waist height, supporting her with his elbows placed under the crook of her knees while she hangs on by throwing her arms around his neck.*

● *"In the Manner of the Bull" is a recommended rear-entry position which consists*

*simply of the woman
kneeling on all fours, while
the man squats behind her
and draws her to him.*

● *More interesting by far are
the woman-on-top positions,
and most advanced of all is
the position of the Gopala-
girl, "She Who Milks The
Cow"! With the man on his
back, the woman sits cross-
legged above him, seizes his
penis, and thrusts it into her.
She then moves her waist up
and down, while constricting
her vaginal muscles to
squeeze her lover's penis.*

The *Ananga Ranga* promises
that once the art is learned it is
never lost, and that henceforth
her lover "will value her above
all women, so lovely and
pleasant to man is she who
constricts."

A woman who wanted to
give and receive added pleasure
by ensuring that her lover fitted
her tightly could rub her yoni
(vagina) with a concoction
from a certain fruit which
would "contract the yoni for
one whole night".

■ Intimate Intrusion

Fantasy and fantasizing are
vital ingredients for spicing up
our sex lives, and role-playing
strangers can add a definite
frisson . . .

After a party where she's
been admired by all, the
hostess stands in front of the
mirror, admiring herself.
Slowly, in the cool evening
breeze, she slips off her dress to
reveal her naked body.

She caresses her breasts,
rubbing her nipples and
squeezing them hard. Then she
trails her fingers across her
stomach to her vagina, totally
unaware that she has an
audience.

As one hand plays with
the erect nipples, the other
slides over her clitoris and she
slips two fingers inside her
vagina. She is about to climax

when she sees a movement in the mirror.

She looks wildly around the room as the shadow of a man steps out of the darkness and walks towards her. She recognizes him as a handsome guest someone else had brought along to the party. They hadn't spoken but she'd seen him watching her during the evening. She thought all the guests had left but obviously he'd stayed behind to catch her on her own.

Standing silently behind her, he wraps his arms around her, gripping her breasts and grinding his hips against her bare bottom. She can feel his erection and gives in to her desire.

He pushes her gently onto her knees, facing the mirror, unzips his trousers and enters her from behind, penetrating deeply. She watches his face in the mirror, and pushes back onto him fiercely.

With him masturbating her, she orgasms and as she

does, he withdraws, moves swiftly in front of her and pushes his penis into her willing mouth. She sucks him relentlessly and when he ejaculates, she hungrily swallows his semen.

They make love for hours without speaking and when she wakes in the morning she realizes she doesn't even know his name.

■ *Japanese Loving*

The Japanese have a rich sexual heritage. The most erotic of their prints, scrolls and book illustrations are *shunga*, or "spring drawings".

There are two very striking features about *shinga* prints. First, the lovers are rarely naked – the Japanese thought that sensuous, loose-fitting clothing heightened sexual attraction.

Secondly, the sexual organs in all the pictures are grossly exaggerated, the vulvas gaping wide and often dripping, the pubic hair luxuriant, the penises massively swollen, heavily-veined and bristling with hair, to emphasize the sexual act itself, rather than the participants as individuals.

The subject matter of the prints makes clear the completely unrestrained Japanese approach to sex. There are often two or more women making love to one man, or to each other. Everything was natural to the Japanese.

Women are frequently observed masturbating with a dildo, lying or sitting back with the dildo strapped to a foot.

The *shunga* prints present the sexual act in an almost inexhaustible variety of ways. One classic book illustrates the forty-eight positions considered practicable or possible for heterosexual couples to enjoy.

While the ancient Japanese described a whole variety of sexual techniques, they paid particular attention to the importance and value of foreplay and to oral sex as a means of foreplay and an end in itself:

*'Everything can be done with
lip service,
Even love.'*

The descriptions and advice are appropriate, but the language lends cunnilingus a charm all of its own:

*'If the cup is deep
Plunge your tongue into it
several times.'*

Much can be learned from the Japanese delight in sexual matters, and a brief foray into the mystic East with your partner could yield wonderful rewards.

■ *Jungle Fever*

Why not try a bungle in the jungle in the privacy of your

own home with a lick of tribal body paint and a little native wit . . .

Set aside a place in your home to play, perhaps on your sitting room floor, or bedroom. Place a sheet over the carpet and collect leaves and flower petals, then strew them all over the jungle floor. Now take the largest, most exotic pot plants you can find and make a leafy barrier between you and the civilization you are leaving behind.

Paint sensual, colourful camouflage all over your own and your partner's body, using either body paints, love paints from specialist shops, or simply a selection of brightly coloured lipstick and face make-up.

A slow build-up is best for the budding Tarzan and Jane. Using ever so soft and sensual paint brushes, take turns to paint each other from top to toe (don't, however, use paint directly on the genital areas, as it may cause redness and irritation).

Use tantalizing, swirling brush-strokes to create your designs. When you are painted and ready for further action, play some heavy heartbeat music and do a courtship dance together. Pick the sexiest, liveliest records you have – ones with throbbing bass lines and heavy drumbeats, or try sound effects records, or CDs featuring twittering bird sounds and the roaring and purring of dangerous animals.

Dance to attract your mate in an increasingly wild frenzy, almost touching, but then drawing away from each other again to build momentum. Then reach your hands out and slide your fingers teasingly up and down each other's genitals.

Of course, Tarzan and Jane must eventually give in to their irresistible natural desires – as nature intended – and consummate their passion in a coupling that will leave them both exhausted and happy.

■ *Kitchen Capers*

Interrupt the drudgery of washing up to create your own exciting "kitchen sink" drama with some wild and spontaneous sex.

There is endless scope for fun in the kitchen for those who like to play games when they make love. Start with the soapsuds in the sink and clothe your partner with bubbles.

Or raid the refrigerator for goodies such as ice, whipped cream, aerosols and yogurt, and treat your partner like a dessert, spooning on the yogurt or cream and licking it off, while running the ice across nipples, earlobes and genitals.

Or go to the kitchen cupboard and turn your lover into a savoury snack, using spreads, peanut butter or cream cheese.

When it comes to penetration, go all out to make it the highlight of your lovemaking, not just an uncomfortable wriggle on a cold hard surface.

Sweep her up and carry her to the kitchen table. Lay her on the table top, penetrating her deeply from above. If the table is small, you can stand at the end while she lays back facing upwards, or she can bend across the table facing away from you as you take her from behind.

Lift your partner onto a clear space and let her twine her legs around the small of your back. If the work surface is at the right height for you both, you can penetrate her simply by lifting her onto your penis while her buttocks rest on the kitchen worktop.

A great alternative is the washing machine or dishwasher. When switched on, the heat and vibrations generated can add a completely new sensation to your sex life.

Sit your partner on a towel on top of the machine and let them absorb the machine's pulsating energy while you lean up against them. When they are fully charged with the vibrations, begin penetration from whichever angle is most comfortable.

■ Lingering Loveplay

Long and lingering foreplay is the key to a memorable night of passion and for many couples it can take over as the main source of excitement:

● *Sharing a meal and a bottle of wine, or dancing together can be the perfect prelude to making love.*

● *Slowly peeling off your partner's clothes, or your own, while he or she watches, adds an exciting element to your night of passion. Striptease is one of the most erotic ways of arousing your partner.*

● *Anticipation is one of the most powerful sex stimulants of all. What the French call pattes d'araignée – literally spider's feet – takes advantage of this fact. The aim is not actually to touch the skin – merely the tips of the hairs that grow on it.*

● *The lips can be particularly effective in bringing your partner to the height of sexual arousal. Remember that kissing does not have to be restricted to the mouth: a light carpet of kisses or caresses across the whole body can be especially rewarding for both partners.*

● *Water and ice can also have a stimulating shock effect on the skin. Use ice which is on the point of melting to leave deliciously cool, damp trails across the entire length of the body.*

● *Blowing on wet skin produces goose pimples and the resulting tightening of the skin can be a major turn-on. The best way is to moisten the skin with the tongue and blow across the wet area.*

● *Why not indulge in what is known as Turkish-type foreplay? Snuggle at the foot of the bed and slowly work your way up under the covers using your lips, hands and tongue to arouse your partner as you go.*

● *If you attach some soft feathers to the nozzle of your hairdryer, turn it on and run it all over your partner, they will find it difficult to stop themselves exploding in an ecstasy of eroticism.*

■ Love on Tap

The bathroom offers great scope for inventive lovers. With towel rails, basins, surfaces of all different heights, the alternatives are endless.

If you prefer a more conventional, pre-planned night of passion, undress each other while the bath is running and slip into comfortable robes. If the light is too harsh, bring candles into the room – as many as you can find – place them all around the bath and light them.

Fill the bath with scented oil, foaming creme or bath salts to add fragrance to the water and soften your skin.

Start with sex in the rising steam. In any position you choose, anywhere in the bathroom except the bath, masturbate your partner in the sticky heat until you bring them to orgasm, then let them masturbate you.

Once you have achieved orgasm you can each slide into the bath, basking in the afterglow, while the warm scented water laps at your skin, enveloping you in fragrant waves. Don't fall asleep. You will miss out on what is to come.

Lather your partner all over with a rich, creamy soap, starting with the back and chest and finishing with the genitals. Work your fingers rhythmically around the sensitive parts and up into each and every secret place, gently stroking and sliding to explore every magical crease and fold.

Shower them slowly clean with a giant sponge, dipped repeatedly in the warm water and squeezed out over their body.

If there is room, you can take it in turns to perform oral sex while still in the water, bringing your partner almost to the point of orgasm.

When you have each had your turn, you can begin the actual penetration. The best position is for him to lay back in the water, while she eases herself down on top of his penis with her legs close together. This way, you can bring each other to a slippery climax with very little effort at all.

■ Maid and Master

Be sure to dress for your big house play – this is half the fun. Why not go turn of the century and dress the master as a stern, Victorian authoritative figure. He can wear a black suit with a stuffy shirt and high starched collar.

A waistcoat with a crisp handkerchief and watch and chain will complete the look.

The maid must look pleasantly archaic in a starched black uniform with white apron and hat. Of course, every self-respecting serving wench will want to don sexy underwear, a lacy bra or boned camisole with barely-there panties to please her frolicsome master.

She can also wear a suspender belt and sexy, sheer stockings with high heels for a modern touch to mix with the Victorian feel of her outfit.

Start off slowly with the maid going about her daily cleaning in the master

bedroom, where she is taken by
surprise when the master
comes in.

    The master may pretend he
is tired and simply must lie
down on the bed. He exclaims
that he would like his

shoulders massaged, and his
faithful maid sits astride him
rubbing them, her breasts
bulging tantalizingly close to
his face. As he sticks his tongue
out to reach her nipples, she
teasingly draws away and runs

her fingers down his torso. This play can go on endlessly until they are both as hot as they can stand.

The master may then feel that he deserves a special bonus. As he gently nudges her kneeling form up against the bed, she will enjoy his probing leg pushed up longingly between her own.

At the same time, he can cup her breasts in his hands and suck on the back of her neck as he presses his bare chest tenderly against her soft, naked back.

Soon he will thrust his member in fully as they both enjoy the passionate pushing and shoving that completes a happy session of abandoned afternoon lovemaking.

■ Mirror Magic

If you put up a mirror in your bedroom opposite the foot of the bed, or on the wall alongside, or better still if you have mirror wardrobe doors, you can watch yourselves make love.

Just as dancers constantly observe themselves in mirrors to ensure that their posture and steps are correct, so too can you observe your position, and improve your physical technique.

Many people find such self-voyeurism fascinating as it reveals a part of themselves that only their lover sees. But, for other people watching their partner's body from new angles is the real pleasure.

With many sexual positions, getting a good view of your partner is not easy. So much of the body is involved in the sexual act, and each bit undergoes its subtle change during the build-up to orgasm that it is impossible to see and appreciate it all. Added to which, watching your partner's body move in time with yours can be extremely stimulating.

Using mirrors in the bedroom – or in any other

room in which you choose to make love can teach you so much more about one other and improve the harmony of your sexual technique.

If the sight of your naked reflection turns you off rather than on, then it might only take a small adjustment to change the way you feel about mirror sex.

Just as in movies, where it is all a question of clever camera angles and lighting, so it is in your own home, where high-powered and practical bedroom and bathroom lights show your skin in its full, blemished glory.

Dim the lights or use a few carefully positioned candles so you can watch yourselves writhe on honey-coloured sheets, while the flickering flames create highlights and shadows on your bodies.

In such unfamiliar light, your room can take on a strangely timeless feeling, and you can fantasize about being transported back into the past.

■ Moving In

When you are moving into a new home together, why not pack in the unpacking and "move-in" on your partner for some rough-and-ready sex among the boxes.

You'll be wearing casual clothes in which you feel comfortable, but that doesn't mean you can't be sexy at the same time. Jeans are a time-honored sex symbol, and he should be wearing his sexiest pair with a handsome shirt, and maybe a muscle-man vest underneath.

Silky boxer shorts are sexy and comfortable, so wear a pair for this special, informal occasion.

She can wear a well-worn pair of dungarees, and perhaps an alluring body-suit which has poppers on the crutch for easy access. Men love the ease with which they can unfasten and remove dungarees and the sort of little girl charm they imply.

Wear a lacy bra and some provocative panties or, if you're feeling really wicked, wear nothing underneath apart from his favourite perfume.

Take advantage of a coffee break to give your partner a relaxing massage. This is the perfect opportunity for you to pounce on him while his eyes are shut, and have your wicked way! Straddle him fully clothed, then slowly and provocatively unzip his jeans, waiting for him to become excited before you touch his flesh.

You can pull his trousers off slowly, kissing his bare skin inch by inch, and then please him with a little tantalizing oral sex.

Or you may choose to rip his trousers off quickly, and then get on top of him before he knows what has hit him. You can bend backwards and hold onto his legs, and then move forward and pull him up into a sitting position, for a rocking intercourse motion.

In either case, he will be more than happy to assist, making the earth move on a moving day you will both remember.

◼ *Nurse! Nurse!*

Re-enact a sick-bed scene with a sexy twist, as nurse kisses you better in a night of patient passion.

Why not indulge in some hilarious bandage bondage – cover him up in plasters and bandages. You can use bits of cotton sheeting torn into strips, or to be really sensual, use strips of silk or silky scarves.

Slowly wrap his head very loosely leaving eye, nose and mouth openings, massaging the back of his neck with your fingers. Next wrap his chest, seductively rubbing your cheek and lips against it as you go, then perhaps bind one of his legs, kissing and licking the pretend wounds.

Wind bandages round every part of his body, except for his neck, so that he looks like a mummy or the invisible man.

Nurse may need to give the patient a sponge bath, patting her warm wet sponge seductively against his chest and arms.

Or she may dip the sponge in cold water and dab it lightly along his inner thighs. As he squeals with chilly delight, she may be so overcome by compassion that she simply must join him in bed.

Perhaps she will guide his hand up under her uniform, whereupon he discovers that she has forgotten her regulation white stockings and panties.

He may just feel strong enough to beckon her to get on top of him for some special private medical care.

To show his appreciation, the patient may feel obliged to kiss and touch her with his unbandaged mouth. But first he must pull her uniform off completely so that she can feel the full force of his gratitude. Then she can settle back gently and fondle his poor bandaged head as he gives her a spot of healthy oral sex.

To make his stay in hospital memorable enjoy some passionate, deep penetration lovemaking in a bed-rocking finale. Later on, if you are both still in the mood, swap roles and start again.

■ Office Sex

Many men and women find it exciting to sneak their partners into the office after hours for a bit of passion among the filing cabinets. The contrast between the responsibilities you normally have in working hours and the carefree fun of sex can make the experience feel particularly mischievous. And next day, when you're sitting around the boardroom table, you can smile to yourself as you remember what you got up to there the night before! But remember to keep an eye open for security guards and cleaners.

Unless you have an iron back and a passion so great that you don't mind being practically impaled on paperclips and shredders, the actual sex is likely to be what used to be called "knee-tremblers" – you do it standing up, the woman usually supporting her back against the wall.

This has its drawbacks – foreplay will often be minimal and unless you are both much the same height the man's penis may not sit comfortably in his lover's vagina.

If he is strong, he can lift the woman up slightly so that she is almost straddling him, but he won't be able to keep this up for very long.

Lying on the floor is better, but can be very hard on whoever is underneath: throwing a couple of coats down first makes an adequate blanket – be careful not to get them stained.

In this type of situation it's often a better idea not to go for full sex, but to bring each other to orgasm through mutual masturbation or to have oral sex. It's just as satisfying and less of a strain on the back.

Grappling with your passion among the computers is wild and should be fun, but be careful not to damage your hard drive.

■ On the Road

As you drive down the road, why not put the thought of sexy play into your partner's mind by lightly stroking his or her leg in a gentle way so that you will not distract either your own or your partner's attention from safe driving.

Then, head for your own driveway or garage. If you live out of town and it is evening, you may be able to find a secluded spot where you won't be seen. Remember that in some countries, it is illegal to have sex in public places.

Rev up the amorous engine by fondling your partner in a more obvious manner. Rub your hand up and down their trouser leg or skirt, while still clothed. Bite the insides of their thighs.

Put your head in their lap and simulate oral sex through their clothes. It is quite easy to perform oral sex on a man who is sitting upright, but you can playfully tease him to build up excitement.

In the front seat, the woman may straddle her lover after removing her skirt or trousers. The man can unzip his fly and pull his trousers open to be instantly ready for action. She can put her arms around his neck, and he can hold her waist, while she moves up and down on top of him.

For a really sizzling and sexy session, climb into the back seat of the car and tear off each other's clothes. In man-on-top positions, the woman can place one leg across the back of the front seat, and prop one leg against the back window shelf. The man can give the woman oral sex, or penetrate her deeply in this position.

If you have reclining seats, the scope for movement can be greater. The woman can get on top facing the man, or mount him with her back to him if she is careful about where she places her legs!

■ *Paintpot Passion*

A spot of home decorating is an effective way of adding more than a coat of gloss to your love life.

You don't need much. A dust sheet or two, a set of stepladders, some paint-brushes (the softer the bristles the better) and if you're really in the mood, some body paints.

Let him go up the ladder. When he is busy with a brush, come into the room, lean languidly against the ladder and give the sort of look that brings the blood rushing to his cheeks – and the other parts of his body that you have your interior designs on!

When he is safely earthbound, take the brush from his hand and run it lazily over his face with one hand while unbuttoning his shirt with the other. When his chest is bared tease him by running the silky bristles over his nipples and navel.

Now take your shirt off and use the brush to caress your breasts until your nipples stand proud and tempting.

Meanwhile, the home handyman has taken off his jeans and uses his hands to prove they can do more than wield a brush, while you use the brush to bring him closer and closer to the point where the room will be rocking so much that the paintpots will splash their contents onto the dustsheets!

And talking of the paintpots – that's where the added fun comes in. For while some are filled with non-toxic body paints, others could contain yogurt, syrup or other sweet, runny substances that are so sexy to roll around the mouth!

If you want it to end there, that's up to you, but if you can control your climax, continue to drive each other wild with your tantalizing brush technique. After that it's up to you which position to adopt for full-scale penetrative sex.

■ *Patio Sex*

Try and enjoy an afternoon of passion in the privacy of your own secluded patio or sun deck and you'll have only the birds and bees to worry about!

Try awakening your partner's passion with some gentle foreplay. You know what gets them going, but a soft, seductive approach may well surprise them into action immediately.

Outdoor sex can have an entirely different, intense flavour from that which you are accustomed to in bed. To begin with, the traditional missionary position is all but impossible, surrounded as you are with only the hard surfaces of the paved ground and canvas chairs.

Better to use your imagination with what is around you:

Lift your partner onto your lap, while balancing on the edge of the table, or lay her gently back over the table, while you remain standing at the end. Or for those who prefer the eroticism of the rear-entry position, she can bend forwards, supporting herself on a sturdy canvas chair, or even a tub of flowers while you caress her buttocks through her flimsy summer clothes.

If you have a patio swing, or swing seat, this could add a whole new dimension to your lovemaking – she can sit astride you while the swing rocks gently to and fro. You will both feel like you're flying as you climax in mid-air.

Let the experience of making love out of doors take you back to your last holiday in a sunny location, where you made love on the balcony or roof of your holiday home to the sound of the distant waves on the beach, and sipped cool margueritas to quench your thirst in the afterglow.

Alternatively let your fantasies transport you: she can indulge in passionate foreplay with a young, muscular gardener; he can be a plantation owner teaching his young lover the joys of sex.

■ *Pillow Talk*

Pillow fights are a great way to let inhibitions and everyday stresses fly away, and can often lead to something more interesting . . .

Should you fight naked, like a Centurion, or clothed? Should you play a kind of "strip pillow fight", where with each knock, the loser has to remove an article of clothing?

However you play it, make sure that the game lasts just long enough to act as a warm-up, otherwise you will be too tired for the next, altogether more pleasurable stage. Here are some straightforward positions in which the use of pillows really increases the pleasure:

● *Oral Delight. A simple trick to make cunnilingus more comfortable. Just place a pillow beneath her buttocks to raise her genitals a little.*

● *Rear Entry. This classic position really benefits from*

the support of a pillow or two. Place a couple of pillows beneath her stomach to raise her buttocks into the air, and her partner can then lie along the length of her back, entering her at just the right angle for maximum pleasure.

● *Butterflies. Pillows make this position much easier for the man. She should lie on the bed, a pile of pillows beside her. He should kneel upright between her legs, then lift her buttocks towards his penis. She should then quickly place the pillows beneath the small of her back, so that her partner does not have to support the whole weight of her body as they make love in an almost body opposing, butterfly-like position.*

● *Deep Penetration. Don't try this position unless the woman is highly aroused. She then lies on her back with a pillow under her*

buttocks. He kneels between her legs and bends her thighs against her chest as far as possible. He can now place his penis in her vagina, taking care to penetrate slowly to create maximum pleasure.

■ *Rock Star and Groupie*

You should both be very excited about role-playing rock star and groupie – after all, you'll be on a big high. The rock star will just have finished a concert and for the groupie this is the chance of a lifetime.

The rock star knows he's desired, and the groupie knows that the only way to keep his attention is to amuse him sexually, so she'd better be good . . .

He pours himself a bourbon, offering her one too, and he knocks it back in one. He puts some music on, his own naturally, and sings her a love song, walking right up close to her. Feeling outrageous, she whips off her top and asks him to autograph one of her breasts. He does this and at the same time he grinds her hand onto the bulge in his jeans. He undoes his belt and gets out of his jeans.

Holding his buttocks with both hands, she runs her tongue over his hard penis, kissing his inner thighs. She wants this to be the best oral sex he's ever had.

She's only really just begun when, to her surprise, he slips his hands under her arms and pulls her to her feet. He undoes her shorts and lets them fall around her ankles.

Coquettishly he lifts the side of her panties and signs his name on her buttock. He then kisses his way down from her breast to her panties.

Slowly he pulls them down, and begins to perform cunnilingus. She stands above him, and holds his head, directing him to where she needs him most, unable to believe that this is actually happening.

As he begins to enter her, she holds onto the chair and thrusts in time to the music. She takes charge, reversing the roles, pulls him onto the floor and sits astride him. As they both come he calls out her name and you feels a predatory thrill.

■ *Role-play*

In whatever game you choose, one partner must take the lead or dominant role, and the other person takes the passive, submissive role; the key is to transform yourself and your lover from your everyday personae.

Here are a few ideas:

● *The Patient enters the room fully dressed and then the Doctor or Nurse tells them that they will require a full examination and must* remove all their clothes. The sight of one person stripping while the other remains fully clothed can be highly arousing in itself. The Doctor or Nurse then orders the Patient onto the table for an intimate "examination" of the genitals including long, internal examinations of the woman about which the Doctor then comments in detail.

● The sexual liaison of the lady of the manor with her chauffeur, gardener or other servant has always been a popular theme. The sex-starved Lady Chatterley and her earthy, sensual gamekeeper were often to be found engaged in embraces outdoors in the woods and fields. They had special pet names for their genitals and other body parts, and often wove wild flowers into their pubic hair as they spent long, lingering, sunny afternoons making love in the open air.

● Some people have crushes on their aerobics teachers – that seemingly endless stamina and those perfectly tuned bodies; the way they come over to correct your position during difficult or new exercises and stand over you watching to see if you get it right. You can play out this type of fantasy by re-creating a gym class in your own living room. One person takes the lead as the Teacher, the other the enthused adoring Student. Both partners should don tight, revealing gym clothes. The Teacher can then pop an aerobics video in the video recorder, or simply play some fast-paced music and begin the work-out by calling out the exercises. He or she may then comment on the heat in the room, and nonchalantly starts to strip off their tight, lycra clothing. This display of exhibitionism, combined with the natural juices already flowing, is bound to *make you both eager for a little "extra-curricular" activity.*

■ Roman Romp

With a few props and very little planning you can create the atmosphere of ancient Rome in your own home, submitting to an orgy of pleasure.

Run a warm bath, and sprinkle it liberally with scented oil. Take it in turns to soak in the perfumed water, or if the tub is big enough you can bathe together in true Roman style.

Next on the agenda is a Roman body massage with rich oils. Take turns to cover each other's body with the scented oil. Make it an invigorating, firm massage and, once the whole body is glistening, take a small, blunt scraper and gently scrape the oil off the body in soft movements in the direction of the heart. This exfoliation should leave the skin tingling and feeling super-smooth.

Now you are ready to put on your Roman clothes. Tunics covered by simple draped lengths of fabric are among the easiest of costumes to emulate.

Next comes the great feast. Romans ate their meals while reclining on couches, so recline on a low sofa, and place trays of food on a coffee table on the floor.

Go for bread rolls, cheese, cold meat, small sausages, squares of pâté on toast, or anything for that matter that you enjoy. Make sure there is plenty of fresh fruit – peaches, pineapples, pomegranates, passion fruit, figs and, of course, lush juicy grapes. Serve everything with copious quantities of chilled wine in goblets!

Revived by the food and wine, you can enjoy each other's bodies again. This time you can undress each other completely if you choose – a simple tug should free each of

you from the restriction of your robes.

Comfortable on a bed of cushions, you can experiment with athletic positions, or, satiated with food and sex, resort to the easiest and most gratifying. Whatever you get up to, make it a romp to remember!

■ *Sex Toys*

Special catalogues are available from which you can choose

from any number of sex toys and paraphernalia, then purchase them by mail order. Alternatively, you may want to shop for sex toys together.

Penis-shaped vibrators come in an amazing variety of sizes, textures and colours. From the small-sized – about 6 inches long and 1.5 inches wide – to the deluxe jumbo-sized 12-inch-model, they are made to suit every woman.

Some designs are hard and non-porous, while others are soft, with a spongy flesh-like texture. A few have knobbly bits on the outside for added stimulation in the vagina, and some have clitoral stimulators attached to the base of the penis shape.

Many come with assorted attachments such as a G spot massager and an anal stimulator. There is even a model moulded in the shape of a finger and thumb.

Penis rings are another way to give a woman pleasure. They are usually made of plastic and are placed over the man's erect penis before intercourse.

Oriental love balls (little plastic or metal balls with strings attached for safe removal) are inserted into the vagina; as the woman moves, so do the balls, stimulating the walls of the vagina and her G spot.

Why not put yourselves into a silly mood with glasses which sport a willy nose? Or at times you may desire your lover so much that you just want to eat them all up. Edible fruit-flavoured panties and condoms can help you in your quest to "devour" your loved one.

With the aid of sex toys like the strap-on dickie penis and pussy air-pump vagina, you can swap sexes with your partner and pretend you have become each other. Sex-swapping can lead to great role-play fun as you discover many of your lover's secret amorous desires by watching how they act as a member of the "opposite sex".

■ *Shampoo and Sex*

It's not unusual to fantasize about making love with your hairdresser. They are after all included in the short-list of people, like doctors and dentists, who we allow to touch us in an intimate manner . . .

As you discuss your client's needs, tantalize him or her by standing close to examine their hair, looking provocatively into their eyes. Let them feel your body heat and smell your scent before backing away.

Now wash, or pretend to wash, the client's hair. Using gentle pressure rub the head in circular motions with the tips of your fingers.

As you service your client try making small-talk about every day things like the weather, then subtly steer the conversation to more sexual matters.

Tell them the kind of things that turn you on – you can create all kinds of fantasy scenarios here. Some people get really stimulated by talking erotically like this – make it as steamy as you and your partner are comfortable with. Allude to your prowess in massaging other parts of the body: flirting is a powerful aphrodisiac.

By this time you'll barely be able to keep your hands off each other. Your "hairdressing salon" will be full of inspiring items that can be used as sex aids.

Pick up a portable hairdryer and alternately kiss and blow warm air on the nipples and genitals of your partner. The mixture of wet and dry can be incredibly arousing.

If your partner gets pleasure from vaginal penetration with sex toys, you can perhaps excite her with the smooth rounded end of a hairbrush.

Perhaps you can then go on to tease each other with all-over skin stimulation using hair rollers of various sizes.

The possibilities are endless . . .

■ "Shedding" Inhibitions

There are relatively few places close to home where you can hide yourselves away from the kids, pets and neighbours and even parents, but one such is the tool shed or garage.

The dry, dusty odour of cedarwood, creosote, old canvas and potting compost could even be quite an aphrodisiac.

If you want to take your partner by surprise, you will either have to pounce while they are actually working in the shed, or make some excuse for them to join you there. Either way it is up to you to lure them to your den. If the shed is large enough you may be able to make some rough preparations such as laying out a rug or setting up a canvas chair.

Once inside, shut the door and wedge it so that they can't escape – if they are still unsuspecting of your motives, make it clear with a big kiss on the lips.

Give them the sexiest kiss imaginable, one that cannot fail to turn them on. Slide your arms about them to still any final protest and run your hands over their erogenous zones down to the penis and clitoris.

If there is room, you can perform oral sex, kneeling while your partner stands. Otherwise bring them slowly to the point of orgasm by hand. Your partner may never look upon gardening or DIY in the same light again.

If you have a greenhouse, sex among the plants can be another thrill. Barely hidden by the lush greenery of tomato plants, geraniums or fuchsias, there is the added danger that someone might glimpse through the glass. Let the thick, heady scent of the foliage transport you to hotter climes – you might be in a jungle or on a tropical island. Either way, the sensual heat in the height of summer will tempt you to linger longer beneath the glass and take your time with your lovemaking.

■ Shower Power

Make your showertime an assault on the senses. Pick your

favourite music and play it in a nearby room. Meanwhile, both you and your partner can soap up and dance with your arms locked together, your bodies pressing against each other under the warm spray.

Giving a man a shower can be an exciting way to bring him to the verge of orgasm. Wash his back first and then his neck, splashing or spraying water on him throughout.

Soap his front gently, lathering his chest, and slowly circle down towards his genitals. Then wash the back of his legs and his buttocks. Now, turn him around again and wash his testicles. Use featherlight strokes, keeping up a slow, but persistent pressure. Make a ritual of this, perhaps washing and rinsing his penis twice. Gently pull back his foreskin and then, using the slipperiness of the soap, simulate masturbation – but only as a teaser. After you have finished ignore any of his pleas to continue. Now it's your turn to enjoy the warm sensation of shower play . . .

Women have an infinite variety of erogenous zones. Start by washing her hair using your fingers to rub in the shampoo and make the rinsing as sensuous an experience as you can.

Play her soapy fingers right down your body until you reach the most pleasurable spots. Pay special attention to her breasts, spending as much time as you both like. Kiss her wet body and press your body against her soapy back.

Save the rinsing of her genitals until last. Hold the shower attachment pointing towards her, cleansing her gently with a slow steady spray. Make sure it's not too hot, and take care not to direct the water right up her vagina, as this can be dangerous.

The shower is an ideal place for oral sex. The active partner can kneel on the shower floor while the passive partner remains standing.

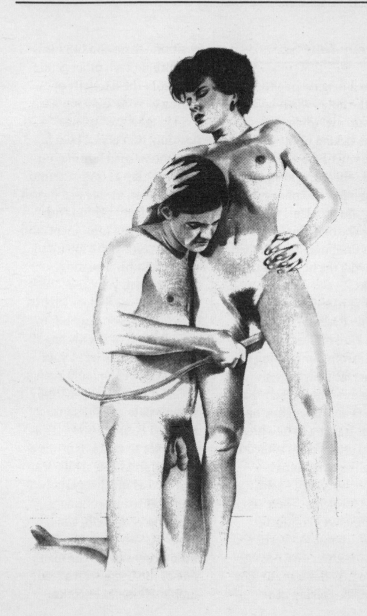

■ Sleepy-time Sex

There is a magical quality about the hours when no one else is stirring, when there is only the ticking of the clock to remind you of the world outside. There are no children causing havoc, no phones ringing, no problems to be solved. The only thing that matters is enjoying each other and having the best orgasm possible.

Lying in each other's arms as you go to sleep has its own special kind of intimacy – one that, far from diminishing over the years, actually grows.

It may seem unlikely that wearing your old nightie or pyjamas is going to be a great turn-on, but there is something especially sexy about a desirable body clad in such prosaic garments. There can be something very comforting about the innocent feel of good old flannelette.

You may not want to move very much, so lying in a

position where you can easily masturbate each other gently will avoid the necessity of having to wake up completely.

Lying in the "spoons" position, that is side by side with the woman "sitting" on the man's lap as they curl into one another, means that he can enter her from behind with very little extra movement, and she can control the force and strength of his thrusting.

Sex when you are practically asleep does have its drawbacks – you tend not to use any kind of sex toy or aid, so any inadequacies in your technique will be more evident.

Also, in your wonderfully drowsy state you might forget all about contraceptive. It's a good idea to make inserting a diaphragm, if you are likely to have sex, as much a part of your night-time routine as brushing your teeth, and condoms can always be kept as close as possible to the man's side of the bed – with a ready supply of tissues of course!

And remember that being sleepy is no excuse for fitting any contraceptive device sloppily.

■ *Slippery Sex*

Imagine your favourite scent – sweet warm vanilla or fresh tangy lemon; the rich texture of oil on your skin; the feel of your lover's hands gliding firmly down your back. Such is the pleasure of sensual massage.

To make the most of sensual massage, and be sure of a climactic result, you need to make it more active. And in order to do this you need extra oil, more space and a few simple props.

Active massage tends to make more of a mess than a standard massage, so to prevent any seepage and stains, and make it more fun, you will need some towels and a large sheet of polythene.

Clear a space in the middle of the bedroom or lounge, and lay towels two or three deep in that space. Then lay the polythene on top of the towels and weight the edges with furniture or heavy books.

Start with each other's neck, rubbing the oil around the front and back, then move onto the shoulders and upper arms. Any other part of the body is out of bounds while you work away the stress in the muscles. Spend at least five minutes on this area, particularly the neck and hairline, as this is one of the great erogenous zones.

One of you can then turn around and sit between the other's legs. While one partner works on the other's back, the other can work on the feet. Be generous with the oil. Cover the back and rub it all over. Smother the feet and calves, working between the toes and round the ankles.

When the skin is glistening and the muscles refreshed, start on the rest of the body. Use plenty of oil – spread it liberally over the chest and breasts.

Warm it first in your hands or drizzle it straight from the bottle. Don't restrict the massage to your hands – move every part of your oiled body against your partner's.

■ Storytime

As it gets close to bedtime, turn to your partner and suggest that you read him a story in bed – but not quite the way that mummy used to do it. Make him get undressed, wash, brush his teeth then slip under the bedcovers. You should sit on top of the covers wearing a loose robe, and holding the book of your choice.

Everyone has their own favourite stories – some may prefer modern scenarios but why not try your partner with the short pieces of erotica by Anaïs Nin in *Delta of Venus* and *Little Birds*; or *Fanny Hill*

by the eighteenth-century English author John Cleland; or *The Pearl* and other stories by anonymous Victorian writers.

As you read, you may like to stroke your partner through the bedcovers, or loosen your robe and let him touch you, but nothing more is allowed until you reach the end of the story, and close the book.

■ Striptease – Her for Him

The basic principle of striptease is to save the best bits – the tease – until last.

Start by dancing around to music, as if you were dancing at a disco, but emphasize your breasts, legs and bottom. Run your hands down the outside of your hips and thighs, over your arms and your breasts. Run your fingers through your hair, and cover your body with strokes, as though it were your man doing it.

Slowly undo your blouse in a teasing way to reveal more of your breasts. When all the buttons are undone, turn round with your back to him, tease down the top of your blouse, remove it and throw it over to your man.

Undo the waistband of your skirt, and wriggle out of it, letting it fall to the ground. Step out of it, and kick it over to him.

Sit on a high stool or chair and slowly undo your stockings from the suspenders. Roll down one stocking at a time to the toe, and remove it sexily. Once you have removed your stockings, put your shoes back on – this enhances the shape of your legs. Now you are wearing only bra, panties, suspenders and shoes.

Stand up, and dance some more. Emphasize your breasts, because they are to be the next center of attraction. Remove one brassière strap, then the other, and with your back to your man, undo the clip

behind. Now, to the music, do a peep-bo with first one breast and then the other. Finally toss the bra over to him with a flourish.

Remove your stockings, panties and suspender belt as sexily as you can.

Lie down on the floor and writhe around to the music. Facing him, open up your legs and stroke your vulva. Lie on your tummy then get on all fours, and caress your bottom so that you are totally open to his view. Wet a finger or two and moisten your nipples, then caress your clitoral area. From here on it is likely your partner will want to get in on the action as he will have been teased quite enough.

■ Striptease – Him for Her

Stripping for your lover can be a wonderful way to boost her sexual interest. You may want to surprise her with an impromptu striptease, or lead her on through the day with naughty little hints.

Start your striptease session fully clothed, and if possible, in your very best suit. Begin by throwing your keys and wallet on a chair with great abandon. Unbutton and pull your jacket off slowly, one arm and then the other. Wriggle out of it and throw it behind you nonchalantly.

Now loosen your tie. Make a show of pulling it off and twisting it round your lover's waist or lightly whipping her with it. Be sure to keep up good eye contact with her throughout.

Slowly unbutton your shirt, moving to the beat of the music. As you remove your shirt, move your chest close to her face and ask her to lick it. When her tongue has nearly touched your skin, pull away teasingly.

Bend over with your backside facing her and take off your shoes – then remove your socks. Unbuckle your belt and pull it quickly from your waist. Whip it into the air, perhaps jumping over it as you flick it across the floor.

Now smoothly rub your hands over your chest and down towards your crotch. Insert one hand into the waist of your trousers and simulate masturbation.

Move teasingly close to her after you have unzipped your fly. She may wish to reach out to you at this point, but tell her that she can look but not touch. Dance seductively out of your trousers to reveal the skimpy G-string you are wearing underneath.

Now is the time to let her experience her desire fully. Let her fondle your genitals for a while before pulling away and removing your G-string.

■ *Telephone Sex*

You and your partner may be apart but by setting the wires

alight with passion and making love over the phone you can still turn each other on.

If your partner is away from home you could phone in the evening, when he is getting ready for bed. Pamper yourself with a fragrant bubble bath and then dress in your sexiest underwear or night clothes.

There may be no-one to see you but if you look the part you are bound to feel more sexy. Ring your partner and tell him how much you are missing him and then describe in detail what you are wearing.

Ask him what he's doing and then describe to him what you would do if he was there next to you. He'll probably be in bed but if he's not, get him to transfer the call to somewhere he won't be disturbed.

Ask him to describe his favourite lovemaking scene: what exactly he would like you to wear and what he would like you to do to him. You may be in for some surprises.

People who may be quite shy about sex face to face can really let themselves go over the phone.

By this stage you should both feel pretty passionate and you may not be able to resist caressing yourself. Don't be afraid to tell him exactly what you are doing – he's probably doing the same and what better way to ease the frustration of being apart than to orgasm to the sound of one another's voice.

Of course, with the increase in the use of portable phones, it's possible to contact your partner practically anywhere, anytime.

But beware! It could cause an extremely embarrassing accident if you phoned him whilst he was driving and it's worth checking your partner hasn't put his office phone on "hands free" – you may find your naughty, loving words broadcast to his surprised, and envious, colleagues!

■ *Togetherness*

To guarantee a truly memorable night, you have to start preparing during the day. Wake up a little earlier than usual and spend time kissing, cuddling and simply turning each other on.

You won't have time to make love, but that's the point – by the time you both leave for work, you'll be aching to see each other in the evening.

Prepare yourself physically with some pampering during the day; a workout or a facial perhaps. Ensure that you will be undisturbed in the evening by children or flatmates. Stock the refrigerator with favourites such as champagne and strawberries. And take the phone off the hook . . .

Wear an outfit that you feel sensational in – one that you know your partner loves you in or maybe something you've bought especially for tonight, and very sexy underwear.

Eating at home can be romantic but for a special treat, book a table at your favorite restaurant. Arrive separately so it feels like a date; flirt with each other; play footsie under the table; enjoy each other's company; feed each other suggestively.

After the meal, catch a cab home and smooch in the back seat. Cab rides can be incredible turn-ons.

Home alone, you can really get into each other. Take a candlelit bath together and spend ages soaping and caressing your bodies. When you are ready, towel each other dry. Take a bottle of champagne into the bedroom, pour a glass each, put some music on, light the candles and lie down together.

But don't start making love yet. Indulge in a relaxing, sensual oil massage. Stroking each other lovingly is the perfect prelude to sex.

When you do start making love, aim to make it last for

hours. Tonight isn't about quickie sex – it's about hours spent together, enjoying and relishing each other.

■ *Truth or Dare*

First of all, both of you should write a number of instructions on little pieces of paper, to serve as dares. They should all be things that you would like the other person to do to you. For example, instructions could read "Smear honey on my nipples and lick it off slowly and thoroughly", "Put me over your knee and spank me", "Give me a back rub", "Blindfold me and trace a pattern with an ice cube all over my naked body".

Fold the pieces of paper in half and put them in a hat.

The first person starts by asking the other "Truth or dare?" If they choose Truth, they have to answer any question put to them truthfully – and you should make the questions as awkward and revealing as possible.

If they choose "Dare" they have to pick a piece of paper from the hat and read out the dare on it. The other person then gets to choose whether the dare is done to them, or they do it to the chooser.

Make sure your dares are as imaginative as possible!

■ *Vampire*

If the vampire legend inspires you, let your imagination carry you to dark foreign crypts. Or, you can set the scene in your own home for a night of gothic passion.

Wait until dark, and extinguish all the lights in the house, replacing them with candles which diffuse a dancing, golden glow.

Let the "victim" lay upon the bed with their eyes closed as if sleeping. The foreplay starts, as in all vampire movies, with a bite.

Lean down over your "sleeping" lover, and brush your lips gently against the exposed skin of their neck. Move slowly upwards, and whisper your desires into their ear.

Then work your way around the lobes, the line of the hair and down to the throat, nibbling with your lips, stroking with your teeth and tracing the contours with your tongue.

Make them wait. Once you have begun to arouse them, continue downwards, undressing if necessary to reveal their breasts or chest. Caress with hands and tongue, biting the nipples and skating across the curves with your teeth.

Move ever downwards with your hands, scratching back and front with fingernails, and easing your lover out of their remaining clothes.

Slide your hands around their hips, thighs and across their genitals. Slip your fingers over her clitoris or around his penis and masturbate your partner into a sexual frenzy, while your tongue darts wickedly from neck to ear.

Just before they reach the peak of their pleasure, withdraw. Wait silently for your unseeing victim's breathing to return to normal, then approach them again, now offering the gift of oral sex.

When again they approach climax, withdraw, and wait. Then come to them a final time for full sexual intercourse. Make love to them with wild abandon, and at the moment of orgasm, bite their neck, but not hard enough to draw blood, nor leave a trace of a bruise.

■ *Video Fun*

Much of the pleasure in making a video will be the preparation.

First, you both need to familiarize yourselves with the

workings of the camera. Try firing off a few feet of video on test shots. It will not be wasted as you can always record over it again.

Next, rehearse certain scenes and take up various positions with your partner without leaving the frame.

Decide on the location. Probably you will want to use your own house as you are going to need privacy, so plan out which corners are going to suit the action.

In the absence of any powerful and expensive artificial light you are going to have to rely on sunlight, so use the room with the biggest windows.

Interesting shots can be achieved shooting upwards from the floor, or down from the ceiling – or reflected in a strategically placed mirror.

Keep your shooting script handy throughout filming and try to stick to it. But if something exciting occurs, capture the moment on tape.

It may be better than anything you had planned.

The easiest scenario to film is a straightforward striptease – simply because one partner can handle the camera while the other supplies the action.

Panning slowly across a naked body, from head to toe – or from toe to head – can have a lingering eroticism, as can panning slowly across the scene to find a nude in a far corner.

What is not seen is often more erotic than what is – such is the power of the imagination. If the camera follows the feet of a subject upstairs while clothes fall around them on the steps, the viewer will draw only one conclusion.

Once you have edited your movie and have the final version ready, close the curtains, dim the lights, and watch. You may find that you want to relive some of the highlights of your own personal lovetape!

■ *Voyeurism*

Window cleaning may be hard work, yet it can have certain benefits that many have never considered. If he is cleaning the windows she can opt for the strategy below; and if she is cleaning the windows he will have to adapt the seduction scene with a Chippendales-style performance to suit her.

As soon as he steps outside with his bucket and chamois leather, you have to spring into action. Take a quick shower or bath, cover yourself with fragrant body lotion or perfume, then change into your sexiest underwear with a slinky silken robe or similar in order to look as seductive as possible.

Before he begins to clean the windows of your room, draw the curtains or blinds so that he cannot see inside.

Then, once he is on the final polish, pull them open to reveal yourself, at your dressing table combing your hair, sipping a glass of wine in the dining room, or even with a tray of tea and biscuits in the kitchen or lounge.

Once he has recovered himself, move towards the window and coax him inside. If the windows are still closed, he won't be able to hear you until you deign to open them, so you will have to encourage him with your actions.

Carry on with your chosen activity, then let your robe open revealing your underwear. Stand up and walk around, letting the robe slip slinkily away. You could pretend to have dropped something, bending over to give him a really good view of your buttocks.

If he is showing signs that he cannot wait any longer, open the window and haul him in. And now is the time to put your striptease skills into action. One thing is for certain, cleaning the windows will never be the same dull household chore again!

■ Wrestling

Why not become sparring partners for a night and wrestle your way into bed with a stimulating session in the ring?

Set up a mock ring in your living room or bedroom. Place a rubber sheet on the floor to mark the wrestling arena, and put on your sexiest and most alluring gym clothes.

Ring a bell to indicate the start and end of each match. Decide the timing and the rules for each round. You may want to play a sound-effects record or CD with crowd noises to give you the kinky feeling of being watched.

Try a few simple moves at first. Hop around and move in and out of your partner's space. Play a teasing game of coming up close, almost touching, and then moving away. You can use your hands to block and touch, grab and probe your partner.

Now lock arms as you push and swerve with each other.

Get yourselves in a head-butt situation and try to outwit your lover into being the first one to make a false move. Pull him or her to the side and gently force them down on the mat. Slither your chest against theirs and get as close as you dare.

Make plenty of skin contact. Try wedging your leg in between your partner's, then flip from side to side. Be rough, but not so rough that you hurt them.

At the end of the match take a cloth or a big sponge dipped in cool water scented with a drop or two of essential oil. Pat it across your lover's forehead, cheeks, neck and shoulders.

At this point you may want to start removing each other's clothes and sponging down the breasts, chest and legs. Leave the best bits for last. Then you can squirm around together on the rubber mat, oiled and ready for further love play.

❖

Index